Essays in Honour of Grant Notley

Socialism and Democracy in Alberta

Grant Notley, who died in a plane accident in October 1984, was one of Alberta's most respected and able politicians. He was also a socialist. Although just 45 when he died, he had been active in the provincial New Democratic Party for 25 years and its leader since 1968, and he left his stamp on Alberta's political life.

The ten essays written for this tribute to Grant Notley deal with the man, the history of the progressive movement in Alberta, Notley's role in opposition from 1971 until his death, and the two great questions that dominated his thought and activities—socialism and democracy in Alberta and Canada.

The essays were written "in honour" of Grant Notley, and the authors have taken this to mean that they should do more than justify the man and the party. The book contains material that is sharply critical of social democracy and of the NDP—a stance that is entirely in keeping with Grant Notley's own realism and honesty.

Essays in Honour of Grant Notley

Socialism and Democracy in Alberta

Edited by Larry Pratt
with a Preface by Ray Martin

NeWest Press   Edmonton

Canadian Cataloguing in Publication Data

Main entry under title:

Essays in honour of Grant Notley

ISBN 0-920897-02-9 (bound) — ISBN 0-920897-00-2 (pbk.)

1. Alberta - Politics and government - 1971- *. 2. Alberta New Democratic Party - History. 3. Notley, Grant, 1939-1984. I. Pratt, Larry, 1944- . II. Notley, Grant, 1939-1984.
FC3675.2.E8 1986   971.23'03   C86-091529-8
F1078.E8 1986

Credits

Cover design: S. Colberg
Photograph of Grant Notley: Susan Mayse
by permission of The Provincial Archives of Alberta
Typesetting: K. Wilson, M. Albert
Printing and binding: Jasper Printing, Edmonton

Financial Assistance

Alberta Culture
The Alberta Foundation for the Literary Arts
The Canada Council

NeWest Publishers Ltd.
Suite 204, 8631 - 109 Street
Edmonton, Alberta
Canada   T6G 1E8

Table of Contents

Foreword   *Larry Pratt*   ix
Preface   *Ray Martin*   xi
Introduction   *Larry Pratt*   xv

Chapter 1
Grant Notley: Politics as a Calling   *Larry Pratt*   *1*
Chapter 2
Dreaming a New Jerusalem in the Land of Social Credit:
The Struggles of the CCF in Alberta   *Olenka Melnyk*   *40*
Chapter 3
Social Democracy in Alberta:
From the CCF to the NDP   *Robin Hunter*   *57*
Chapter 4
Opportunity and Constraint:
Grant Notley and the Modern State   *Allan Tupper*   *88*
Chapter 5
Oil, Class and Development in Alberta   *Ed Shaffer*   *112*
Chapter 6
Insults to Democracy during
the Lougheed Era   *Ron Chalmers*   *131*
Chapter 7
Intraparty Democracy
and the Alberta NDP   *T.C. Pocklington*   *146*
Chapter 8
Grant Notley and Democracy in Alberta
   Frederick C. Engelmann   *172*
Chapter 9
From Consensus to Competition: Social Democracy and
Political Culture in Alberta   *Gurston Dacks*   *186*
Chapter 10
Class and Class Politics in Alberta   *Garth Stevenson*   *205*

Contributors   *239*

For Grant Notley (1939—1984)

For famous men have the whole earth as their memorial: it is not only the inscriptions on their graves in their own country that mark them out; no, in foreign lands also, not in any visible form but in people's hearts, their memory abides and grows. It is for you to try to be like them. Make up your minds that happiness depends on being free, and freedom depends on being courageous.

*Pericles' Funeral Oration
as recorded by Thucydides*

Foreword

Grant Notley died in a tragic plane accident in October 1984. At the time of his death he was just 45 years old, but he had been active in Alberta politics for a quarter of century and leader of the provincial New Democratic Party since 1968. A myth had already been created—not without Notley's subtle encouragement—that the Alberta NDP had virtually been founded and nurtured by a single individual, and that this had happened despite the historical weakness of the Alberta Left since the 1930s. Notley's tenacity and his contribution were indeed formidable, but there were other leaders and socialist activists who were present at the creation of the party, and still others who have carried on its work since Notley's death. When Alberta's New Democrats finally made an electoral breakthrough in the provincial general election on 8 May 1986, capturing 29 per cent of the popular vote and increasing their seats in the Legislature from 2 to 16, the outcome was the doing of thousands of party activists, organizers and candidates. That they had built on Notley's foundation was generously acknowledged on election night by the present leader of the Alberta NDP, Ray Martin, whose personal appreciation of the man opens this collection of essays. But the party is also a movement, and the movement has never depended on the fortunes of one man.

The future of Alberta politics and of the Alberta New Democratic Party is now less certain than it has seemed since 1971 when the Lougheed Conservatives unexpectedly swept Social Credit from power. NDP optimists believe that their party will do the same to the Tories in the next provincial election; but skeptical observers note that the outcome in 1986 was more the result of a record low turnout than a sudden surge in favour of the NDP; further, the Liberals have also begun a revival in Alberta. About all that can be said is that politics is inherently unpredictable; Machiavelli guessed that fortune rules about half of human affairs and he advised his Prince that he would need an iron will to exercise mastery over the remainder.

There are many debts of gratitude to be acknowledged. The preparation of the essays in this collection would not have been possible without the cooperation of the Alberta New Democratic Party. Access to its historical records at the Provincial Archives of Alberta was indispensable in the research for the historical chapters on the NDP and CCF in Alberta. We also thank the provincial archivists for their patience and assistance. Colleen Dempsey of the Public Archives of Canada helped us to locate important papers on the struggle over the founding of the Alberta NDP in the early Sixties. We thank the national NDP for providing access to these records.

The Central Research Fund of the University of Alberta generously provided us with financial assistance for research of this book. Ellen Nygaard's excellent reportorial and research skills allowed us to complete most of the research in the summer of 1985; we gratefully acknowledge her many contributions.

A large number of NDP activists and friends of Grant Notley were interviewed as part of the research for this book. Some generously provided us with their personal papers and documents on the organization and development of the Alberta NDP. Among many, we are especially grateful to Ken Novakowski, Ray Martin, Neil Reimer, Nellie Peterson, Tony and Betty Mardiros, Ted Chudyk, Kevin Peterson, Geoff White, Keith and Kathy Wright, Reg Basken, Gordon Wright, Ivor Dent, Bill and Myrna Glass, John Worton, Jean McBean, Winston Gereluk, Joyce Kurie, Lawrence Radcliffe, Ed Shaffer, P.J. Ryan and Roy Jamha. Transcripts of most of these interviews are available at the Department of Political Science, University of Alberta.

Professor Henry Kreisel of the University of Alberta was kind enough to read these essays in manuscript form and to offer valuable advice plus some gentle reproaches concerning academic jargon and literary excesses. The flaws that remain are entirely the responsibility of the authors and the editor.

Finally, we wish to thank the Board and the staff of NeWest Press for their consistent support for this modest tribute to Grant Notley.

Larry Pratt, May 1986

Preface

Ray Martin MLA

"Some people strengthen the society just by being the kind of people they are."

John W. Gardner

Outside of my family no one has had a more profound influence on my life than my late colleague Grant Notley. My first recollection of meeting Grant was at a party function in Calgary soon after I had joined the party in 1970. He was at that time the new leader of the Alberta NDP, having been elected to that position in 1968. While I found him at that meeting to be a very intelligent person he did not leave a strong impression upon me, perhaps because I didn't think of myself as a potential politician and felt his concern to be beyond my sphere. This was soon to change, however, starting with the provincial election of 1971 when he was first elected to the Alberta Legislature. I grew to know him well and respect him more and more during the period between 1971 and 1975, as I became involved in political organization and opposition to Peter Lougheed's Conservative government.

Obviously my closest association with Grant occurred between 1975 and his death in October 1984 during which time I served as Provincial Secretary of the New Democratic Party, as President of the New Democratic Party and as his colleague in the Alberta Legislature.

The 1975 election saw the Conservatives grow even more powerful in the province, but Grant managed to hold his seat in spite of a determined bid by the Tories to unseat him in a two-way fight. I myself had run in that election in Calgary McKnight and thought I had done my bit in fighting for social democracy in Alberta. Grant Notley, however, had other ideas. He and the retiring Provincial Secretary, Howard Leeson, decided that I should become Provincial Secretary of the party, a paid position which required an inconvenient move to Edmonton. Needless to say, I ended up as Provincial Secretary in Edmonton—taking a $6,000 pay cut for the dubious privilege.

People who knew Grant well know how persistent an arm-twister he was. It was almost impossible to say no to him. He won again in 1979 when he insisted that I take on the position of party president. These two examples say a lot about Grant's best attributes as a political leader—determination and persistence. This determination and persistence were demonstrated throughout his political career.

What would have happened to the Alberta NDP without Notley? One must understand Alberta politics during the time Grant was leader of our small party. It was a time when Premier Lougheed and the Conservative Party were all-powerful and the petro-dollars flowed in the province because of the oil boom. Very little attention was given to an alternate point of view. Grant Notley was the lone voice in the province and in the Legislature giving an alternative point of view that most people simply didn't want to hear. It was an extremely lonely position and there were many disappointments, election after election. Only a person with Grant's determination, persistence and inner strength would have continued this seemingly hopeless struggle over those number of years. I personally believe the NDP in Alberta would not have survived as a viable party if Grant Notley had not been there. There now would be an NDP, but probably it would be not much more than a theoretical organization that would put up a handful of candidates at election time just to remind people that a socialist view was still around the province. Certainly the New Democrats would not be the Official Opposition in this Province and the main alternative to the Conservative government at the present time.

This position did not come about through good luck but through Grant's tireless efforts after the founding of the party in 1962. He and I travelled throughout the province between 1975 and 1979 in what we laughingly called the Grant and Ray show. Grant would give the speech and I would give the traditional pitch, i.e. asking for money for the party (another party tradition—never having enough money). During this time Grant became more than a politician and the Leader of the party to me—he became my closest friend and confidant. Spending that much time together really allowed me to know him as an individual. Perhaps the part of Grant Notley that many Albertans did not see or perceive was his sense of humour. Nobody enjoyed kibitzing or laughing at himself and those close to him more than Grant. Over the years we teased each other unmercifully and laughed at each other's speeches and personalities; all in good humor. In fact, I am sure it was the jokes that kept both of us going during those years.

People have asked me about Grant's politics over the years. By this they wanted me conveniently to place him on a spectrum of left to right.

However, people do not conveniently fall into nice little niches on a political spectrum and certainly Grant Notley did not. If there is a mainstream in the New Democratic Party, Grant epitomized it. As far as I am concerned he represented what was best about our movement in the progressive tradition of Coldwell, Douglas and Lewis. Grant didn't care whether you called him a democratic socialist or a social democrat—he was comfortable with both labels. He was more concerned with issues that affected ordinary Albertans and how government could best enhance the lives of citizens in this province. He was accessible to people, and he strongly believed that the New Democratic Party was the vehicle to bring about desirable social change.

While all people in political life need healthy egos to survive, Grant Notley's main concern was not the building up of himself in public opinion; in truth he had already achieved enormous respect from Albertans all over the province. This was certainly proven by the reactions of Albertans after his death. How often did Grant and the rest of us hear the following, "He is a good man but he is in the wrong party." That reaction was deeply frustrating for Grant because his prime goal was the growth and success of the party.

There was considerable speculation in the media after Grant's tragic death in October, 1984, about the future of the NDP in Alberta. Some commentators suggested that the party had died with its leader. What this overlooked was Grant's legacy and the strength and commitment of the thousands of progressive men and women who remained to carry on his life's work. The first test was decided in our favor when the NDP dramatically increased its share of the popular vote—from 19 to 29 per cent—and its seats in the Alberta Legislature—from two to 16 seats—in the provincial election of May 1986. As I said on election night, this could not have happened without Grant Notley's years in the wilderness, building the party and earning the respect of the people of Alberta. In the next election we expect to win power, to give Albertans the government they deserve, and to begin the building of the type of society Grant Notley fought for.

Ray Martin, MLA for Edmonton Norwood, is leader of the Alberta NDP and Leader of the Official Opposition.

Introduction

Larry Pratt

There is a marvellous story about the fierce tenacity of prairie settlers that seems to explain something of the psychology of the late Grant Notley and many of the older generation of Alberta socialists. The story, Henry Kreisel's "The Broken Globe", concerns a conflict between a father, a Ukrainian farmer, and his son, a scientist, over whether the earth moves. The father's world, fixed for him by "some medieval priest in the small Ukrainian village where he was born," is the static centre of the universe. That the earth is flat and immobile is beyond debate. One day the son arrives home from science class to announce heretically that the earth is round and moves about the sun. "Stop your ears! Let not Satan come in!" shouts the father, and he beats his son. But the boy insists, "She moves, she moves," and soon the estrangement is total.

Years later, the academic narrator of Kreisel's story visits the old farmer, still fierce and fixed in his views, to bring him greetings from his son, now a scientist in England. The father recounts the story of his bitter conflict with his son and concludes quietly: "When I die, there will be nobody to look after the land. Instead he has gone off to tamper with God's earth." The narrator takes his leave.

> When I was about to get into my car, he touched me lightly on the arm. I turned. His eyes surveyed the vast expanse of sky and land, stretching far into the distance, reddish clouds in the sky and blue shadows on the land. With a gesture of great dignity and power he lifted his arm and stood pointing into the distance, at the flat land and the low-hanging sky. "Look," he said, very slowly and very quietly, "she is flat, and she stands still."

> It was impossible not to feel a kind of admiration for the old man. There was something heroic about him. I held out my hand and he took it. He looked at me steadily, then averted his eyes and said, "Send greetings to my son."

> I drove off quickly, but had to stop again in order to open the wooden gate. I looked back at the house, and saw him still standing there, still

looking at his beloved land, a lonely, towering figure framed against the
darkening evening sky.[1]

I do not wish to imply a connection between the medieval superstitions
of Kreisel's Ukrainian farmer and the beliefs of prairie socialists.
Socialism, after all, is a product of European rationalism and science,
and the old man—unlike his son—stands for a rather brutal pre-
scientific ignorance. Yet, as portrayed by Kreisel, he is also admirable;
against the landscape of sky and prairie, he has both dignity and power;
he is a lonely, towering figure, inseparable from the grandeur of his vast,
beloved land. Far from being pathetic or an object of ridicule, Kreisel's
farmer evokes our sympathies because of his passionate commitment to
his unorthodox beliefs, notwithstanding Galileo and conventional opinion. And it is here, I think, in the capacity to dissent and to hold unorthodox views in a climate of overwhelming conservative orthodoxy—to be
a pariah among parvenus—that we may find our parallel between Henry
Kreisel's fiercely independent settler and the stubborn rump of post-
1935 Alberta socialism which Grant Notley exemplified. Both were products of a stern prairie puritanism which flowed from the initial con-
quest of the land and the dream of building a moral community in
Alberta—a New Jerusalem in the dominion of Social Credit.

For a brief moment in the early Thirties it appeared to some
observers that Alberta would be the first beachhead of socialism in
North American capitalism. The signs of radicalism and incipient revolt
were everywhere. Calgary, previously a stronghold of the One Big
Union, was the founding place of the Cooperative Commonwealth
Federation (CCF) in 1932; Alberta's labour party was growing; the
industrial working-class, small but militant, was engaged in conflicts in
the coal mines of the Crowsnest Pass and the packing house plants of
Edmonton; thousands of unemployed workers clashed with the police
along Jasper Avenue in Edmonton; and the farmers of the West were
desperately looking for a solution to the crisis of the Depression. Conditions seemed ripe for an upheaval.

It was not however the left to which the destitute and desperate
turned in the 1935 provincial election. Rather, it was William
Aberhart's Social Credit movement that swept the United Farmers of
Alberta (U.F.A.) from power in a landslide, decimating the parties of the
left almost as an afterthought. Socialism in Alberta has never recovered
from that shattering defeat. Some of the reasons for the CCF's failure in
1935 are reviewed by Olenka Melnyk in her colourful essay in this
book, but William Irvine, the party's dominant leader in Alberta,

analyzed the debacle with characteristic bluntness in a speech to the CCF Clubs in July of 1936.

The 1935 election had convinced Irvine of two basic things. First, "when economic pressure threatens life, people will act." Second, "fear, anger, hate of good-will, in short, emotions, are the vehicles of mass action rather than reasoned knowledge. The average man is not a potential professor of economics but he may be counted on to respond quickly to a sense of economic danger." The leadership and program of the CCF had become intellectually removed from the ordinary experience of the people, doctrine had become a fetish, and mass organization had been neglected. An effective program "must reach the people where they are living. Let the program be sound, let it be honest, let it be fundamental and far-reaching, but let it reach the people."

Sounding for all the world like a disciple of Aberhart, Bill Irvine called for an electoral appeal to people's hearts and their immediate interests. The Regina Manifesto, like the Rock of Gibraltar, was magnificent but useless for strategic purposes. People wanted practical solutions and strong leadership. "While it is true that we must have navigators who can guide our ship across a trackless sea, it is not necessary that every sailor should have a master's ticket."[2]

Bill Irvine's appraisal of the 1935 debacle suggested that Aberhart's victory was based, first, on Social Credit's vastly superior political organization and, second, on its mass psychological approach. Unlike many socialists, Irvine grasped the importance of the religious and irrational appeal of Social Credit: its blend of pre-millenial fundamentalism, charismatic leadership, and promises of immediate economic relief offered an explanation and a sense of meaning to desperate people.

As the historian John Irving, our most perceptive student of the Social Credit movement, observes, thousands of Albertans were not simply oppressed by financial difficulties by 1935; "they were also suffering from feelings, often deep-seated, of guilt or of personal inadequacy for being unemployed or on relief. The meaning of their world, as far as that world was constituted by their economic and social environment, had often well-nigh vanished." Aberhart helped these people to regain their self-respect by providing them with a (false) explanation of the collapse of the economy and by involving them in a programme of social action. "They could adjust to their environment by transforming that environment."[3]

However, the adjustment was not a tolerant affair. Nor did the new politics nurture democratic values. The first Social Crediters were a very intolerant band of dogmatists. No matter that Social Credit could not transform the capitalist environment, people believed in Aberhart and his promise of immediate debt-free solutions and they shouted down those who dared support the other parties. Those who criticized Aberhart the Prophet were often threatened with violence. So bitter were the cleavages that rural churches divided into Social Credit and U.F.A. factions; families split apart. Social Credit was a movement of believers led by a charismatic leader who supplied an ideological faith in return for unquestioning obedience. However illogical its doctrine and unconstitutional its remedies, once an individual converted to Social Credit he had only to refer to the little blue *Social Credit Manual*, written by Wm. Aberhart, B.A., for answers to all of life's "puzzling questions." For example:

> What effect will basic dividends have upon the drink traffic?
>
> **Answer**—There is no real relationship between dividends and the drink traffic. Discouragement and discontent tend to the drowning of sorrow. Contentment and happiness will lead men and women from debauchery. The control of the drink traffic is separate and distinct from the economic problems of to-day. Men could not be allowed to spend the whole of their basic dividends on drink, and thereby be without proper food, clothing or shelter.[4]

This passage (and many others) from Aberhart's blue book are suggestive of another of Social Credit's traits: its deep-seated authoritarianism. Aberhart, wishing to reassure his followers that the monthly $25 dividend will not worsen the drink traffic, informs them that prosperity encourages temperance rather than debauchery—he did not live to witness Alberta's oil booms—but then goes on to say that men "could not be allowed" to spend the whole of their dividends on booze. The right to a dividend, in short, is conditional upon an individual's behaviour conforming to moral standards defined by a paternalistic leader. Aberhart's oppressive political system, revealed subsequently in his illegal efforts to muzzle a critical press, offered the convert a freedom of sorts: the freedom to submit, conform and repress dissent.

Fortunately, some rebelled. The ten essays in this volume are a tribute not only to Grant Notley but also to his socialist predecessors who fought to rebuild the shattered progressive movement in Alberta in the years after 1935. Chester Ronning, Bill Irvine, Elmer Roper, Nellie

Peterson, Aylmer Liesemer, Stan Rudnycki, Floyd Johnson, Tony and Betty Mardiros, Harold Bronson, Neil Reimer, Pat Lenihan, Roy Jamha, Ed Nelson, Bob Carlyle, Ivor Dent, Art Bunney, Pat Ryan, and others: although divided on many issues and on organizational questions, they had in common a commitment to democracy and socialism in Alberta and Canada. Against orthodoxy and conventional opinion they dissented. Electoral success eluded them, as it eluded Notley, and the CCF was plagued with sectarianism in its last years. But it was because of their political efforts that the progressive tradition remained (barely) alive in Alberta, despite the hegemony of right-wing ideas, the Cold War and the invasion of American resource capital after World War II. Grant Notley personified that tradition, but he was also a product of it: he stood on the shoulders of J.S. Woodsworth, Irvine and the older generation of prairie radicals, and like them he was rather proud to be against the tyranny of the conservative majority.

The question is addressed more than once in this book: why did Notley and his CCF predecessors keep struggling in the face of such overwhelming odds? A plausible answer is suggested by Nellie Peterson, one of the strongest CCF leaders, at the end of Olenka Melnyk's essay. It was not our time, she says—the left was not making headway anywhere. But there was "a hope you kept alive, a little spark anyway"; and if all one could do was "to be there and say, 'This is right and that is wrong,' then it's worthwhile." Notley's answer might have been less solemn—he was in it for fun as well as duty—but he confronted his conscience and came to the same conclusion as the formidable Mrs. Peterson. In an imperfect world a moral person is not entitled to withdraw, to run away, or to remain silent. There were many things about contemporary Canada and Alberta that Notley disliked, but he never succumbed to the temptation to turn his back on civilization and, like Huck Finn, drift away down the river on his raft. Escapism was no solution to the dilemmas of our time.

Notley is remembered by some as an agrarian socialist who sought to convey a populist vision of politics to Albertans, but failed in the face of a rising urban middle class whose banner was carried by Peter Lougheed's Conservatives. This is a romantic view that has to be rejected. Notley certainly saw himself in the tradition of progressive prairie politics, and he represented a rural Peace River constituency during his years as an MLA (1971-1984), but he was basically a mainstream social democrat building a modern party organization—a machine, as he put it—around a coalition of urban and rural interests.

There were two models which he rejected. The first was the old CCF approach emphasizing ideological purity and a focus upon the remnants of agrarian radicalism. This was hopelessly sectarian. The second was the view that the NDP should be the political arm of organized labour and concentrated mainly in the urban working class constituencies of Edmonton and Calgary. This would confine the Alberta NDP to permanent marginal status. After winning the party's leadership in 1968 Notley pitched his appeal to the cities as much as to the farms, and if he never won over the new Alberta middle class it was certainly not for a want of trying. In many respects his policies on energy, economic diversification and a strong interventionist state were nearly indistinguishable from those of Lougheed's party; as Allan Tupper notes in his incisive critique of NDP policy, this left the voters with little incentive to vote for Notley rather than the Tories. The problem was not so much that the Conservatives were too interventionist as it was that the NDP was insufficiently socialist.

In the larger scheme of things, the distinctions between the ideas of Peter Lougheed and Grant Notley on, say, the oil export tax or the National Energy Program are probably not very interesting. There are more important things than the price of oil. What *is* important is that Notley never lost sight of the human dimension of political decisions and changes in the economy. He kept one eye on the underside of the boom, and when the boom and Alberta's ambition collapsed in the early Eighties he attacked the indifference and injustice of Conservative policies which redistributed wealth from the public to the petroleum industry. He did not much care for the acquisitive new money of Calgary and Edmonton and its equation of the misery index with the price of crude oil. And it did not care for him.

His final address in the Alberta Legislature, on October 18, 1984, stressed "the primacy of people over things"—an echo of the call by the Catholic bishops and the Pope for a restructuring of the economy and "the human primacy of the human person in the productive process." He pointed to the worsening unemployment, farm foreclosures, the growing incidence of suicide and wife-battering, and raised once again the death of a young native boy, Richard Cardinal, who had taken his life after setting down in his diary an unbearable description of his abuse by the foster care system in Alberta. For Notley and many other people the boy's suicide and his testament were a much more compelling indicator of a society's basic decency and its moral purpose than the Premier's smug recitation of big projects, White Papers and drilling statistics.

Notley looked across the aisle at a front bench of complacent, smirking Cabinet ministers and angrily put the blame for the boy's suicide, not on overworked social workers, but on Lougheed's government: ". . . the tragedy of Richard Cardinal is an indictment of a process for which this government is responsible." To which an honourable Conservative member shouted, "Where were his parents?"[5]

On the evening of the next day, October 19, 1984, Notley and five other people died in a plane crash near Lesser Slave Lake.

The ten essays which follow were written some months after Notley's death as a tribute to the man, and a number of them were discussed at a small conference at the University of Alberta in the Fall of 1985. They deal with Grant Notley's public life; the Alberta CCF and the origins of the NDP; and the two central themes of Notley's vocation in politics—socialism and democracy in Alberta. If in places their tone appears sharply critical of the NDP and of social democracy generally, readers should know that they were not written to celebrate or to justify particular politicians or policies. The unsentimental treatment of Grant Notley in several of the chapters is entirely in keeping with the man's wry and flinty realism, and it can also be seen as an attempt by the writers to respect his own determination to face the music. There are, said Albert Camus, some people who prefer to look their destiny straight in the eye.

---

[1]Henry Kreisel, "The Broken Globe," in *The Almost Meeting and Other Stories*, (Edmonton, 1981), pp. 146-7.

[2]"A Call to Action," Address of William Irvine to the First Annual Convention of CCF Clubs, Edmonton, July 14-15, 1936.

[3]John A. Irving, *The Social Credit Movement in Alberta*, (Toronto, 1959), pp. 263-4.

[4]Wm. Aberhart, *Social Credit Manual: Social Credit as applied to the Province of Alberta*, (Calgary, 1935), p. 43. In reply to the question: "What if a citizen squandered his dividends and was hungry or improperly clothed?" Aberhart wrote: "The Credit House Inspector would warn the citizen that he was abusing his rights and privileges and that it must be stopped or he would lose his dividends. If necessary, he would be put on an Indian list." In other words, he would lose his citizenship.

[5]*Alberta Hansard*, October 18, 1984, pp. 1204-5.

Chapter 1

Grant Notley: Politics as a Calling

Larry Pratt

The first thing you had to understand was that if he was a socialist—and the jury's still out on that one—he was a *prairie* socialist. His roots were in the West, and it was in Alberta that he would fight for what he called the renaissance of the progressive movement of farmers and workers. His heroes were men such as J.S. Woodsworth and William Irvine, two of the greatest leaders of the western progressive movement whose portraits had pride of place in his office on the main floor of the Alberta Legislature. He admired their commitment and idealism and shared their love of parliamentary debate, but the renaissance he had in mind was not so much a resurrection of their policies as it was an effort to recapture their state of mind—their thirst for knowledge, their love of culture, their commitment to democratic politics. Of Irvine he remarked that "Bill would stand and be counted whether the public acclaimed him as a hero, or condemned him as a menace to society" (it was frequently the latter), and it was fitting that Grant Notley would open his maiden speech in the Legislature by evoking the name of the founder of the democratic socialist movement in Alberta, almost as if he was trying to conjure up the spirit of the progressives and the early CCF and to banish the reactionary ideas which had ruled the province since 1935. If and when he retired from active politics—and who could imagine that?—he said he planned to immerse himself in the sources and write the history of the progressive movement in Alberta.

That rather nostalgic image of pre-Social Credit Alberta was never allowed to stand in the way of the job of building a modern social democratic party run by professionals. He was a full-time party man, not a dilettante, and for him the New Democratic Party was not an extension of the old CCF alliance of agrarian populists and urban intellectuals; it was a different organization reflecting changing social and political circumstances. Speaking in his role as provincial secretary to the 1964 Alberta NDP convention, he called on the party to "abandon many of the old practices" when formulating organizational plans." "Forty years ago," he said, "a meeting called in the local schoolhouse or town hall would attract the whole neighbourhood. Today, public meetings are generally poorly attended, and at times so few people turn out that meetings must be cancelled. The decline of the public meeting merely serves to illustrate one essential point, in the sixties we must take our message to the people, not wait in a vain hope that they will come to us."[1]

Notley was a professional career politician who combined in modest measure the three qualities which Max Weber deemed essential to politics as a calling: passion, responsibility and a sense of proportion. He also possessed a fourth attribute, a sense of humor, without which progressive individuals soon wither in Alberta's reactionary climate. "Not summer's bloom lies ahead of us, but rather a polar night of icy darkness and hardness." For Notley, politics as a vocation meant the ruthless subordination of every facet of his private life to the building of a party machine oriented to electoral success. Winning wasn't everything, but it was the first thing. As Bill Irvine had put it: "Our first objective is to attain power. The first step in that direction is organization."

Within the party and the social democratic movement generally, he was known as a man who always looked for the unifying principle. That found its origins mainly in his temperament which was tolerant of divergent views, but it also stemmed from the situation of the Alberta NDP: a small social democratic formation operating in a deeply conservative province and fighting against overwhelming legislative majorities. Alberta's "quasi-party" system imposed its own limits: the party could not afford sectarian divisions, nor could it risk isolating itself from the federal NDP—despite the intermittent tensions between the western regionalists and the urban social democrats of Ontario. As a leader Notley practiced integrative politics, and he had the gift of involving people—trade unionists, farmers, professionals—and making them feel they were important to the coalition he was building. He could be utterly Machiavellian in running the party's affairs and, as will be seen, the Alberta NDP left much to be desired as a democratic organization. And yet Notley did not conceive of politics simply as a struggle for power and domination. Power was based on co-operation: it came into being when people would get together and bind themselves through reciprocal pledges and covenants. Legitimate power was based on mutuality and community, and it was the calling of the politician to build the coalitions that could bring a progressive society into being.

These three themes—his western progressive roots, his vocation as a professional politician, and his practice of integrative politics—are fundamental to understanding Grant Notley and the party he shaped. His perceptions and political ideas shifted over the years in response to changing circumstances, but from the date of his entry into politics in the late 1950's until his death in 1984 there is an underlying continuity to the man's thought and actions. In his vocation he sought to gain and use political power; yet he was not a vulgarian seeking power for its own sake. There was a purpose to his political life, a sense of service behind his tenacious ambition.

Building the New Party

The Alberta CCF never recovered from the debacle of 1935 when William Aberhart's Social Credit movement, drawing upon a blend of religious fundamentalism, ideas of monetary reform and appeals to mass psychological needs, swept the ruling United Farmers of Alberta into oblivion. The UFA and the labour parties failed to gain a single seat. The CCF was badly compromised in the voters' eyes through its associations with the UFA, a conservative farmer's government beset with scandals and seemingly helpless in the face of the worsening Depression. The argument that the CCF's defeat in 1935 was an "accident of history" caused by a series of contingent events and circumstances that might easily have been otherwise is totally unconvincing. Social Credit was a powerful mass movement well before it entered politics: it combined strong leadership, the skillful use of radio and propaganda, and a province-wide grass roots organization that reached into every community in Alberta. Resembling the religious sect from which it sprang, Social Credit offered a sense of psychological meaning to lower middle class people and farmers ravaged by the Depression, and this combined with the pledge of monthly dividends promised immediate relief; against this the CCF held out the post-millenial earthly kingdom of the Regina Manifesto—a document which a chastened Bill Irvine in 1936 described as sound, impregnable and magnificent as the Rock of Gibraltar, and every bit as useless. "An effective program must reach the people where they are living."[2]

Foremost among CCF organizers who took to the dusty roads and back-lanes of Alberta during and after the Depression to "reach the people where they are living" was Nellie Peterson, a formidable socialist and women's activist from a farm community north-west of Edmonton. Of Peterson—with whom he had many political differences—Grant Notley remarked that, "Nellie was a person who would have made an absolutely outstanding member of the legislature and was one of the people in the old CCF who had the ability to have actually been premier of the province. I think very few of them did, but Nellie had the ability to be premier."[3] The voters were less impressed. She ran in several elections but never won—in 1944 the CCF expected a major breakthrough and Peterson's riding was considered a sure thing, but even her farm neighbours couldn't bring themselves to vote against Social Credit.

She organized for the CCF north of the Red Deer line, concentrating on the farm communities and the towns where one could expect to find left-wing labour and ethnic groups. Peterson developed pockets of CCF support in the Peace River country (insulated by distance from Aberhart's radio broadcasts), in Vegreville, Lac St. Anne, Redwater, and the Edson-Hinton-Jasper region—generally the same areas where the NDP has done relatively well since 1963. Edmonton, especially in the north-east region around the big packing plants—now largely closed—was good CCF territory, given the modified system of proportional representation used then in provincial elections. But organizing against Social Credit was like chiselling through granite, and Peterson learned to focus on those who were well enough off that they could take the longer view:

> Generally I went around and picked out the nicest looking homes and barns that there were in the area and knocked on the door, told them who I was, that I was having a meeting in the area that evening, and that's where I got the response from. I never went to the rundown places. I learned from experience that they were Social Credit. I couldn't make a dent on them. But the well-to-do farmers: I wasn't very often disappointed. Why? Because generally speaking I think they didn't need a party that promised them immediate relief. They were not the people who had wanted twenty-five dollars a month so badly that they could taste it . . . . The CCF was never able to say, Tomorrow we'll have everything fixed.[4]

Nellie Peterson, who became provincial secretary of the CCF, Irvine, Chester Ronning, Elmer Roper, Floyd Johnson and others waged an uphill struggle against a regime which used religion, Cold War ideology and the prosperity of oil to maintain its hegemony. The CCF never succeeded in electing more than two members to the Alberta Legislature, and through the 1950s membership declined and the party came to seem less and less relevant to progressive people. The leadership of the CCF, disappointed by years of defeat, took less and less interest in provincial affairs and spent most of their time on international relations—the Cold War, Korea, the nuclear arms race, and Canada's involvement in alliances such as NATO. It was to their credit that they insisted that these were legitimate issues for provincial politicians to debate (although Irvine was the antithesis of a parochial provincialist), and the brand of socialist internationalism being preached by the Alberta CCF was more far-sighted than the hackneyed anti-communism then being peddled by David Lewis and the national party. However, there was more than a little truth in Gad Horowitz's assertion that the Alberta CCF had by the late Fifties "declined into a powerless sect with minimal support from both farmers and workers," and "was controlled by exponents of a brand of socialism so extreme that it made most British Columbia 'leftists' seem mildly liberal. The leadership's relationship with the CCF unionists in the province was neither close nor friendly."[5]

Leaving aside the alleged "extreme" brand of socialism being advocated in Alberta, it is perfectly true that relations between the CCF and labour were based on mutual mistrust. The Alberta CCF, like the Saskatchewan and Manitoba sections of the party, reflected an agrarian petit-bourgeois attitude to organized labour and "union bosses." Labour was right-wing and backward, the argument went, and the trade unionists would seek to dominate any political grouping by using bloc voting and other tactics. The party leadership, in Alberta and elsewhere, feared a watering down of the CCF's socialism; which the unionists invariably referred to as "doctrinaire socialism." Few of the leading labour men in the province were active in the CCF, believing it to be more interested in the future of the Soviet Union than that of Alberta. They dismissed the CCF leaders as "armchair socialists" who enjoyed losing elections. One prominent unionist recalled dropping in on Woodsworth House in downtown Edmonton, the CCF's headquarters, on elections night in 1959 when the party lost its two seats and dropped to five per cent of the popular vote. There sat the socialist leaders of Alberta happily playing bridge and telling their visitor that "the people of Alberta will vote for socialism when the time arrives." These tensions between labour and the CCF were by no means confined to Alberta: they existed in every province and were especially sharp wherever the farmers controlled the party. Neil Reimer, the tough realist who organized for the International Oil Workers Union in Saskatchewan and later moved to Alberta to head the Oil, Chemical and Atomic Workers, (OCAW), took the view that agrarian legislators were not so much anti-labour as incapable of understanding the gulf between farm life and that of the industrial labourer. "I understood the difference: the work ethic on the farm, and then all of a sudden you had somebody between your own philosophies and God. And that's the boss, who now assigned your values to you."

At a CCF National Council in early 1956 Tommy Douglas warned that the movement must be deepened and broadened. The core of socialist activists must reach out to the labour congresses, the farm unions and other groups, or perhaps merge in a new alignment of the left; otherwise, "we will continue to be a diminishing group, a small well-respected, highly-thought-of minority, with increasingly less influence."[6] Labour was a main target in broadening the base of the social democratic left, and at the founding convention of the Canadian Labour Congress in 1956 (at which the Trades and Labour Congress of Canada and the Canadian Congress of Labour merged) the call went out for a "new party: comprised of CCF activists, labour, farm organizations and other liberally-minded people." Discussions continued between top-level CLC and CCF officials, but it was not until the massive Diefenbaker sweep of March 1958—in which the CCF held just eight of its twenty-five seats in Parliament—that the final decision was taken to transform the CCF into a broadly-based, labour-oriented party. "It was the culmination of some twenty-five years of effort on the part of David Lewis, above all, to make the CCF into a Canadian version of the British Labour party."[7] A new party resolution was enthusiastically endorsed at the 1958 CLC convention, and Stanley Knowles, who had lost his parliamentary seat, was elected to the executive of the Congress. It was Knowles and CCF national secretary Carl Hamilton who headed up the National Committee of the New Party, which initiated seminars, forums and conferences across the country at which CCFers, unionists, and "liberally-minded" persons could debate the idea and aims of the new party. The so-called liberally-minded were encouraged to join New Party Clubs, which sprang up like dandelions in every province—much to the alarm of the CCF.

These were the changing political circumstances on the left when Grant Notley, a young history student at the University of Alberta, became involved with the CCF after 1958. Notley was born in Didsbury, about fifty miles north of Calgary, and was raised on a dairy farm in the Westerdale district west of the town of Olds. This was hardly fertile ground for socialism—Olds-Didsbury remained stubbornly Social Credit until 1982 when it sent Alberta's first separatist MLA to the Legislature—but Notley's father, Walter, was active in the Farmer's Union of Alberta and the co-operative movement and his mother, Frances Grant Notley, was a school-teacher in the area for many years. They may have voted CCF but—as Nellie Peterson used to tease

Notley—they were never members; and, Notley would retort, there was no active CCF organization in the area. In any event, it was probably not Olds and Didsbury that he was thinking of when he evoked the western progressive tradition in his later speeches.

What issues drew him into politics? The Cold War, disarmament and the peace movement: these were (and still are) the great political problems of the day, and it seems plain that Notley was attracted to the CCF because it was that party's leadership that was taking the clearest stand on international problems. In 1958, his second year at university, he and his close friend, Keith Wright, and a handful of other socialist students reactivated the Campus CCF Club and then set up the Edmonton CCF Youth and the Alberta Young CCF. Notley was the acknowledged leader of this small but growing band of activists, and even then his organizing abilities were impressive. He was a rather awkward public speaker who had to memorize his speeches to overcome a stutter, but he had the gift of mobilizing people and keeping them active; and he knew how to "count noses" before a vote was taken, and when to back off in the face of a divisive issue. It was said of him after he became provincial secretary of the NDP that if Notley was in the hospital and the executive voted to send flowers, he would somehow finesse a seven-six split.

While Notley grew critical of the Alberta CCF leaders, especially Irvine and Peterson, for giving up on provincial politics and spending too much time on international affairs (he and others also felt that Irvine was much too indulgent of the Soviet Union), the young CCFers were equally caught up in world politics. Like the student generations who followed them, they marched for peace and disarmament, demanded South Africa's expulsion from the United Nations, protested nuclear weapons tests and argued over whether Canada should be in NORAD and NATO. Notley sported a large peace button on his coat and always began his speeches with an appeal for money for Norman Alcock's Canadian Peace Research Institute. He disliked the Cold War and the conservative climate which accompanied it, but as he pointed out in the Campus CCF newspaper, *The Progressive Student*, the challenge of peaceful co-existence—"this new war of economics"—posed a real threat to the West. "The supreme confidence of Soviet leaders is not without reason, for the picture of capitalism in peacetime is a dreary landscape, blemished by many an inflation, and scarred by countless catastrophic depressions." To the challenge from Russia, "we in the CCF say, 'Let's institute Democratic Socialism!'" And what, to him, was

Democratic Socialism? It involved "social planning and above all, the realization that the rights of a few to make money must always be subordinate to the rights of the people as a whole." If that was socialism, it was a rather tepid, inoffensive version that posed no threat to that "dreary landscape" of capitalism.

Notley had a single-minded preoccupation with politics, and it left certain facets of his personality somewhat undernourished. He and his best friends, Keith and Kathy Wright, went out to see Hitchcock's *Psycho* and he sat there, while everybody around him was screaming and crawling under their seats, and he finally asked in a bored voice: What's all the excitement about, this thing has no political message. They socialized a lot but the activity always had a political aim: they were the Young Pioneers of the Alberta left. They discovered that the CCF owned an old property down at Mulhurst on Pigeon Lake, and so they spent many summer Sundays down there swimming, building camp-fires and singing the standard left-wing songs. The others would wince at Notley's off-key rendition of the labour anthem, "The Worker's Flag is Deepest Red", which he had laundered to "The Worker's flag is deepest pink/It's not as red as some folks think." At Mulhurst Notley first met the future premier of Manitoba, Howard Pawley, who was then a leading opponent of the new party movement. But Notley spent much of his time at the beach trying to keep everyone's mind off sex, segregating the men and women, and warning them that the movement had to maintain a clean image. There was always a strong puritan streak in Notley, common among prairie politicians, that rather disapproved of people who did things like go on holidays or spend time with their families when they could be doing political work. And then there was his attitude to money. In a word, he was cheap. He simply hated spending money on things like clothes and shoes: and it showed. In the early Sixties Notley visited the Wrights, then living in Montreal, and the three of them went out to a night-club. The Wrights paid for the drinks, leaving the standard tip for the waiter, and this set Notley off on a lengthy harangue against the evils of tipping: it encouraged the employers to exploit their staff by paying minimal wages. Notley finally offered to pay for a round and paid the waiter, who had heard the lecture, and in a gesture of fraternal solidarity added a dime for a tip. The waiter looked at the dime, gave it back to Notley and said, "Sir, I really think you need this more than I do."

Notley was enthusiastically behind the movement for the new party, and this was to isolate him from the left-wingers who ran the provincial CCF. They referred to him as an opportunist and "a pimply youth with backward ideas," but his view was that the CCF had given up on serious political activity and had become a debating society and bridge club. He called them "the 7th Street bridge clique" (Woodsworth house, headquarters of the Alberta CCF, was located on 107th Street in downtown Edmonton), and his principal criticism of them was that they appeared positively to *enjoy* losing elections and telling one another that conditions were not ripe for democratic socialism in Alberta. If you campaigned on *that* as a platform, you could bet you'd lose elections. It was not so much that the CCF leadership had lost touch with the membership; the membership had atrophied. Most of the constituency associations were inactive. Notley was more impressed with the arguments of men such as Reimer or Ivor Dent, both of whom were ex-Saskatchewan CCF and took the view that politics means organization. Every cause requires a machine. Dent, like Reimer, was to play a major role in building the new party in Alberta, and subsequently became the party's president from 1963 to 1968 (and then mayor of Edmonton). "When we came here from Saskatchewan," Dent recalled, "we found there was no organizational aspect of politics in the CCF. People sat down and they philosophized. We found after a considerable time that they resented us terribly because we wanted to disturb them . . . and begin to be active and organize constituencies and polls."[8]

Notley often talked about political clout; you didn't have to be the government, but to have influence over policies and decisions you needed leverage. That entailed the "organizational aspect," the building of a strong party machine. And it was this, and not an interest in policy or program, that became his *raison d'etre* and the focal point of his vocation in politics. In the debate over party vs. movement, he came down on the side of the machine:

> You know, there are people who think the emphasis should be on the movement element, and there are others who say, "No," you know, "a movement is only effective if it has some political muscle." There are other movements on the left too, that really are marginal because they have no political muscle. The NDP or the CCF has only been effective when it has some political muscle. During the 1940's for example, the party had a great influence on Mackenzie King because it had the clout to be effective. I don't think that was necessarily true as much in Alberta in the last stages, because when the party in 1959 got—what, 5% of the vote? . . . the kind of things we talked about didn't influence the opinion leaders very much because they didn't see us as a relevant force. You've

got to be able to scare the dickens out of the other side in order to get them to see the light. And so that's where the political aspects, the partisanship, the building of a machine come into play in my judgment.[9]

Notley was actively involved in the new party movement from about 1959 until May of 1961 when—to his everlasting credit—he left Law School at the University of Alberta and went to work as a provincial organizer for the National Committee of the New Party; after the national founding convention of the New Democratic Party, he kept organizing for the NDP until the founding convention of the provincial NDP in January, 1962.

Notley's task as New Party organizer was to attract people to the right of the CCF into New Party Clubs while keeping communists out. His correspondence with the national office shows that he spent an inordinate amount of time worrying over alleged communists who might be entering the Alberta clubs. In the Crowsnest Pass, for example, where there was a real potential for the New Party to expand, the communists still had a strong organization; but Notley had arranged for the local United Church minister "to be a watchdog, and report to the office any moves the local communists make in regard to the New Party." In Calgary, where the Rev. Ed Mullen was the dominant force in the New Party movement, there was concern over the past communist activities of Pat Lenihan, a Vice-President of the Alberta Federation of Labour and one of the key unionists in the province. Lenihan was viewed by Notley as the most popular New Party person in Alberta, with powerful friends in the union movement, and not somebody to mess with— openly. "After conferring with Reverend Mullen, we both agreed that a witch hunt would be both undesirable and at the same time unsuccessful. Knowing the character of the Alberta movement, I'm sure you will agree that a witch hunt would only backfire. However, I have decided to follow Reverend Mullen's advice and let a few people know of the doubts raised about Pat. This will be done with extreme caution."

Notley was fortunate indeed to find such decent men of the cloth to cleanse the New Party of heretics, but he fretted through the summer of 1961 over the delicate situation in Vegreville where a young director of the Farmers' Union of Alberta named Ted Chudyk was busily organizing New Party Clubs. "Chudyk has had communist connections in the past. He apparently has been a member of the World Federation of Democratic Youth, which, as you will no doubt recognize, is a communist dominated organization. He went to the World Peace Conference in 1956 . . . I learned that Chudyk is regarded locally as a communist.

Unfortunately, he is not a card-carrying member, nor has he taken any public role in the communist party itself. Consequently, it is almost impossible to prove that he is a communist." A month later Notley wrote that, after checking with the Reverend Mullen, he could find no evidence to confirm the rumours about Chudyk and he therefore reluctantly recommended that his credentials be accepted. "If Chudyk is genuine, as I am inclined to think he is, he could be an extremely valuable addition to our movement."[10]

Notley had powerful patrons in men such as David Lewis, Carl Hamilton, Reimer and other New Party supporters, and within the province he found allies among labour leader such as Henry Tomaschuck, formerly of the Packinghouse Workers and later a CLC representative, Roy Jamha of the OCAW, Howard Mitchell and Jim Russell of the Steelworkers, Norm Atkin of the Railway and Transport Workers, and Jack Hampson and Norm Riches of the very active Packinghouse Workers. Labour's support was spearheaded by Reimer's OCAW—he and Jamha and Pat Lenihan were among the most active union leaders behind the New Party—but there were key farm activists involved as well: Art Bunney, a yeoman farmer—radical and independent (and who much later became involved in the "Farmers for Peace" mission to socialist Nicaragua); Bob Carlyle, president of the CCF; and, above all, Ed Nelson, then president of the Farmers' Union of Alberta. The FUA had earned the lasting respect of Jamha and the Packinghouse workers in the late Forties during a bitter strike at one of the large Edmonton packing plants; the Social Credit government, trying to play farmer against worker, asked the FUA to arrange for strikebreakers. The FUA obliged by sending food and provisions to the strikers. Henry Young, founder and first president of the Farmers' Union, became active in the NDP and worked with Nelson and unionists such as Roy Jamha to promote farm-labour unity.

Notley's job was to help organize the so-called "liberally-minded people"—professionals, small businessmen, co-op and credit union workers—into the New Party Clubs. This was done via a series of seminars held around the province. Another New Party organizer, P.J. "Pat" Ryan, recalls that Notley did a lot of listening and not much talking at these meetings; that he was "very astute" and keenly interested in the process. Bill Irvine, however, was "very disturbed" at what he saw in the New Party Clubs because he could see "the middle class people smothering his socialist ideas."[11] Anti-labour sentiment was stronger in the liberal New Party Clubs than it was among the farm element. It was about this time that Irvine, dying of cancer and totally unrepentant in his radicalism, delivered a blistering attack on those who would sell the socialist principle down the river and settle for the "mixed economy": "Make no mistake. In a mixed economy the bank accounts of the wealthy will not be mixed with the bank accounts of the wage earners. . . . We may rest assured that as long as capitalism dominates the economy any mixture will be like the famous hamburger made from one horse and one rabbit."[12]

The Alberta CCF attacked the proliferating New Party Clubs, arguing, in Nellie Peterson's words, that "we are joined by an ever growing crowd of people who themselves are uncommitted to anything of a specific nature"; the purpose of the clubs, she protested to Carl Hamilton of the National Committee of the New Party, was "to move the new party right up to the edge of the old line parties." That was perfectly fair. Notley reported to Ottawa that he took the greatest pride in the Central Lethbridge club, a group of 40 ex-Social Creditors, "with a smattering of former Grits and Tories." The Alberta CCF caustically dismissed the NCNP's draft program as vague and meaningless—which was generous—but the party fatally weakened its critique by implying that the status quo was preferable to revitalization. Neil Reimer of OCAW was so angered by the provincial CCFers that he attempted to deny them the right to representation at the national founding convention.[13] It was a gratuitous gesture; the CCF was a spent force, and not just in Alberta.

Utterly disillusioned with developments, and particularly with the Ottawa national founding convention of the NDP in August, 1961 ("Nellie Peterson cried all the way home," one of her best friends remembered), the Alberta CCF dissolved itself and created the Woodsworth-Irvine Socialist Fellowship, devoted to socialist education and study. It represented a retreat into political irrelevance. Notley, who was prone to comparing the CCF to an old age pensioner's debating society, remained wary of Nellie Peterson, whom he never underestimated, and worried that she would remain in the NDP "and make a last-ditch effort" to control it. The CCF's assets, including Woodsworth House, were transferred to the WISF, not the NDP, and this deepened the split and also ensured that the new party would lack the grouping that was the very ideological base of the CCF. That was perfectly acceptable to Reimer and probably Notley, but as one critic noted: "The failure of this group to maintain an active and contributory role in the leadership of the NDP, in effect, resulted in an end to ideology in the political left of Alberta . . . and left the NDP in the hand of a new leadership—a leadership more concerned with organization and electoral success than with political education and socialist action at all levels of society."[14] Given the deep political rift, which was overlain by bitter personality feuds, no reconciliation was possible and it was not until the Seventies that the WISF was even permitted to affiliate with the NDP.

Notley and other New Party organizers set up about 65 New Party Clubs in Alberta by the time of the provincial founding convention in January, 1962. "The combined membership in these groups," Notley wrote to Ivor Dent, "is somewhere in the neighbourhood of a thousand people. Although some are from the CCF, the majority are new people."[15] The preponderance of labour and New Party people was much in evidence at the founding convention, held at the Macdonald Hotel in Edmonton on January 21-22, 1962: of a total of 379 delegates, 172 were labour, 93 from New Party Clubs, 85 from the CCF, and a few from youth and other. Although most rural ridings sent a single delegate, the composition of the convention was overwhelmingly urban: about one-third of the delegates were from Edmonton alone. Organized labour appeared to be firmly in the saddle.

Neil Reimer was chosen first president of the Alberta NDP, but no leader of the party was selected at the founding convention. There was still some lingering fear of "labour domination," and there was also some concern that one of the CCFers might run for the leadership. Finally, Ivor Dent, one of the most likely candidates for leader, was out of the country. So Reimer became *de facto* leader until 1963 when he defeated Dent at a leadership convention; he then led the party, and arguably led it tolerably well, for five difficult years. For most of that time he also acted as local director of his union, and it was the OCAW that paid Reimer's salary and expenses as NDP leader.

Reimer had made it known *in no uncertain terms* that he wanted Grant Notley in the key post of provincial secretary, but the CCFers wanted their man, Pat Ryan. At the first provincial council, held immediately after the convention, both men were nominated and sat outside the door while the storm raged within. This was, in effect, a trial of strength to determine whether the Reimer organization-electoral wing or the Peterson educational-movement side was going to run the party. There are several versions of what happened. Some say that a vote was taken and that Ryan won by a slim margin, and that it was overturned after Reimer threatened to quit. Others say that the council was split down the middle, that a good deal of arm-twisting ensued and that Ryan finally withdrew. All agree that Reimer made a strong "union boss" speech in which he refused to work with Ryan and demanded a vote in support of Notley. "I didn't make any friends that night," Reimer admitted. That Notley had earned the job is beyond question, but there is also no doubt that he owed Reimer.[16] One of the active unionists boasted of the weekend's struggle, "The CCF got skunked," while Notley wrote to his pal, Keith Wright, that the convention was an "outstanding success" and that "the 7th Street bridge clique has once and for all been annihilated."[17]

The Organizers

There had been no formal merger of the CCF with the NDP, and many of the former constituency associations had been inactive since the late 1940s or mid-1950s. Notley, Reimer and a few part-time organizers faced the mammoth task of building up federal and provincial constituencies, fighting the 1962 federal election, raising funds, planning the 1963 leadership convention, and doubling the party's membership from about 2,300 to 5,000. The NDP also had very ambitious plans to make a healthy contribution to the national party's "victory fund." But where was the money to come from?

They had a strange attitude to spending and fund-raising. Driven on by the manic enthusiasm of some of the organizers, who were always convinced that a "breakthrough" was imminent, the party tended to bankrupt itself in every provincial election. At that point the provincial office would be closed, organizers would be laid off, and the structure would atrophy while all available energy was poured into the reduction of the debt. On the other hand, Reimer wanted the NDP to project an aura of success, not the subsistence psychology of the CCF, and so conventions were held in the best hotels with all the trimmings. "We were out of the Dirty Thirties": even Nellie Peterson had to admit that Reimer was right. People wanted to dress up and have a party, not spend a weekend in some dowdy community hall discussing the difference between social democracy and democratic socialism. But it was not only the old lefties who were appalled by the way the party's executive spent money, always putting politics before book-keeping and running the party on credit.

The party qualified for a small annual subvention from the federal NDP, it received donations from the Alberta Federation of Labour, the

OCAW and several other affiliated unions, but it relied heavily on monthly deductions and donations from individual members. At one convention in the mid-1960s Ted Chudyk, who had just been appointed a full-time organizer with the NDP, was confronted by an enthusiastic little woman from Calgary named Irene Dyck. She congratulated him on his job, pressed a hundred dollar bill in his hand, and said, "Now, don't tell my husband."

"Doesn't he like the NDP?" asked Chudyk.

"Oh, of course he does. But if you don't tell him, you can get another hundred out of him." And she became one of Notley's greatest admirers and the party's most important benefactor in years to come.

Notley took up the question of finances, party organization and electoral strategy in a memorandum entitled "Four-Year Plan," which was presented to the provincial executive in January, 1964, and discussed at the annual convention in February. The document is vintage Notley and, curiously, is one of the very few actually written by him on the strategy of the party. The four-year plan was needed, he told the convention, for several reasons: first, planning was required "to boost morale among members and supporters"; endless appeals for money and memberships would "bear a small return, unless we convince supporters of this movement that we are planning for the future in a positive manner'; second, the plan was an attempt to focus attention on attainable goals, such as regular constituency meetings, increased membership and political education; third, the plan tried to integrate activities and delineate the responsibilities of the executive, council and convention; fourth, the plan set out a strategy for using the media; and, finally, he said, "I believe that the four-year plan offers more democratic control," adding however that such control would be exercised via the annual convention. In fact, the thrust of Notley's strategy would be to place more power, more discretionary control over organizational policy, electoral decisions and finances, in the hands of the leading members of the executive—sometimes known (in a phrase from union organization) as the "table officers." Far from suggesting a re-structuring of conventions into policy-making bodies rather than staged pep rallies or a process of making his own position and Reimer's accountable to provincial council and the convention, Notley proposed to centralize power and to make the party less democratic internally.

Many of Notley's specific targets and goals, set out in the four-year plan, had the specific purpose of strengthening his own provincial office. Though he cautioned that central planning should only set broad objectives and not undermine the autonomy and initiatives of local constituencies, most of his financial and policy proposals were intended to increase the authorities of the executive and his own office. For example, he agreed that the party must balance electoral activity with political education, but what was meant by "political education"? It meant the creation of a political action fund, with a budget of $30,000 by 1967, most of which would be devoted to television advertising. Control of the funds obviously would reside with provincial office. Political education, in short, would be from the top down to the membership via short TV messages. With the CCF obviously in mind he warned: "Endless discussion and philosophical debate, undisciplined by an accompanying responsibility to actively build and support the party is dangerous, for it may result in a party organization composed of people with little sense of political reality." You could develop a better sense of reality by turning on the TV set and waiting for a five-minute message from the leader.

He was brutally realistic in outlining the weaknesses of the party organization. "Our organizational picture in Alberta still represents a rather confused muddle, with a few people going in different directions. While certain differences may be inevitable, the extent of these differences at the moment is great enough that we must provide some form of definite leadership to straighten this out." The provincial constituency associations were a mixed lot: most of the rural ridings were inactive, while some of the urban constituencies were showing more initiative. But "few of our constituencies are showing much imagination in drawing up a program of interesting activities and events." Communications between the centre and the constituencies were unsatisfactory, and "there is no integration of activity" within the party, "no logical relationship between our financial year, membership year or constituency organizational year." And finally, the provincial office must be placed on a stable financial basis: it could not continue to operate on a feast or famine approach. "It is impossible to provide any form of intelligent, consistent planning on the central level, when subsistence has to be the order of the day."

Although Notley had identified a basic weakness in the party's structure that would outlast him—namely, the absence of involvement and commitment at the base or the constituency level, especially between elections—his remedies were almost entirely aimed at political and financial centralization. The result would be to reinforce the hierarchical and bureaucratic character of the NDP: real power was increasingly concentrated in the hands of a small party oligarchy, while the illusion of democratic accountability was sustained by the elaborate structure of party councils and the annual rituals at the convention. Thus he called for a large increase in the budget of his office so that full-time organizers and a director of research could be added to staff and a subsidiary office opened in Calgary. A major effort must be made to increase memberships and monthly donations—all of which would be dedicated to the regular income of provincial office. Control of all funds was to be tightly centralized. The electoral strategy outlined in the four-year plan was correctly based on the assumption of a provincial election in 1967. He viewed *federal* campaigns from a purely tactical standpoint, arguing that rather than attempting to win votes the NDP should use federal elections to sign up members and strengthen the provincial organization. "It is of paramount importance that we do not allow the demands of a federal campaign to undermine the effectiveness of our provincial constituency structure." The provincial election strategy would be "based on the theory of concentration within the framework of an all-out effort." This meant that, first, all constituencies must nominate candidates, if only to show the party colours and raise the overall vote; but, second, a number of concentrated or priority ridings would be selected for special organizing effort and money. In principle, the idea of focusing on key constituencies is sensible and obvious, especially for a small party with scarce resources, but the question arises: who decides and on what basis? Should there be a balance between urban and rural, or north and south; should those who give election donations, such as trade unions, have the right to designate a labour-oriented riding as a priority; suppose a party dissident is running in a priority constituency: is he or she entitled to special assistance? The answers are by no means self-evident. Notley put it this way, adding a small Stalinist flourish: the provincial council would, on the advice of the executive, choose half a dozen ridings for concentration. The criteria used in selecting the priority ridings would be past voting record, membership activity, and the relative strength of other parties. "Once the decision on constituencies is made, all members of the provincial council must accept the discipline imposed by this decision. Any attempt to disrupt the party, or to incite differences, will be dealt with by the provincial disciplinary committee." There was of course no such committee, but the party oligarchy had its own way of dealing with dissidents.

Notley loved being on the road organizing. He drove an old Plymouth, which was never washed and on which he logged more than

200,000 miles in those early years. There was no full-time organizer at
the time, and so Reimer and Notley drove from one end of the province
to the other—holding meetings, twisting the arms of potential candidates, and trying to set up constituency associations. "Some places we'd
only have one person coming out and he'd be a Social Crediter watching
us," recalled Reimer. "But I said to Grant, everything starts with one, so
we practiced our speeches in front of Social Crediters." Notley's heroes
were people who had "acquitted themselves well in the House of
Commons"—Woodsworth, Irvine, M.J. Coldwell. Reimer knew some
of these people and he also educated Notley about labour's problems
with the Saskatchewan CCF. The car trips were briefing sessions for
Notley. Reimer thought Notley was a fine organizer and that he had
phenomenal energy and endurance—"the only guy that ever tired me
out"—but he also felt that he lacked confidence because of the split in
the party. In the first year, before Reimer became the leader, Notley was
constantly being whip-sawed between the "outs" and the "ins": Reimer,
as party president, got tired of it and said, "Grant, don't call me
anymore. I'll keep the wolves off your back; you don't need to worry
that I'm going to sneak up behind you. Just do your job and I'll look
after the dissidents." That gave him confidence, thought Reimer, "and he
also knew that if there was a fight, the casualties would not only be on
our side." Reimer thought that "Grant had a great desire for recognition," and that his involvement in the NDP gave him "a lot of his thrust,
maturity and beliefs." But it did not do much for his appearance. His
scruffy green jacket was much shorter than his shirt sleeves, his pants
rode up below his knees, and his shoes were full of holes: "He hadn't got
what you would call natural charisma."[18] On the other hand, it was Notley, and not Reimer, who finally gained a voice for the New Democrats
in the Tory-dominated legislature.

The left-wing families of the Vegreville-Mundare-St. Paul area of
Alberta have made a splendid contribution to the progressive side of
prairie politics over the decades, but they overdid it when they sent Ken
Novakowski and Ted Chudyk into the NDP. They could hardly have
been more different—Novakowski the radical firebrand and conscience
of the socialist left, Chudyk the hyperactive organizer and bagman of
the party, the man who could settle the party's accounts with a bottle of
rye whiskey and a fresh deck of cards. They personified the "movement" and "organization" wings of the party, and they also shared a few
gifts. Both were masters of party in-fighting and knew how to count

noses as well as Notley. They were great organizers capable of instilling devotion and enthusiasm in the troops. They were activists and not intellectuals, although Novakowski was a clear-headed Marxist who was more than competent in theory. And both were suspected of being communists—falsely. Had it been true in Chudyk's case, it would have amounted to a terrible slander against Karl Marx.

Ted Chudyk came into the new party through his connections in the farm movement, and he was elected as one of the NDP's first vice-presidents at the 1963 leadership convention. Notley, according to Chudyk, orchestrated his election by playing up his farm union connections; the purpose of the maneuver was to defeat Nellie Peterson's candidacy and to remove her once and for all from any position of authority in party. The stratagem, which succeeded, was undoubtedly linked to Reimer's selection as leader and Notley's determination to consolidate their power.[19] Chudyk loved party intrigue almost as much as Notley, and he enjoyed watching the young party secretary at work on the convention floor—trying to defeat a resolution, say, in favour of nationalization of the oil industry—or counting noses at provincial council. "He didn't care whether he won unanimously or by one vote. He just counted noses and if the noses were short it would be amazing how that meeting got delayed and delayed until somebody drove up from Calgary."

People were always wondering where Chudyk got his money, but there was no big mystery. When he first got out of school he and a friend took a winter to follow the prairie curling circuit all the way from Calgary to Whitehorse. After a bonspiel was over, the cards and a few bottles of whiskey would come out: the farmers usually had sneaked two or three hundred dollars out of their bank accounts for the poker games that followed the curling. Chudyk's pal was supposed to keep bidding the pot up, and Chudyk would take it: simple as that, they didn't cheat. They netted about $2,000 per night, and when the tour was over Chudyk took a trip to Europe, bought himself a turkey farm and put $10,000 in the bank. He was a fiend with a deck of cards, and he subsequently earned an international reputation as a poker player. He also had a shrewd eye for real estate and investment: was there something wrong in being a *rich* social democrat?

Chudyk was fanatical about the need for organizing (by which he meant signing up people and emptying their wallets). After a few drinks he would tell Notley that they should sign up fifty per cent of the population plus one and go for union certification; forget about elections. He and two other organizers went on salary with Notley's office in 1966, and memberships went up sharply in the next two years. But the organizers were mostly signing up members and raising money for central office, and little attention was given to building a strong grass roots organization. Ken Novakowski was not unfair when he said later that, "the high membership is largely indicative of the hard work of Provincial Secretary Grant Notley and his team of organizers since the staff enlargement in early 1966. However, the high membership figures are no indication of the organization of the party across the province. Memberships went up, particularly in rural Alberta, as organizers crossed the province raising money for the central party office so that their salaries and expenses might be met. In few cases did the organizers leave behind functioning constituency organizations." Novakowski linked the absence of a strong grass roots organization to the dominance of the four table officers on the executive—Reimer, party president Ivor Dent, Notley and treasurer Roy Jamha—and he argued that the top-heavy structure of the party was responsible for the NDP's lack of a coherent and progressive ideology. "Acquiring power, without the support of a strong, conscious grass roots movement will mean very little if the NDP hopes to bring any changes to the social and economic structure of Alberta."[20]

During the long, wearying car trips criss-crossing the province with Neil Reimer, Ted Chudyk and others, Notley's mental landscape was shaped in subtle ways by the society and its geography. His contact with Alberta's physical and social environment moved and matured him, leaving him with an abiding sense of obligation to the place and its people. Though he disliked the hegemony of conservative beliefs which he encountered throughout the province, he seldom questioned the authenticity of those beliefs or disparaged the individuals who held them. In truth, Notley himself was a conservative man shaped by a conservative society in certain fundamental ways: in his conception of a decent political and moral community; in his notion of civic duty as a virtue; and in his implied view of legitimate power as something that came from citizens acting in concert through political associations. The purpose of a party was to integrate, to help people "act in concert"; power corresponded to the human capacity not just to act but to act collectively. He might well have agreed with Edmund Burke, "that no men could act with effect, who did not act in concert; that no men could act in concert, who did not act with confidence; that no men could act with confidence, who were not bound together by common opinions, common affections, and common interests." Notley had a strong aversion to political abstractions and seems to have believed that the improvement of the human condition depends in the first instance upon the creation of a community. "The human being who has lost his place in a community, his political status in the struggle of his time, and the legal personality which makes his actions and part of his destiny a consistent whole, is left with those qualities which usually can become articulate only in the sphere of private life and must remain unqualified, mere existence in all matters of public concern."[21]

Organizing this community involved ventures into unorthodoxy. In spite of his well-known aversion to parting with his own money, Notley could usually be inveigled by Chudyk or one of the other organizers into a political bet. The prize was a bottle of Canadian Club, and the bet typically involved a test of the organizing skills of Notley and his comrades. One boring afternoon Chudyk challenged Notley: Grant should choose a poll, any poll, and Chudyk would sign up at least fifty per cent of the people he was able to contact. Knowing this was ludicrous, Notley accepted the bet and chose a rural poll near Mayerthorpe, north-west of Edmonton, in which the NDP had collected exactly two votes in the previous election. Chudyk had never set foot in the poll, but the party did have a friendly contact in the district and it was agreed that he would accompany 'the red from Vegreville' on his mission, if only to protect him from the solidly Social Credit farmers.

They set off down the road early Monday morning and before long were in sight of the first farm. Chudyk ordered his friend to turn into the lane.

"We can't stop here," he was warned. "The woman who lives here is the secretary of the Social Credit League."

Chudyk could feel the panic rising, but there was no way out. The terms of the wager demanded that he call on every farm. So in they went. The old couple, in traditional prairie fashion, invited the men in for coffee, and as they sat around the kitchen table Chudyk told them of his great admiration for Social Credit and Mr. Aberhart. If he, Chudyk, had been a young man in 1935, he would have worked for Social Credit, too. The farmers of Alberta were right to throw out the U.F.A. and to vote for radical change. But—and here there was a long pause—what had Mr. Aberhart's movement turned into? What was Social Credit in the Sixties? There were some very highly-placed politicians getting wealthy while they held office. They had their deals with the oil companies and the banks—why the same banks that Mr. Aberhart had denounced!—but what were they doing for the average person, for the farmers? Chudyk allowed that he was not against religion, but he had the feeling that Social Credit was now using the gospel to protect their privileged position and to prevent change. Now, all the NDP was attempting to do was to improve the lot of the small farmers and the working people . . . and suddenly Chudyk noticed that the old man was nodding his head in vigorous agreement.

"I don't care what you do," said the old farmer to his wife. "I'm signing up with these fellows."

"Well," said the secretary of the Social Credit League, "now that you mention it, I think I will, too."

For his part, Neil Reimer was preoccupied after 1963 with a political strategy for the annihilation of Ernest Manning's Social Credit regime. Reimer, who detested Manning, was perfectly prepared to sacrifice his own political career in order to begin the destruction of Social Credit; and it must be said that he advanced his objective and also paid the price. Reimer held the view that Alberta was a closed society, that it had all the markings of the fascist concept: in his speeches he frequently compared Social Credit to the inefficient but brutal one-party states of Latin America. Manning held power by encouraging apathy on the part of the electorate, by gerrymandering in favour of the rural areas, and above all through the manipulation of religious values. The image projected by Manning and his Cabinet ministers was that they could do no wrong because they had been anointed by God; that they got their strength from the Bible, and it was blasphemous to criticize them.

Reimer, who was more than competent in class analysis, did not confuse the ideological and political hegemony of Social Credit with a homogenous or single-class society. He sharply criticized any suggestion that Alberta's social structure lacked the usual cleavages of a capitalist system: "We have a very strong establishment who rule and will stop at nothing in order to continue that rule. Their motto: 'Socialism for the wealthy, but private enterprise for the poor.' We have a much larger middle class than ever before. We have thousands upon thousands who have a marginal and sub-marginal existence. They have no say; they have no union; they have no organization; they do not feel a sense of participation." Organized labour and the progressive farmers, acting politically through the NDP, had to mobilize this large pool of disenfranchised men and women. But the first step was to re-establish democracy in Alberta: the heavy smog of fear and apathy that had seeped into all walks of life must be blown away and replaced by free thoughts, free speech and free political exchange.

In plainer language, Reimer intended to blow the bastards out of office and he was not fussy or about to lose any sleep over the methods. Through his large number of contacts in the labour movement, he began to acquire information concerning the business and other affairs of Social Credit cabinet ministers, including the pious Manning. He found some friends in high places and he even boasted that he had infiltrated the Cabinet. Power, he discovered, ran from Manning's office directly to the deputy ministers. Reimer suggested publicly that people in high public office should divulge their corporate interests and business dealings, but the shocked Premier replied that such action would imply that someone was crooked. When Reimer subsequently informed the provincial council of his plan of attack, the few remaining ex-CCFers protested and reminded him of what had happened to the Liberals after their mudslinging attacks on UFA Premier John Brownlee in 1934—Aberhart had wiped them off the political map. Manning was held in high respect, especially in rural Alberta, and a strategy of muckraking and personal attacks would harm, not advance, the struggle for socialism. But Reimer repeated that he was prepared to sacrifice his own career to attack "the establishment of this Province" and, as he put it in 1968: "If this Party and its leadership cannot speak out against corruption; against the rape of this Province; abuse of office, then we will also be very unconvincing that we have the guts to establish the policies and programs that we want for Canada and Alberta."[22] That was Reimer— the tough uncompromising street-fighter who gave no quarter, expected none in return, and never apologized for his actions.

If Neil Reimer's tactics were debatable, his analysis of Social Credit and the political economy of Alberta was fundamentally sound. His was by no means the only voice decrying what one newspaper called the "total extinction of democratic government in the province."[23]

A Calgary editorialist noted in 1964 that to the dedicated Social Crediter "government is not a matter of giving expression to the free play of variegated social and political forces. It is nothing more than a form of corporate authoritarianism administered by infallible leadership." Under Social Credit's blend of "business-like" government and quasi-fascist ideology, the voters had developed a "superstitious fear" of voting for another party. Such was the influence wielded by the "strange, almost mystic ideology" of Social Credit. It might be that "just short of total submersion in totalitarianism" the people of Alberta would restore democracy to the province, but to do this they would have to "heighten their sense of vigilance lest their democratic rights be eroded beyond the point of no return before they decide to act."[24] This was precisely's Reimer's point, as it was to become Notley's theme from 1971 to 1984. Without an open, democratic political system, there could be no progressive movement in Alberta; and it was this, not just electoral expediency, that led both leaders to stress the "democratic" side of democratic socialism.

In March of 1965, Reimer came within ninety votes of gaining a seat in the Legislature when he ran in the Edson by-election. The Edson constituency sprawls westward to Hinton and Jasper and contains a fairly large body of organized labourers. Union men, particularly the railroaders from Jasper and Reimer's own OCAW, poured into Edson, and every labour family in the district was press-ganged into active duty. In his speeches Reimer pressed for a higher minimum wage and called for an opposition voice in the Legislature; all Social Credit members, he remarked caustically, were used to thinking alike but few could think for themselves. On the eve of the election, Manning arrived in Edson to promise the voters a pulp mill, but the Social Credit candidate was soundly trounced. The Liberals won, and after the celebrations were underway somebody tied a coffin to the back of his car and dragged it around the town of Edson. On the coffin appeared the unkind inscription, "Rest in Peace Neil Reimer." The Jasper railroaders took exception and there ensued a dust-up which was seen by some as a small setback for the forces of reaction.

If Edson was a near miss for the NDP, the Pincher Creek-Crowsnest by-election in October, 1966, was a major turning-point for the party, Notley, and—in a number of ways—the political development of Alberta. Pincher Creek set off a chain of events that helped set the forces of change in motion; forces that would eventually undermine the Old Order of Social Credit and sweep Peter Lougheed's Conservatives into power. The New Democrats played a part in this by attacking Manning, but in so doing they discredited their own approach, and Lougheed was waiting to grab the brass ring. They then compounded their problems by insisting that the Conservatives were, after all, merely an updated version of Manning's party.

Pincher Creek, lying in the south-west section of Alberta, was a long way from the traditional strongholds of CCF-NDP support—all of which lay north of the Red Deer line: Edmonton, the Peace River country, Vegreville, etc. The NDP had just 31 members in Pincher Creek-Crowsnest at the time of the by-election, but the decision was taken to make an all-out organizing effort to win the seat for the party's candidate, Pincher Creek lawyer Garth Turcott. The NDP was thought by some media observers to be gaining ground on Social Credit and another strong showing in a by-election could influence voter psychology in the coming provincial election. But more importantly, Notley and his organizers wanted to use Pincher Creek as a laboratory in which they could test the new door-to-door canvassing techniques, the debriefing, recording and polling methods which were being used in other sections of the NDP. They could lose the by-election, as one of the organizers put it, but they would not lose the experience.

Ted Chudyk, who organized for the NDP all across the country, recalls Pincher Creek as the model: "the only perfect campaign I've been involved with." The NDP's Prairie Organizer, Clarence Lyons, was brought in from Saskatchewan to run the campaign and Notley and his organizers were each assigned different parts of the riding. Notley was given Coleman, Chudyk was responsible for Blairmore, Ken Kerr had the Frank area, and so on. The competition among the organizers, particularly between Chudyk and Notley, was fierce; their reputations were on the line and Chudyk was of the view that anyone who lost his poll should throw himself on his sword. Intensive door-to-door canvassing had rarely been used in Alberta elections—the voters were used to waiting for a heavenly sign from the Premier—and the reaction was one of bewilderment. Chudyk, who was really running against Notley rather than the other parties, had his canvassers contact each voter four times: the first reaction was disbelief; the second time it was: "Buzz off you guys!"; the third contact was often greeted with: "You guys are really serious, aren't you?"; and the last response was: "Hell yes, we're with you." Two observers of these techniques who were impressed with what they saw were Joe Clark, a Conservative organizer, and the new leader of the provincial Conservative party, Peter Lougheed. Lougheed learned a good deal from the NDP's organizing methods in Pincher Creek, and then applied it in the next two provincial elections; Lougheed's canvassers *ran* between houses, they wore three-piece polyester suits, and they smiled a lot. Have a nice day and so forth.

Reimer worked on convincing the large Hutterite colonies near Pincher Creek that their traditional rejection of politics and voting was against their interests. Speaking quietly to them in their own language, Reimer told the Hutterites that Social Credit used religion to keep people apathetic and intimidated. You are, he told them, an oppressed minority; you may not vote NDP, but vote.

The NDP brought in federal leader Tommy Douglas for a series of rallies with Neil Reimer and Garth Turcott, and Chudyk wanted to string a huge banner—**Welcome Tommy Douglas**—right across the highway leading into Blairmore. But the town council vetoed the idea, saying they couldn't endorse any candidate. A couple of mornings later Chudyk walked out in the street, and there was this great sign strung across the road between two telephone poles: **Vote Hanrahan Socred.** Chudyk fumed all day, worrying about how this might affect his chances against Notley, and that night, after a few drinks and hands of poker, he shinnied up the pole with an axe in his mouth, hacked away at the thick rope, and brought the reactionary thing down. He'll tell you that it's buried out there in the Frank rock slide, although at the time he thought it was entirely possible that the Conservatives were responsible. Turcott won the by-election, and for a brief moment it seemed to many that the NDP's star was on the rise in Alberta.

The Politician

By the mid-Sixties it was evident to many observers of Alberta politics that Social Credit was slipping. The Liberals and the NDP had both scored by-election upsets and the long-dormant Conservatives were being revitalized by Peter Lougheed, a Calgary corporate lawyer with strong links to the petroleum industry. It was however the Liberals, who had elected fifteen MLAs a decade earlier, that preoccupied Reimer's NDP: the Liberal strategy was to drive the NDP further to the left and to open up a vacuum in the centre of the spectrum. "Any major move to the left by this party, I predict," Reimer warned the NDP, "will see a resurgence of the Liberal Party in the Province of Alberta." Thus, when the Liberals came out for nationalization of Calgary Power in the expectation that Reimer would be forced to outdo them by advocating, for example, public ownership of the oil industry, the NDP, to whom ideology and policy were subordinated to electoral tactics, refused to take the bait and even derided the idea of taking over Calgary Power. In effect, Reimer, Notley and other party leaders were consciously taking up positions to the *right* of the avowedly capitalist parties in the vain hope of winning over small business and conservative voters. The strategy seems superficially clever but it invariably alienates activists and traditional party supporters for whom socialist principles are not to be traded off against votes and the interests of reactionary small businessmen. There were in Alberta many social and economic issues crying out for the NDP's attention. The appalling scandal of the province's mental health system, the degradation of Alberta's large, neglected native population, the impact of rapid urbanization on housing, land prices, education and social services, the growth of the public sector and the need to unionize white-collar workers, the impact of farm mechanization and agribusiness on rural Alberta, the underpricing of the province's natural gas and low oil royalties, and the need for an independent industrial strategy—these were the issues of the day which the NDP neglected in its obsession with corruption in high places. The principle that those in public office must not use their office for personal gain is of course fundamental in a democratic society, and Reimer's NDP were right to make it an issue; but they allowed it to occupy their whole agenda until it appeared that the real issue was Neil Reimer's vendetta against Premier Manning.

The "Turcott affair" and the subsequent Commission of Inquiry by Justice W.J.C. Kirby concerned allegations that two prominent Social Credit politicians, former Treasurer E.W. Hinman and Minister of Municipal Affairs A.J. Hooke had engaged in business and land dealings which were in conflict with their public duties. Although NDP MLA Garth Turcott was the first to make the allegations in the Legislature, there was not much that was new in the charges. Hinman had been dropped from the Cabinet by Manning in 1964 over conflict-of-interest charges in the press, and following Hinman's resignation *The Edmonton Journal* had launched its own cloak-and-dagger investigation of Alf Hooke, tracking him to Victoria where he was found in an apartment owned by Edmonton millionaire Charles Allard. The *Journal*, itself a model of probity, alleged that Hooke used his office to engage in land speculation and entered into business deals with Allard. Turcott raised these matters upon his entry into the Legislature in late 1966 and then tabled documents during his reply to the Speech from the Throne in February, 1967: Turcott demanded a judicial inquiry into Hooke and Hinman's affairs.

Garth Turcott was a reluctant muckraker. He clearly was acting at the direction of Reimer and Notley, and he was to be sacrificed, if needed, in their attack against "the establishment"—i.e. Manning. Turcott and Reimer told the NDP executive in November, 1966, that raising the issue in the Legislature was "a dramatic move to attract public attention" and that "the move was a good one from the viewpoint of political strategy."[25] But Manning turned the tables, forced a vote of censure against Turcott, and called an election. Predictably, Manning accused "the leader of the socialist party" of leading a smear campaign—an act of impiety if not sacrilege. Subsequently, he was forced to set up the Kirby Inquiry. Kirby's report of October, 1968, provided a mass of documentation concerning Hooke's and Hinman's business affairs but unaccountably concluded that neither used his office for personal gain.[26]

Our interest in the Turcott/Kirby affair is only in its impact on the NDP. In the 1967 provincial election, which the NDP mainly fought as a "negative" campaign against corruption, the party captured 16 per cent of the vote but won no seats. It was a major blow for the NDP leadership. Turcott, Reimer, Notley—all were soundly defeated. Lougheed's Conservatives, by contrast, took half a dozen urban seats. The NDP had thrown everything into the election and borrowed heavily to finance the campaign, and the outcome was a fiasco. Reimer accused the other parties of making deals to keep the NDP out, but a more plausible explanation is simply that the party had a) been overly optimistic in its reading of the by-election results (Notley told the 1966 party convention, "If you take the results in Pincher Creek and apply them across the Province, we would win 35 seats in the next election"); and b) failed to offer a constructive and progressive alternative to the right-wing parties. "Mr. Reimer," wrote a left-wing critic, "neglected to tell the people of Alberta just what he proposed to do in Mr. Manning's place and how the election of an NDP government would bring changes to the economic situation of the province. He spent too much time and effort tearing down Mr. Manning and his regime and too little time and effort building up Mr. Reimer and the NDP."[27] The party had borrowed $20,000 from a credit union to hire a Toronto ad agency to prepare negative "Point Ads," which probably did the NDP more harm than good. If the attacks on Manning rebounded to anyone's advantage, it was Peter Lougheed's, as even an unrepentant Neil Reimer admitted:

> Today it can be said, and possibly with some accuracy, that the Conservative Party took advantage of the work of the New Democratic Party. Be that as it may, none of these winds of change that we see today, nor the growth of our Party, could have been possible unless someone got into the fight. . . . The establishment of this Province was challenged for the first time in thirty years.[28]

The second impact was financial. In order to intervene at the Kirby Inquiry, the NDP was forced to pay legal fees on the order of $25,000, and this at a time when it had already borrowed up to the hilt to fight the election. Manning had his revenge on the NDP when he refused to have the Inquiry cover the party's costs. As we shall see, the debt and its retirement so preoccupied the party leadership after 1967 that critical debate of ideology and policies was largely confined to the small but well-organized left-wing of the NDP. Further, the severe austerity measures later undertaken by party treasurer Reg Basken forced the closure of the party office, the laying-off of the organizers and many smaller tribulations: not even the IMF wielded so sharp a knife!

The third impact was on Grant Notley's conception of leadership. Deeply involved in the Turcott affair, he henceforth avoided like the plague any idea of muckraking opposition politics or any temptation to indulge in *ad hominem* attacks on party leaders (even though he suffered many himself in his later years in the Legislature). One example will suffice. In 1974 a disgruntled employee of Syncrude Canada Ltd. donated several boxes of confidential files to an NDP researcher; the files displayed a relationship between the Alberta Government and the multinational oil companies that put Premier Peter Lougheed in a rather embarrassing light. Though the documents were of a political rather than a personal nature, Notley adamantly refused to make them public or to associate himself with their use. Why? Because he was determined "not to become another Turcott."

In the aftermath of the rout of 1967, Notley and Chudyk met to assess the damage. The first clue was that their typewriter was being repossessed. They appeared to be close to $100,000 in the red, and the Kirby Inquiry expenses were yet to come. Notley and Chudyk had persuaded the executive to "go for broke," rather as Chudyk did it in Reno, and now they had to account for the results. "I've got a one-way ticket to Brazil," said Chudyk. "It's suicide to stay here." But Notley was thinking of the next election, not Brazil, and he was scheming. "Ted, we should sell debentures in the party." Chudyk was skeptical and called up a guy at the securities commission to check it out. "Well, what'd he say?", asked Notley. "I can't tell you 'cause he wouldn't stop laughing long enough to answer." Notley took that for approval, so the party issued some $30,000 in debentures to upright true believers and downright stupid fools, and they became the NDP equivalent of Aberhart's famous $25 monthly dividend. The difference was that everybody voted for Aberhart and nobody got a cent, while hardly anybody voted for the NDP but if they did they also got to buy a worthless debenture in a bankrupt party *and* turn back the annual dividend to Chudyk's collection agency. An idiot could see it was cheaper not to vote.

Notley had also set up an incredible 120-day marathon of meetings for himself and Chudyk. They started in the deep south and worked their way town by town to the north. Notley would open each meeting by giving the membership hell. They hadn't done enough. "They would sit there with their heads bowed," said Chudyk, "and he just raked them over. Then I'd get in and they'd pull out their wallets. It was unbelievable." There was a meeting every night, and two on Sundays and Saturdays. Chudyk learned to sleep with his eyes open, hearing that same speech over and over again. By the end of the tour he hated Notley. After one of their last meetings up north, they came back to their hotel and Chudyk spotted a couple of attractive young women in the bar. My Lord, thought Chudyk, that's just what I need to settle my nerves. "What do you say, Grant, should we try for it?"

Notley took a long, cool look at the women and turned back to Chudyk. "I don't know Ted, do you think we can sign them up?"

Party documents and the personal files of NDP activists reveal that a major breach developed in 1967 between the leadership and the left-wing members of the New Democratic Youth, led by the redoubtable Ken Novakowski. After 1969, the NDY activists of Edmonton and Calgary became the dominant element in the small Alberta section of the Waffle caucus of the NDP. Novakowski came from a left-wing family in Mundare (his father was a member of the Communist Party), and, like Notley, he first became active through campus politics at the University of Alberta. In 1965 the NDY moved out of its earnest mock Parliament phase and went off campus, leafleting high schools, organizing in support of a packinghouse workers' strike, and demonstrating against American aggression in Vietnam. Unlike many student radicals of the day, Novakowski was contemptuous of the anti-politics of the New Left and preferred to operate within the NDP—indeed, as a member of the provincial executive—and to fight to make it more democratic and much more oriented to urban working class interests. Notley and his organizers, who were barely keeping the party afloat, had little use for the NDY radicals: "You know Ken," Chudyk would say. "He'd rather be right than successful." Which was a roundabout way of saying that Chudyk would rather be successful than right. And Notley, Chudyk insisted, was also in the game to win, to gain power. "Grant undertook to mobilize and take the principles and the issues and get them into a position of power. Power didn't mean anything to Ken Novakowski."[29]

Novakowski had great respect for Reimer's gutsy, street-fighting style (he was far less impressed with Notley), but the NDY wanted radical changes in the structure and policies of the NDP. It was another round in the old fight between the presbyterians and the congregationalists: the realist presbyterians, led by Notley, wanted to preserve the pyramidal structure of the church/party but were willing to admit almost anyone to the membership; whereas the congregationalists, led by Novakowski, wanted to get rid of the bishops, let each congregation/constituency be its own church, and promote a religion of true believers. "Not until the party leadership realizes that involvement at all levels is an essential pre-requisite to any broadly based movement, can the party hope to make any significant organization gains," wrote Novakowski. He vented his dissatisfaction to *The Calgary Herald* and was attacked by Reimer as "totally irresponsible" for washing the party's linen in public. Novakowski retorted that the party was drifting to the right; the election campaign was too negative; the NDP ought to stop describing itself as social democratic; the party should be active at all levels, not just in electoral politics; and "the provincial executive make too few of the really important decisions. These decisions are usually made by the Table Officers or the staff."

Circling their wagons round the leader, the rest of the executive denounced the dissident, ignoring the entire critique of the party. "Some concern was voiced by executive members at what was termed a dangerous tendancy (sic) on the part of the NDY to replace "social democratic" terminology with the exclusive use of the word socialist. It was pointed out that the NDP is democratic first and socialist second. Several executive members warned that neither they or (sic) the labour movement would have any part of a movement that smacked of [the] totalitarian left."[30] If anything confirmed Novakowski's argument that the Alberta NDP was neither socialist *nor* democratic, it was this sort of bludgeoning of intra-party dissent. The party's public image—the stress on the open society, accountability and democratic opposition—masked a structure that was deeply undemocratic and resistant to reform.

Reimer and Novakowski did agree on one crucial point of political strategy: that the party must "move from the country to the city" and concentrate its efforts in the industrialized urban ridings. Rapid urbanization was undermining Social Credit's base, and the NDP must fight the Conservative party for control of the cities. Shortly before stepping down as leader, Reimer told a 1968 policy conference of the Alberta NDP that the party must focus its electoral efforts in the cities, and he was sharply critical when his successor declined to take the advice. Novakowski and the socialist left, to whom Social Credit personified the political idiocy of rural life, also wanted to build "a truly conscious labour party in Alberta" based on the cities. Novakowski and Reimer both argued that the party committed a "classic error" in 1967 by failing to concentrate resources and effort in north and east Edmonton. Concentration of organization by the central office, Novakowski argued, "has always been in rural areas. The NDP in Alberta has not developed any significant urban orientation indicating that the party leadership still feels an NDP victory will come as a result of rural support. The NDP, consequently, failed to make an issue out of the fact that urban Alberta is grossly underrepresented in the legislature. Eventually, redistribution will become a demand of growing urban centres and the NDP will still lack an effective labor base in the cities, unless it changes many of its current organizational practices."[31]

Notley disagreed. He had a very unsentimental view of Alberta's working class. He never believed the New Democratic Party could become a labour party, and particularly not in Alberta. The strategy of building a socialist working class party had been attempted by the Labour party in the 1920's and early 1930's, and it scored some notable successes in municipal and provincial politics, but Social Credit won over the working class as well as the agrarian vote after 1935. Notley, ever the hard-headed realist, was skeptical of the thesis that the NDP could build on such a narrow class and sectional base. It was the new middle class, not an industrial proletariat, that was swelling the cities. Since Calgary was hopeless, Reimer and Novakowski were in effect advocating a concentration upon Edmonton's industrial belt. But having himself lost in Norwood, a predominantly working class riding in Edmonton, Notley was even less sympathetic to this view, and after 1967 he never again ran in the city. He would not turn his back on the pockets of strong NDP support in the rural areas, such as the Peace River country; nor would he elevate the class interests of organized workers above those of farmers, tenants, professionals or small business. The party must practice integrative politics, he believed, building coalitions among the disaffected and attracting the most able individuals into the leadership. They way to power in Alberta did not lie in David Lewis's formula. Having said that, it must be added that although he was not of labour, Notley was invariably *with* labour in its political struggles with Lougheed's Conservatives. Whether labour was with Notley is another question.

Neil Reimer was appointed Canadian director of the OCAW and in July, 1968, he announced his decision to step down as leader of the Alberta NDP. Who would succeed him? Grant Notley was not an obvious choice. He was only 29, he was unknown to the public, and within the party he was regarded as an establishment appararatchik and wirepuller. In the party, one friend recalled, "the toughest job Grant had was to establish himself as leader because he had for so long established himself as joe-boy of the party, as secretary, as the manipulator, the guy who caused things to happen." He agonized over whether he had the stature, the right stuff to make the transition and gain the party's respect. Even Chudyk wondered whether the young kid with the brushcut, short pants and long shirt cuffs could fill Reimer's shoes. When Notley finally decided to run, Chudyk and Reg Basken forced him to go to a tailor to be fitted for a couple of suits. "If it means that much money," he moaned, "I don't know if I *want* to be leader." As he stood there being fitted for his leader's threads, he looked at the bill and huge tears were rolling down his cheeks. George Cadbury, the multimillionaire Fabian who served as treasurer of the federal NDP in the early Seventies, once took Notley aside and told him, "Grant, you're too damn poor to be a socialist."

"Notley," said Chudyk the image-maker, "You don't swear enough. You have to curse if you want respect." So they taught him the right phrases, and he'd practice in his office. "Oh, the clouds are coming out again, God—damn—it." And so the methodical shaping and grooming of the outer man proceeded, but his ideas and principles—the reasons why he was running—were entirely his own. He argued, first, that the party needed a full-time leader, a professional politician; and second, he wanted to use the NDP to revitalize the older prairie progressive movement. These were authentic themes. Politics was Notley's only vocation and calling, and he always saw himself as part of that greater tradition of left-wing western radicalism and protest.

An odd "stop Notley" coalition developed around the only other serious leadership candidate, Edmonton lawyer Gordon Wright. Novakowski managed Wright's campaign, and Reimer, though publicly professing neutrality, also supported Wright. Jamaican-born and British-educated, Wright had arrived in Alberta in the early Fifties and entered the NDP via the New Party Clubs. The Alberta CCF/NDP, unlike its Saskatchewan counterpart, does not have a Fabian tradition, but Gordon Wright was cut from that cloth. His diffidence and accent led some to conclude that he was in politics out of *noblesse oblige*, yet he was probably the most progressive senior person in the party. A perennial candidate and party workhorse, Wright admired Notley but felt a good leadership race would be a tonic for the party. (A wonderful photograph of the two, taken during a later campaign, reveals Notley and Wright in impeccable attire on a voter's doorstep. Wright is down on his knees, humbly begging for electoral favour, while a laughing Notley shakes the hand of a woman who is probably thinking, "These guys *have* to be the NDP.")

At the party's seventh annual convention, held in Calgary on November 9-11, 1968, Grant Notley defeated Wright on the first ballot. The hard years lay ahead. The NDP's worsening financial situation forced the executive to let the party's organizers go (Ted Chudyk left for Manitoba in 1969), and finally it was decided to close the provincial office: for two years the party's office was treasurer Reg Basken's desk at the OCAW. Notley refused to run in an Edmonton by-election, but chose instead to try for a seat in another contest in Edson in 1969. Unlike Reimer, he obtained scant labour support in Hinton, Edson and so on, and Basken held money back from Notley's campaign. It was, Notley said much later, "the biggest setback of my political life. I ran third among four candidates, and so that was probably the hardest time because I was the leader of the party and we had done badly in the by-election and there was a big debt and we had to try to keep the party afloat and it was probably the time that took the most courage. People say it takes courage to be a member of the legislature and I'll only tell you, dealing with the Tories was a rather easy task compared to trying to revive a little life into an organization whose party had run third with a debt of almost $100,000 and the provincial office had to be closed down; and so I was the leader and the fundraiser and the organizer and collected memberships and paid the bills, and so I wouldn't want to go through that again."[32]

It must have been a lonely, dispiriting three years, and only a person with Notley's grit could have endured the job. He did not yet have strong support within the NDP—many members saw him as an interim leader—and the party no longer interested the media or the public: all eyes were on Lougheed's Tories. Notley was a virtual unknown. The party was almost paralyzed by its lack of money. Financial exigencies affected every decision, and the structure of the central office with a staff of full-time organizers had collapsed under the sheer weight of the debt. Most of his close allies in the party had left for greener pastures in the other western provinces, and then in late 1969 the NDP's unity was strained by the creation of the Waffle group. Led by Novakowski and a few university students and teachers, the Alberta section of the Waffle was very small but vocal and it soon raised the ire of organized labour with its nationalistic attacks on international unions such as the OCAW. The Alberta Waffle—which was really a branch-plant of Waffle Central in Toronto—was peddling southern Ontario economic nationalism in the most conservative prairie province, and the main plank in its platform was a call for the complete nationalization of the oil industry. Notley, by contrast, was emphasizing the capture of economic rents via higher royalties and gas prices, reduced exports to the U.S., an oil marketing agency and selective public ownership for resources such as the tar sands—all of which came to pass. Like Lougheed, Notley wanted to use the economic value of oil and gas resources to build an industrial base in Alberta, and this required tougher bargaining with the oil industry and tighter controls on the pace of development. Nationalization was neither necessary nor feasible. So when the well-organized Waffle came to the 1970 and 1971 annual NDP conventions armed with radical resolutions calling for the creation of a public oil corporation which would "direct the usage of all sources of energy within the province" and "have as its charter the nationalization of all the energy resource industries of Alberta," Notley started counting noses in a hurry. To adopt such a policy, he thought, would be tantamount to electoral suicide. The arguments were mustered, the votes mobilized, and the left was defeated. But it was not Notley's way to purge the Waffle. Novakowski thought that Notley accepted it as "a legitimate point of view but he disagreed politically because it was too left-wing. The Waffle here [Alberta] never underwent the same kind of vicious attack that it underwent in Ontario. That was partly because we were legitimate New Democrats before and were therefore thought by the party to have a legitimate voice."[33] The Alberta Waffle was occasionally a source of creative ideological tension within the NDP, but the group faded away following Novakowski's departure for B.C. in 1971; and nationally it disintegrated into irrelevant sects.

Notley's principal concern was to gain the party a voice in the Alberta Legislature. In September of 1970 the federal secretary of the NDP, Cliff Scotton, and provincial secretary Hart Horn quietly polled four constituencies in northern Alberta—two in Edmonton and two in the Peace River country—in a bid to identify a winnable seat for Notley. Their research turned up ominous signs of the growing shift toward the Conservatives, notably in the urban working class ridings of Beverly and Norwood (where the P.C.s seemed to have 40 per cent of the vote vs. about 15 per cent for the NDP). Unemployment and the cost of living were the main issues in the urban ridings; however, in the northern ridings of Smoky River and Spirit River-Fairview there was a great deal of discontent among farmers with both the federal and provincial governments.

The NDP had run strongly in the Peace in 1967 (the party had more than 500 members in Spirit River alone), but Scotton and Hart Horn were cautioned that there was a swing to the Conservatives in the Smoky River riding and that NDP supporters were moving over to Lougheed's candidate; the NDP could only hope to win with a candidate who would "meet the aspirations of the strong ethnic [i.e., French Canadian] vote" in the Fahler area. It was generally agreed that it "would be too risky to commit the Leader, Grant Notley, to running in the riding." On the other hand, the Social Credit incumbent in Spirit River-Fairview was seldom to be found in his riding, he was out of touch with farm issues, and there was an evident mood for change. The Conservatives had no power base as yet in Spirit River, and the NDP stood a good chance in a two-way fight with the Socreds. The constituency had a progressive tradition, the National Farmer's Union was growing, and the NDP had a good organization in Rycroft and Fairview. Thus, they concluded that "all other things being equal, it would appear that he [Notley] has the best chance of securing a seat in the Provincial Assembly by way of Spirit River constituency."[34]

Notley's decision to take this advice was characteristically unsentimental and hard-nosed. Despite pressure from Reimer, Basken and the left, all of whom believed in an urban strategy of concentration, Notley began to pour money and manpower into his Peace River policy and in so doing implied his acceptance of an old CCF formula: depend on the farmers to be more radical than the workers. Had electoral success been possible, Notley would probably have run again in Edmonton, but, despite the NDP's organizing efforts, the conservative industrial working class was transferring its allegiance from Social Credit to Lougheed. He would run in Spirit River to win, as the first step on the road to power. That was the ultimate goal, the purpose of his vocation in politics, and he never allowed ideology or sentimentality to deflect him from his course.

There was a good deal of grumbling over the priority given to the Peace River during the 1971 campaign, but one morning that hot summer three dapper men walked into the office of a credit union in downtown Edmonton. Neil Reimer, Ivor Dent and Reg Basken took out a large loan for the NDP election fight, putting up their houses for collateral, and because they had sworn to keep it a secret from their wives you could say they had put their lives, as well as their homes, on the line for the cause. Fortunately, Notley was elected by a margin of 147 votes in Spirit River-Fairview, despite a major sweep of Conservatives elsewhere in the province. It was a beginning.

Let us conclude with a simple question. Why did Grant Notley persevere in the face of such overwhelming odds; why did he remain in Alberta where the chance of success was so slight? He had many opportunities to leave the province that consistently rejected his ideas and party, but he always stayed. Why? Notley confronted a dilemma that has concerned men and women of conscience in every age, including our own. It is the question of what responsibility a principled person owes society. If he considers his society morally wrong and corrupt, should a man withdraw to preserve his principles, or should he stay and fight to reform the society? There is no simple answer to that dilemma, but Notley adopted what may be called the Puritan stance: a righteous man is not permitted to turn his back on this imperfect world; rather, he is required to live in the world, no matter how much he disapproves of it, and to use his power to build a society based on higher ideals. It is then not a choice, but an obligation to society and God to take up politics as a calling, and we may say that while Notley failed to attain power he met that larger obligation. As for his unwillingness to leave Alberta, an ordinary explanation would be that he had found his place. To borrow Elizabeth Spencer's moving words, he felt "the need of a land, of a sure terrain, of a sort of permanent landscape of the heart."[35]

---

[1]"Four Year Plan - Report to Convention 1964." Acc. No. 84.178/470. Alberta New Democratic Party Archive. Provincial Archives of Alberta (PAA).

[2]"A Call to Action," Address of William Irvine to the First Annual Convention of CCF Clubs, Edmonton, July 14-15, 1936.

[3]Grant Notley interview with Barbara Evans, July 31, 1982, at the 50th Anniversary of the CCF, Calgary. By permission of Barbara Evans.

[4]Nellie Peterson interview, May 22, 1985.

[5]Gad Horowitz, *Canadian Labour in Politics* (Toronto, 1962), p. 216.

[6]CCF National Council Minutes, January 13-15, 1956; cited in Horowitz, p. 173.

[7]Walter Young, *The Anatomy of a Party: the National CCF* (Toronto, 1969), p. 133.

[8]Ivor Dent interview, May 19, 1985.

[9]Grant Notley interview with Barbara Evans, July 31, 1982.

[10]Grant Notley to R.D. Sparham, letters of June 13, July 18, 1961, and Notley's organizational report to Carl Hamilton of the NCNP. CCF/NDP papers. MG 28 IV, vol. 379. Public Archives of Canada.

[11]P.J. Ryan interview, June 5, 1985.

[12]A. Mardiros, *William Irvine* (Toronto, 1979), p. 244.

[13]Horowitz, op. cit., pp. 216-17.

[14]Ken Novakowski, "The NDP in Alberta: A Critique," Confrontations, n.d.

[15]Draft of an undated letter from Notley to Dent. Acc. No. 84.178, Box 1. PAA.

[16]Interviews with Neil Reimer, P.J. Ryan, Nellie Peterson and Ted Chudyk, May-June, 1985.

[17]Notley to Keith Wright, 16 February, 1962. Acc. No. 84.178, Box 1. PAA.

[18]Neil Reimer interview, May 29, 1985.

[19]Ted Chudyk interview, June 6, 1985; and Minutes of ANDP Leadership Convention, January 26-27, 1963. Acc. No. 84.178/469. PAA.

[20]Ken Novakowski, "The NDP in Alberta: A Critique". n.d. Personal files of Ken Novakowski.

[21]Hannah Arendt, *The Origins of Totalitarianism*, revised ed. (New York, 1968), p. 301; the quotation from Burke, cited in Arendt, pp. 254-5, is from his, *Upon Party*, 2nd edition (London, 1850).

[22]Report of Provincial Leader to the Alberta New Democratic Party Policy Convention, March 22-24, 1968. Personal files of Gordon Wright.

[23]*Red Deer Advocate*, January 21, 1964.

[24]*Calgary Herald*, January 21, 1964.

[25]Provincial Executive Meeting Minutes, November 27, 1966. Personal papers of Ken Novakowski.

[26]The Report of the Honourable Mr. Justice W.J.C. Kirby In the Matter of an Inquiry by a Royal Commission into the matters set out in Order-in-Council 861/67, (October, 1968). A copy of the Kirby report is in the Alberta Legislative Library.

[27]Ken Novakowski, "The NDP in Alberta: A Critique", op. cit.

[28]N. Reimer, Report to the Alberta NDP Policy Convention, March 22-24, 1968. Personal files of Gordon Wright.

[29]Ted Chudyk interview, June 6, 1985.

[30]Minutes of Provincial Executive Meeting, December 20, 1967. Personal files of Ken Novakowski.

[31]Neil Reimer, Report to the Alberta NDP Policy Conference, March 22-24, 1968. Gordon Wright papers; Ken Novakowski, "The NDP in Alberta: A Critique", op. cit.

[32]Grant Notley interview with Barbara Evans, July 31, 1982.

[33]Ken Novakowski interview, July 19, 1985.

[34]C. Scotton and H. Horn, "Report on Findings in Smoky River and Spirit River", September 2, 1970. The report also contains polling results and discussion of Norwood and Beverly. Acc. No. 84.178/366. PAA.

[35]Elizabeth Spencer, 'A Southern Landscape', in *The Stories of Elizabeth Spencer* (New York, 1981), p. 52.

Chapter 2

Dreaming A New Jerusalem in the Land of Social Credit: The Struggles of the CCF in Alberta

Olenka Melnyk

When I first became politically active it didn't seem impossible to me that we could change the world within a relatively short time. I remember coming home to my parents' farm during the summer holidays once when Bill Irvine came to visit. Irvine had known me since I was a little girl. He asked me how long I thought this would take, or something like that. I had been at it—the CCF—about two or three years, and I said that I didn't think it would take very long. "Twenty years, maybe less than that." Perhaps, I'd said ten; I can just remember him saying, "you better quit now if that's what you expect because I don't think I'll see it in my lifetime and I very much doubt you'll see it in yours. You can make the world a little better, but don't think you'll change it." "That's a devil of a thing for an organizer to come up and say!" I told Mother when we were alone together. And Mother said, "It's a very wise thing. Unless you realize you're up against a tough fight and it's going to last a long, long time, don't bother starting because that's how it is."
Nellie Peterson

The truth of those words was slowly to sink in as Nellie Peterson drove her Ford coupe over thousands of miles of rural Alberta roads, organizing and speaking on behalf of the Cooperative Commonwealth Federation (CCF). The New Jerusalem which Peterson so optimistically envisioned as a young country school teacher during the Depression failed to materialize, of course. Her years as a tireless and largely underpaid party worker were not rewarded by any significant increase in public support at the polls. Despite several runs at political office, Peterson—who according to the late NDP leader Grant Notley possessed the ability to become premier of the province—was not even able to get herself elected. Like the NDP (until its dramatic May 1986 electoral breakthrough when the party won a record 16 seats), the CCF was never able to wheedle more than two legislative seats out of Alberta voters although it did manage to make a greater electoral impact in other provinces, notably Saskatchewan where it formed the government for 17 years, and in British Columbia, Ontario and Manitoba where it had been the official opposition.

Why did CCF activists keep struggling despite the overwhelming and continuing odds in Alberta? And why weren't they more successful there?

The Lost Dream

Alberta may be regarded as the bastion of small c-conservatism today, but socialism was not always considered such a lost cause in that province. Surprisingly enough, the founders of the Cooperative Commonwealth Federation envisioned Alberta, not Saskatchewan, as the future CCF stronghold in Canada. This conviction was shared by Saskatchewan politicians, including Tommy Douglas's future Minister of Finance, Clarence Fines:

> One of our greatest disappointments was that the CCF movement in Alberta had never been able to get off the ground. At our founding convention in Calgary in 1932, we had expected and hoped for more enthusiastic leadership and support from Alberta. At that time the UFA government was in power there and the majority of federal members from Alberta, known as the "ginger group," were UFA members. It appeared certain that Alberta would be the centre from which the CCF would spread to the rest of Canada.[1]

The founding of the CCF marked the culmination of several decades of effort by scattered and fragmented progressive parties across the country to win a voice for the farmer, the worker, the elderly and the unemployed. It was Alberta farmers, nevertheless, who through their UFA representatives called together western farm, labour and socialist groups in Calgary on August 1, 1932 for the express purpose of building a new and radically different political party. That same day, more than a thousand miles away in the nation's capital, the RCMP dispersed a demonstration of the unemployed—remnants of the "On to Ottawa" trekkers—with boots, clubs and fists. Meanwhile, in his office up on the Hill, Prime Minister R.B. Bennett dispensed with their leaders by pounding his fist and denouncing "those who would destroy law and order and democracy."[2] Sniffing a Bolshevik plot in the air, the press reported the Ottawa disturbance as the work of the "Reds" and the birth of the CCF as "Pinkish Soviet Plan Launched."[3] Delegates to the

Calgary conference included 15 farmers, 20 construction workers, six teachers, one miner, six homemakers, six railway workers, one motion picture operator, three nurses, two union executives and 19 unemployed men and women—decidedly not the sort of crowd to be seen floating around Tory or Grit circles of the day. The CCF's debut upon the electoral scene profoundly changed the face of Canadian politics, laying the foundation for much of the social welfare legislation, including medical care, unemployment insurance and old-age pensions, we take for granted today.

When the depression arrived, Alberta was not hit as badly as Saskatchewan, where two thirds of the population was forced onto the welfare rolls, but conditions were grim enough. As the price of No. 1 wheat dropped to 20 cents a bushel in 1932, hard-pressed Alberta farmers found it increasingly difficult to meet their mortgage payments. When the banks and machine companies began to foreclose, farmers were not about to simply sit back given their well-established tradition of agrarian revolt. Alberta's burgeoning, agrarian populism had been heavily influenced by the class-conscious, farmer-based Non-Partisan League which elected a majority to the North Dakota legislature in 1916. Following the example of their American counterparts, Alberta farmers began organizing themselves against the "rapacious" Eastern banks, railroad monopolies, grain elevator companies and manufacturers. Equally disillusioned with the old-line parties which they felt represented Eastern rather than their own best interests, they kicked out the tired, old, patronage-ridden Liberals and swept in their own government, the United Farmers of Alberta, on July 17, 1921. In the subsequent general election, they delivered an even more emphatic message to Ottawa by electing UFA candidates to fill all 12 federal seats. UFA Members of Parliament lost no time in aligning themselves with the radical Progressives who defended the rights of farmers and workers under the leadership of J.S. Woodsworth; six of the eight members of the so-called "Ginger Group" were UFA representatives in fact, including Bill Irvine who later helped found the CCF. The UFA laid the groundwork for the Alberta Farmers' Co-operative Elevator Company in 1913, a co-operative system of marketing grain to protect farmers from unscrupulous grain handlers.[4]

Three years after the Calgary conference, the CCF's dreams of a rosy future in Alberta were dashed when voters, in an abrupt about-face, chose a fundamentalist, Bible-thumping preacher and his "funny money" party to lead the way out of the Depression. Saskatchewan, meanwhile, stuck with the Liberals until the war was nearly over before turning to a Baptist minister and his social gospel party to save it from near-bankruptcy. Comparisons between the two provinces are inevitable: Why did Alberta veer to the right, politically, and Saskatchewan to the left?

Ironically, the UFA did more to bury the CCF cause in Alberta than its worst enemy. By the early Thirties, the UFA government had lost its progressive impetus and deteriorated into an increasingly reactionary force against the very farmers and workers it was supposed to represent. When Blairmore miners struck against the appalling conditions in south-western Alberta coal mines, for example, the Brownlee government heavy-handedly responded by dispatching the RCMP to deal with the situation. The government was equally callous in its handling of the December 1932 Hunger March, once again summoning the RCMP to the rescue. A cavalry of baton-swinging, mounted policemen charged through the crowd of 2,000 marching destitute farmers and unemployed workers before they were able to reach the steps of the legislature. The UFA's already tarnished reputation was completely blackened by the sex scandals implicating Brownlee and one of his cabinet ministers. In those days, Alberta was the spawning ground of more weird and wonderful evangelical sects than any other province in Canada; her straight-laced, deeply pious populace was shocked at the very idea of possible sexual misconduct among her leading citizens. Even if the UFA government had entered the Thirties with an unblemished record, it is highly unlikely that it could have survived the Depression when governments everywhere floundered helplessly in the face of the Great Economic Disaster. In his *Agrarian Socialism*, S.M. Lipset convincingly argues that had the Social Credit formed the government in the early Thirties, it would have been as ignominiously turfed out as the United Farmers.[5] Who were unhappy farmers to use as scapegoat, if not the government? They couldn't very well boot out the banks unless they were ready to storm the barricades; political parties, on the other hand, were much easier to depose.

The UFA's lengthy flirtation with social credit monetary theories also seriously undermined the CCF's chances in Alberta. Nellie Peterson, a UFA supporter and later CCF provincial secretary and organizer, comments:

> I don't think you can neglect the fact that one of the major themes of the UFA in Alberta was the whole issue of money. We often said later that we sharpened the axe that cut off our own head. Long before Social

Credit came on the scene, I remember Alberta politicians, men like Spencer and Irvine, going around lecturing about monetary realities—the effect of gold on monetary standards and the lack of ownership of the banking system, because until we had control of the financial instrument that represented the wealth we had produced, we would not be able to do very much to help ourselves. The control of money was very much recognized as being an important thing in Alberta. I remember quite well one of the stories that came up at almost every meeting. A farmer walks into the bank to borrow some money with a couple of pigs under his arm as collateral. He walks out with nothing but squeal; the banker gets all the rest.[6]

Both the CCF and Social Credit preached monetary reform as part of their respective populist programs, appealing to deeply entrenched, western grievances against the "vested interests" of Eastern big banks and big business. Beyond that point, however, the two ideologies diverged although it is important to understand that both parties were considered genuine populist, protest movements on the prairies. The major difference between the CCF and Social Credit was that the former proposed fundamentally to restructure the existing political and economic system, while the latter had no major quarrels with capitalism, aiming instead to make it work better in the West by shifting control of the financial institutions from the East and by issuing more purchasing power to western consumers.

Prairie farmers were not always able to distinguish between the two. "Only the very politically and economically oriented or astute could recognize that there was much difference," explains Nellie Peterson. "And farmers didn't have any idea of how the banking system worked." This confusion was particularly acute in Alberta where monetary reform theories had been circulating among farm organizations since the days of the Non-Partisan League, one of whose main objectives was the public ownership of banks. CCF leaders in Alberta did not prove immune to the easy appeal of social credit either. The federal UFA members, who later became the strongest CCF supporters in the province, were also the most vigorous proponents of monetary reform. Bill Irvine, "Ginger" MP and founding member of the CCF, spearheaded the monetary reform faction within the UFA and continued to regard social credit as a radical, albeit misguided, alternative well into 1939.[7]

After his election to Parliament, Irvine focussed on reform of the banking system as one of his main goals. He even visited Major C.H.

Douglas, the British founder of social credit, in England in 1923. Back in Canada, he successfully lobbied the federal government to undertake an inquiry into banking and credit, and arranged for Douglas to appear as a witness. The Major failed to impress the Standing Committee on Banking and Commerce, but Irvine was not to be so easily dissuaded and continued to champion Douglas's theories in the UFA. The idea of social credit and monetary reform began to receive widespread support among the UFA locals during the early Thirties as farmers became increasingly disgruntled with the "banking racket."[8] At its 1934 annual convention, the UFA passed a resolution requesting the government to conduct an inquiry into Aberhart's theories. Bowing to pressure, Brownlee's cabinet heard both Aberhart and Douglas out, and then submitted a decidedly negative report on the prospects of social credit in the province. The monetary reform faction persisted, however. Aberhart was invited to expound his ideas at the UFA's convention the following year. Delegates unanimously voted against supporting Aberhart and his social credit theories in the upcoming provincial election. But the next day, in a curious turn-about, they passed a resolution put forward by Irvine requesting the government to engage Major Douglas as a "consulting engineer in the matter of financial reform."

If the UFA seemed to be confused, the public was even more baffled. Why was Aberhart's social credit considered no good for Alberta, and Major Douglas's imported brand more appropriate? The benefit of the doubt went to Aberhart. Aylmer Liesemer, a UFA supporter who taught under the Social Credit leader in Calgary's Crescent Heights High School, saw the 1935 UFA convention as a great propaganda victory for Aberhart.

> I think it was part of Aberhart's tactics to go the the UFA and make a pretence of offering them his ideas, knowing that they wouldn't accept them. Then he could say to the rank and file, "Well, I tried and your leader wouldn't agree. Now, I've got something which is going to cure the depression and I'm turning to you." The UFA leaders spoke against him and carried the delegates with them, but the same delegates went home and joined his party.[9]

Social Credit also enjoyed support among Saskatchewan farmers who favored a union between the Socreds and the CCF. Joint candidates were run in a number of ridings for two years. Tommy Douglas was among the candidates who were singled out for support by both the CCF and Social Credit (although Douglas wisely refused to accept the latter's endorsement) in the 1935 federal election in which the Socreds edged out the CCF in the Saskatchewan polls. Despite Social Credit's early lead in the province, Saskatchewan's dalliance with the party was not destined to blossom into a full romance; CCF provincial leaders determinedly and successfully wooed first the party and then the farmers away into the socialist fold. Saskatchewan farmers were impressed with Aberhart's failure to deliver on his promises next door.

The UFA had initiated the 1932 Calgary conference, but the party leadership was reluctant to relinquish power to the new party (as the CCF would later resist the transition to the NDP). The following year, UFA delegates to the CCF's annual convention in Regina, along with Ontario farmers, were the most opposed to the idea of forming one unified party. As Robert Gardiner, UFA leader and MP, emphatically stated: "The UFA is not going to give up one iota of its autonomy. This is in no way a political party. It is a federation of interested organizations."[10] UFA MPs may have been strong CCF supporters, but this was certainly not true of Brownlee and his cabinet. The ringing rhetoric of the Regina Manifesto, with its declaration that "no CCF Government will rest content until it has eradicated capitalism and put into operation the full program of socialized planning . . ." was not likely to strike a sympathetic chord in the heart of a premier who had previously made his living as a corporate lawyer. UFA MLAs were also rather lukewarm in their endorsement of the CCF. Aylmer Liesemer, later elected as a Calgary CCF MLA, recalls:

> The UFA MLAs were sort of run down and they weren't as enthusiastic in their support. I remember there was a meeting in my parents' house in Didsbury with the local MLA, and I was home from Calgary. I was home deliberately because I knew this local MLA was not too hot for the CCF. And he said, "Well, I go along with the CCF but we mustn't upset the people too much." He just went along because I was there making a big noise about it.[11]

Decimated by a 1935 Socred victory (voters turned out in record numbers to elect 56 novice Social Crediters and not one single, veteran UFA candidate) the UFA opted stubbornly to limp along for another four years rather than throw its support behind the CCF. The party did not vacate the provincial field until 1937 nor the federal until 1939. This seriously hampered the development of the CCF in Alberta which could not very well compete with its provincial parent body for support at the polls. By the time the UFA finally decided to put its tired carcass out to pasture, a good portion of its disgruntled membership had already crossed over to Social Credit.

Nellie Peterson recalls that her CCF club in Edson was barely underway when it was shattered by massive defections. "I think we lost two thirds of our club to Social Credit. I'm sure we did. I guess Social Credit looked very much more likely to do something right away: $25 a month the minute you're elected, which the CCF certainly wasn't promising."[12]

The CCF could draw upon many capable men and women within its ranks in Alberta, but the party lacked a charismatic leader of the calibre of Tommy Douglas to compete with the wildly popular Aberhart. The difficulties of campaigning against a political leader who enjoyed cult status is graphically described by former national CCF secretary David Lewis:

> I always recall with ever-recurring wonderment an experience at a meeting I addressed in a village in southern Alberta in 1938. The meeting, held in a rather dingy hall with wooden benches and little light, attracted no more than twenty-five or thirty people, but we considered it a success in view of the size of the village. I thought I was being careful in my words about social credit so as not to offend anyone, but at one point I made a sharp reference to Aberhart and, to my astonishment, more than half of the audience rose as one and walked out. My mouth dropped as I stared at the retreating figures. When we left the hall, my companion, Bill Irvine, said, "Do you now see what we're up against?"[13]

By posing as a modern-day Christ chasing dastardly Eastern money changers and sleazy politicians out of the temple, Aberhart was able to capture the imagination and support of a demoralized and disillusioned public. What he lacked in economic common sense, Aberhart made up for in moral authority. With his disarming sincerity and God-fearing "wholesomeness," he was able, simply and convincingly, to proselytize nonsensical monetary proposals as if they were part of the Divine Plan. In summing up the character of his former boss, Aylmer Liesemer comments:

> He was a curious mixture. I always said that he had a compartmentalized mind. He could favor one thing in his religion and something different in his politics. They could sometimes be quite radically different but it never seemed to bother him. He was prophesizing the end of the

world on his Sunday afternoon broadcasts from the Bible Institute. My father who was very much opposed to Aberhart used to listen in just to get himself riled up. We heard Aberhart say that the world was coming to an end at such and such a date. I remember saying to Mother and Dad, "What on earth is he going to do when the world doesn't come to an end?" Well, he solved that very easily; he denied ever having said it. As I see it, he had a compartmentalized mind. He could say one thing and live by another. He was constantly confronted with "Where are the $25 monthly dividends supposed to be coming from?", but he just ignored that. He just laughed and got his whole audience to laugh with him. "Well, well, these people don't even know where it comes from. Well, well. Ha. Ha." And that would be the end of it. He was confronted all the time, but he just laughed it off. He was a great, big man physically with a big voice and a big laugh.

With his quixotic blending of politics and religion, Aberhart had an unbeatable combination. No mortal politician seemed up to the task of wrestling the portly Man of God, as he was dubbed by his followers, down to earth. It became impossible, in fact, for his opponents even to question Aberhart or his followers! If they dared to suggest that a program of social credit for Alberta was neither economically nor constitutionally viable, they would be branded as supporters of the hated bankers. If they questioned the propriety of running a political party as an extension of a religious institution, Aberhart simply denied that Social Credit was a political party, insisting that it was an educational and social movement instead.

By the time Aberhart did enter the political scene, he could count on a captive audience, thanks to his popular, widely broadcast Sunday afternoon radio program from the Calgary Prophetic Bible Institute. A forceful, dynamic speaker, Aberhart was a hit on the airwaves in an age when radio was as critical a medium to the politician as television is today. Putting his superb organizational and administrative abilities to good use, Aberhart had also organized hundreds of Bible study clubs throughout the province in conjunction with the Bible Institute. These gradually strayed into more worldly realms as Aberhart began preaching social credit on the air. As the 1935 election campaign swung into gear, Aberhart had a formidable political machine in place.

With its mixture of the social gospel, socialism and Fabianism, the CCF was not short on evangelical fervor either. Its leaders and literature railed against the "Fifty Big Shots," "Worshippers of the God Mammon and the Golden Calf," and "Capitalist Slave Camps and Sweat Shops," and preached the CCF's version of Utopia. The banks would be nationalized. Transportation, utility, communication and medical systems would be run by the state as well. Farmers would enjoy security of tenure and workers, the right to unionize, and receive unemployment insurance and adequate pensions. All this was promised, and sometimes much more! In the early days, many CCF supporters envisioned the dawning of a whole new civilization under a CCF government. As a typical editorial in the party's newspaper, *The Commonwealth*, so confidently put it: "In the social order visualized by the CCF, the field of individual aspiration, training and development would be extended to a degree not hitherto deemed possible!"[14] The trouble was that the CCF was not dangling 25 bucks a month in front of voters' noses. And then, there was the bogey of socialism. Fiercely independent, prairie farmers had always been deeply suspicious of the whole notion of public ownership, particularly of land. The press, big business and opposition parties capitalized upon these fears, doing all they could to convince the public that a CCF government would confiscate "everything from their farms to their toothbrushes." Nellie Peterson recalls the following encounter:

> I remember drinking coffee in one farmer's kitchen. He told me he'd never support the CCF. I said, "Why? What's the matter with the CCF?" "Well," he said, "I know the first thing they'd do is take my farm away." Now it so happened that they lived on a little side hill and the only thing you could see out the window were rocks and trees. It was a hopeless homestead if he ever did clear it out. You know it just flashed through my mind that I'm not going to lose the CCF any support because this man is not going to give it anyways, so I might as well give him a good jolt. And so I said, "To tell you the truth, if I were you, I'd pay somebody to take this farm off my hands!"

Recognizing the problem, the pragmatic Saskatchewan CCF party didn't hesitate long before dropping "socialism" from its 1936 provincial party platform. The term continued to be used in subsequent party debates and literature, but it was downplayed as the provincial party emphasized the social reform aspects of CCF policy, putting together a comprehensive, far-reaching package of social welfare, education, farm security and labor legislation reforms which eventually won popular support. In contrast, the Alberta CCF continued to alarm skittish voters with its strong stance on public ownership.

The Slide to Oblivion
Clearly, the CCF faced enormous handicaps when it made its

political debut in Alberta. Fortunately, CCF activists were far from a faint-hearted lot. A firm belief in the righteousness of their cause fuelled them with a commitment and energy which seem all the more remarkable and refreshing in retrospect. The CCFers did not set their sights on merely winning elections; they really believed they could build a new heaven on earth. Aylmer Liesemer, who sat in the Alberta legislature from 1944 to 1952, chuckles as he recalls his youthful idealism:

> Oh yes, I was very naive. I thought that all we had to do really was to tell people about this wonderful system of socialism and they'd all vote for it. I really thought we were on the verge of a breakthrough to create a new world. It would be a world where there was no suffering, at least man-made suffering. Everybody would have a job. Certainly the very wealthy would have to make great sacrifices through increased taxes and so on. There would be a great deal of public enterprise; and the banks would be taken over in the not-too-distant future. It was the planning of socialism which appealed to me. It seemed like a logical system which would provide a decent livelihood for everybody. Remember this was in the middle of the Depression. You'd see crews of men out with rakes breaking up the rocks on gravel roads. They were getting some relief, but they had to work it out at 25 cents an hour. And some of the jobs were raking rocks back onto the gravel road that the cars had kicked aside. That was a helluva life for people who were capable of doing good work. A scraper could have done that in no time.

As elsewhere in the country, hundreds of little CCF study clubs mushroomed throughout Alberta in the Thirties. Like their Social Credit counterparts, they too focussed on economic matters but with a decidedly different slant. Edward Bellamy's *Looking Backwards*, Upton Sinclair, Sidney Webb, British Labor Party literature and classic socialist tracts were studiously read and discussed. Unemployed or underemployed, many CCF supporters made the most of their time by voraciously reading anything they could lay their hands upon, thus overcoming the deficiencies in their formal education. Groups of ten to fifteen people met in each other's homes once a week in urban areas or in one-room country school houses in rural areas. In 1940, there were 20 to 30 study clubs in her Lac St. Anne constituency alone, according to Nellie Peterson. These clubs faded away during the prosperous post-war years, however, as country roads improved, the country school ceased to serve as the focus of rural community life, and people became preoccupied with their jobs and personal lives.

Campaigning in the rural areas was always a gruelling endurance test for CCF candidates and organizers, particularly during the winter months. Nellie Peterson never set out, for example, without a lantern, extra clothes and foot warmers in case her car broke down on a isolated stretch on the poor country roads. She recalls one particularly harrowing experience:

It was viciously cold, the wind was blowing and the roads were rotten, but I hated to turn back. So I went down to the local garage about ten miles away from where I was going, and asked "Is there anybody in town that you know of that is going out to point B?" The garageman said, "Yeah, there's a chap that just came in and his car has broken down and he wants to get home." And so I got hold of this chap and said, "I'm Mrs. Peterson and I'm an organizer for the CCF. I'm due to have a meeting out in your district tonight." He said, "I don't know if you can get there over these roads." And I said, "No, probably not, but do you want to get home? Now I've got a shovel. Have you?" "No, I haven't," he said, "but if you got a shovel, we'll probably get through." Then he added, "I'm not CCF by the way." "Well, I don't care," I told him. "But when I get to your place, will you help me get to the hall?" He agreed. When we got there, his wife was a nice woman and so were the three teenaged kids. We had a good, hot supper, and then they all dressed up and came out to the hall. And it was a good thing too because when I opened up the door, the smoke just came pouring out. The local group had gotten there early to light the fire to warm up the hall, but for some reason the smoke was not going up the chimney. There was nothing for us to do but take down all those pipes—all 30 feet of them. We didn't find anything until we came to the chimney and that's when we came across the bird's nest. Finally, we got the pipes together again, got the stove going and we had our meeting. But that wasn't the end of it. On the way back, the car got stuck in a drift about a mile and a half from the farmhouse. Nothing would budge it. So we all clambered out of the car and walked to the house, getting frozen stiff in the process. No, it certainly wasn't unusual to get stuck in those days.

Her recompense for her arduous organizing work in the Forties was a munificent "$5 a day, the days I worked." Peterson's salary was raised to $1,000 when she became provincial party secretary, but she resisted any further pay hikes, knowing full well that she would have to raise the money herself!

CCF candidates frequently had to brave the ostracism of their communities and the dirty tricks played by their political opponents. Acquaintances would duck or cross the street when they saw Nancy Zaseybida, a farm woman who ran three times in her constituency of Vegreville in the Fifties, walking towards them. Sexual innuendos were even more painful to deal with. Her husband was frequently taunted with such crude remarks as, "If your wife gets elected she will be in Ottawa only to service the male MPs."[15] It was not unusual for her to arrive at a community hall where she was slated to speak only to discover the caretaker had conveniently gone home with the keys, or that the power had been cut off. Other times she'd find a sign stuck on the door, announcing that the meeting had been cancelled. Candidates were also generally required to underwrite as well as organize their own campaigns since they could expect little help from the CCF's impoverished kitty. For the Zaseybidas that meant an outlay of about $1,000 each time Nancy ran—a sizeable chunk of a farm family's income in those days.

Despite the CCF's dismal Alberta debut, the provincial party dared to hope for a breakthrough in the summer of '44. Nobody expected the CCF actually to *win*, of course, but the bets were on that the party would form a strong opposition to Ernest Manning, Aberhart's successor in the provincial legislature. Their dreams of long-awaited success were even shared by federal party leaders such as David Lewis who expected "a great deal from the CCF in Alberta."[16] They had grounds for their optimism. The CCF was riding a high crest of national popularity as the imagination of a depression and war weary public was captured—if only for a short time—by the CCF's social reform policies. For a brief, heady period in the fall of 1943, the CCF even topped the Gallup polls, inching both the Tories and Grits out by a slight margin with its 30 per cent share of the popular vote. The rosy picture continued into the summer months of 1944 with the CCF's landslide victory in Saskatchewan and as the party edged within striking distance in both B.C. and Ontario. Prospects looked bright in Alberta as well. By the end of July 1944, the provincial party had signed up 11,000 members and collected $12,000 in one month, which represented more bodies and dollars than the party had been able to accumulate over the previous two or three years.[17] It was not to be, however. The CCF did manage to capture 25 per cent of the popular vote in the August 1944 election (never surpassed by the NDP until 1986), but this translated into a meagre two seats. The Liberal-Conservative coalition was able to win three seats and official opposition status after polling only 16.7 per cent of the vote while the Socreds retained their comfortable majority. An article in *The People's Weekly* pointed out that the CCF had to win almost half as many votes as Social Credit to elect two members as compared to the Socred's total of 51. The electoral system again worked against the opposition, producing another overwhelming legislative majority.

The party never recovered, but slowly slid towards political oblivion. The virulent anti-communist hysteria of the Cold War years sadly infected the beleaguered CCF party in Alberta, effectively destroying party unity. The party was split into two factions: one supporting provincial party president, Bill Irvine and the other supporting MLA, Elmer Roper. Irvine got himself into hot water over his 1956 trip to the Soviet Union when Tass quoted his description of Russia as "a new Mecca."[18] A section of the provincial membership wrote to Ottawa asking for permission to secede from the provincial party while retaining national membership. The majority of the party continued to support Irvine, however. A subsequent trip to China did not exactly endear Irvine to either his detractors within the provincial party or to the national leadership.

Nellie Peterson was convinced that a more fundamental issue was at stake, however. To her mind, the CCF had become so fearful of being labelled as "communist" or "Red" that it no longer was willing to risk social censure by taking a strong position on any issue.

> I agreed with Irvine who felt that as soon as you start saying, "Oh well, no, I'm not really a socialist. I don't want to go that far," well, immediately people start saying, "What's the matter with it that you're so scared of it too?" In fact you were defeating yourself by timidity. If you can't strongly support a position you've taken in the CCF as socialists and democrats, if you can't take a stand different from the one which we saw leading to hatred and war among nations, then better quit entirely because you were fouling your own nest. You would try saying to people, "If you've gotten places without ever being called a communist or red, you can't have stuck your neck out very far." For years, if you so much as supported the wheat pool, you'd be called anything up to a Bolshevik.

Membership participation sank to such a low ebb that it was not unusual for only the executive to show up for annual constituency meetings, re-elect themselves and carry on for another year. One former CCF official estimated that two-thirds of the 40 to 50 delegates who attended annual conventions in the latter part of the Fifties had allowed their membership dues to lapse. Provincial party leaders were not wildly enthusiastic about the idea of forming a New Party based on liberal-minded and trade union support, however. In fact, the Alberta CCF was one of the most adamantly opposed sections of the party because it feared the dilution of fundamental, CCF socialist principles as originally laid out in the Regina Manifesto. As one of the architects and fiercest defenders of the New Democratic Party, David Lewis was thoroughly disgruntled with the Alberta doctrinaires:

> There were old-timers who had got used to CCF electoral failures and felt more at home in the role of victims of capitalist greed than they would be as victors in any election battle. Objections from some CCF leaders in Alberta were typical of this group. The party in that province never recovered from the decimation it suffered at the hands of Aberhart in 1935, despite the fact that from time to time we elected to the provincial legislature men of unsurpassed ability and moral quality, like Elmer Roper and Chester Ronning. Yet some Alberta CCFers were determined that their purity in adversity was preferable to any fresh adventures. They represented a small but vocal group[19]

That small but vocal group was unceremoniously shunted aside like a passel of shabby, elderly relations—an embarrassing reminder of past failures—by the enthusiastic supporters of the new party and its new image, however. A handful of diehards did turn out for the 1961 NDP founding convention in Ottawa. But they rode the train home to Alberta deeply disillusioned by the new party's lack of commitment to "socialist" principles on and hurt by the rebuffs they received from its national leaders. They found themselves even less welcome in the new provincial party, launched in early 1962. Bowing to the inevitable, they launched an appeal to pay off their political debts, and then handed over the CCF's old '57 Chevy and $1,000 in assets to Bill Irvine as recognition for his long years of service. Two other long-time workers were rewarded too. The CCF membership lists were turned over to the NDP, but the left-over assets were ploughed into the newly-formed, Woodsworth-Irvine Socialist Fellowship. This made the NDP leaders unhappy, but as Nellie Peterson puts it, they weren't missing out on much. "We didn't have much else except for some old tables, and a rickety typewriter worth about eight dollars and a Gestetner machine we'd had for a donkey's age. At least we disappeared from the party without leaving them with any debts." (Nor did they leave the NDP the old CCF headquarters, Woodsworth-Irvine House.)

The transition from CCF to NDP was hardly smooth and harmonious; and the wounds took a long time to heal. Many old-timers continued to take out memberships in the new party, but for them, the glory was gone. As they quietly buried the old party which represented a lifelong commitment, they were at least able to look back without recrimination or regret. The last word goes to Nellie Peterson, older and wiser than the young country school teacher who plunged into politics with visions of a new Jerusalem dancing through her head.

Did I feel disappointed? Actually, disappointed is the wrong word because one can't be disappointed unless one has appointed a goal that you think is achievable. It was not our time. There was no left-wing movement making advances anywhere in the world. What we did in our little corner in Alberta wouldn't make any difference. But, there was always a hope you kept alive, a little spark anyway, that there was a place for civil libertarians, feminists, and honest trade unionists, a place in the political world for them to go to. And if all you could do was to be there and say, "This is right and that is wrong," then it's worthwhile.

---

[1]Clarence Fines, *Impossible Dream*, Self-published autobiography, Saskatchewan Archives Board (Regina), p. 248.

[2]*Regina Leader-Post* (August 2, 1932), p. 1.

[3]*Calgary Herald* (July 24, 1982).

[4]James G. MacGregor, *A History of Alberta* (Edmonton, 1977), p. 255.

[5]S.M. Lipset, *Agrarian Socialism* (California, 1971), p. 158.

[6]Interview with Nellie Peterson (Mayerthorpe, Alberta, November 8, 1983.)

[7]Anthony Mardiros, *William Irvine: The Life of a Prairie Radical* (Toronto, 1979), p. 150.

[8]John A. Irving, *The Social Credit Movement in Alberta* (Toronto, 1974), p. 147.

[9]Interview with Aylmer Liesemer (Calgary, July 2, 1983).

[10]*The Regina Leader-Post* (July 21, 1933).

[11]Liesemer interview (July 2, 1983).

[12]Interview (November 2, 1983).

[13]David Lewis, *The Good Fight* (Toronto, 1981), p. 109.

[14]*The B.C. Commonwealth* (August 2, 1933).

[15]Myrna Kostash, *All of Baba's Children* (Edmonton, 1980), p. 256.

[16]Lewis, *The Good Fight*, p. 211.

[17]*Ibid.*

[18]Mardiros, *William Irvine*, p. 237.

[19]Lewis, *The Good Fight*, p. 489.

Chapter 3

Social Democracy in Alberta:
From the CCF to the NDP

Robin Hunter

The Decline of the CCF

In the years prior to the creation of the New Democratic Party, the Alberta CCF can hardly have seemed a promising organization to use as a foundation stone for the creation of a new political movement. After the 1935 Social Credit deluge, the party found itself the largest opposition party in the province, replacing the recently-defeated United Farmers of Alberta, while the old-line Liberal and Conservative parties collapsed and ceased organizational existence, only to revive in the decade of the fifties.

In the early nineteen forties, the party underwent very rapid growth. David Lewis, CCF National Secretary at the time, gives the figure of eleven thousand members in July 1944, but suggests growth was so fast that the party's organization was incapable of assimilating or effectively putting to work such an increase.[1] In 1944, the second election the CCF contested, it was the largest opposition party in provincial politics, achieving what was to be its highest proportional vote ever, 25%, but as in 1940, won no seats in the legislature at all.

Important battles were fought in the late forties and nineteen fifties, during which Social Credit abandoned all semblance of its other-than-conventional past, and endeavoured to lock the province into a rigidly orthodox trajectory of economic development. Elmer Roper led the CCF from 1942 until his retirement, after the loss of his seat in the legislature in 1955. A trade unionist and energetic propagandist for socialism, he had first run for election as a Labour candidate in 1921. Using his parliamentary podium as a forum to address the province and pose his party's alternative to the Manning behemoth, he was noted by the press as a lucid speaker and skilled parliamentarian. He challenged Social Credit's policies, particularly around the disposition of Alberta's natural resources. Roper campaigned for higher royalties from crown mineral wealth (later implemented by Peter Lougheed), public ownership and participation in the development of the oil industry, and for publicly-owned electric power. In a manner not unlike Grant Notley in later years, Roper argued in terms free of mystification and humbug, and did his best to persuade Albertans that the left offered a program that made sense in terms of their own lives and concerns.

Initially, the CCF's base of support had been strongest in the rural areas; it inherited organizational readiness and experience from the United Farmers, much of whose personnel came into the CCF as the UFA collapsed. Along with these members, the party inherited the UFA's ethos of radical agrarian populism, and its overriding commitments to the family farm. To ensure its survival, the movement aimed to underwrite the family farm's continued existence by public policy, where necessary intervening in and abrogating the dictates of the capitalist market. The CCF's willingness to advocate these measures, which was of course facilitated by the party's hostility to capitalism, accounts for the continued adherence of so many activists in the farmers' movement during the CCF's decline. Although the organizational descendant of the UFA, the Farmers' Union of Alberta (FUA) never renounced its formal position of nonpartisanship and electoral noninvolvement, its leadership and activist stratum probably had a higher proportion of CCF supporters than any other social organization in Alberta.

The market was not kind to the family farm during the CCF's existence. In Alberta, the number of farm units declined by about a thousand a year, from 100,000 in 1940 to 73,000 in 1961, and would continue to decline to 63,000 in 1971, by which time only 14.6% of the province's population would make its living on the farm.[2]

This decline in the position of the family farm in the province's economy eroded the class basis of the CCF's vote in Alberta, and at the same time undercut the party ideologically. Mechanization in the postwar years led to a gradual rise in the average amount of capital invested in the typical prairie farm. Accompanied by the consolidation of smaller, more marginal farms into surviving units, this mechanization is the hallmark of the transition from farming into "agribusiness", which Richards and Pratt argue expressed itself ideologically in the decline of populist perspectives and the expansion of a capitalist outlook on society and the farming community.[3] The 1950s were particularly lean years for the CCF. Although the party elected a handful of MLA's (never more than two simultaneously) its popular vote declined steadily. By the 1959 election, the party was deprived of any representation in the legislature, and had fallen to just over four per cent of the popular vote.

Along with this process, the CCF membership had, in the space of a decade and a half, become increasingly demoralized, as earlier electoral near-misses became monotonously recurrent defeats. The age of the membership crept upward, as recruitment faded. By the end of the 1950s the increasing frequency of balding heads and whitening hair was visible both at party conventions and constituency meetings. An atmosphere of fatigue often made nomination meetings somber events as party members wondered out loud whether contesting seats which they saw no chance of winning was worth the trouble. The 1959 election saw for the first time the number of seats for which the CCF ran fall below fifty per cent of the total, though in each election since 1944 the percentage contested had dropped. A peculiar mood of fatalism sometimes manifested itself in the members' outlook. There was little feel that the party's activity in itself was a factor in the party's fate, and the sense that a socialist movement could only be successful "when the time was ripe" was often expressed. In the 1950s, silent, acquiescent and self-satisfied (a "me generation" if ever there was one) it sometimes seemed that the optimum which could be asked of those on the left was that they hang on, and keep their politics intact, as a signal to those who might come later of what had been won and aspired to in the past.

It was hard to avoid the feeling at CCF meetings that somehow membership had become an end in itself, rather than a means to an actual social transformation. It is this which David Lewis was getting at when he rather harshly in his memoirs describes the "old timers who had got used to CCF electoral failures and felt more at home in the role of victims of capitalist greed than they would be as victors in any electoral battle . . ." and adds "some CCF leaders in Alberta were typical of this group."[4]

CCFers often opted for philosophizing over politics. It was not rare for a resolution on some practical point requiring action to be diverted to a discussion of "basic principles" which might be abstract speculation about ultimate goals, while the means of acquiring them went quite unconsidered. The objection that the party's internal talk resembled the country store rambling of the "cracker barrel philosophers" was not rare, within certain circles of the party. Grant Notley, speaking to the Provincial Council of the NDP, when that party was less than two years old and still bore the stamp of older CCF methods, reflected this concern. Presenting the Council with a "four-year plan" to lay the basis of an acceptable set of organizational norms and methods for the constituency associations to move toward, Notley was clearly debating with the tenacious ghost of the CCF's habits of operation:

During the course of the next four years, we must induce our constituency associations to find a balance between discussion, education and philosophy on one hand, and the more practical aspects of organization on the other. Indeed, our ultimate political success on the local level lies through reaching a proper balance between these two functions. *Endless discussion, or philosophical debate, undisciplined by an accompanying responsibility to actively build and support the party is dangerous.* It may well lead our members into the false assumption that political success lies in direct proportion to political debate . . . Ideas alone will not build the movement . . . The balanced program of the properly functioning constituency association should involve regular meetings, educational activities, social events, and at the same time, provide for the sale of memberships, the raising of money, and the development of an election organization. There is not, as some may feel, a conflict of interest between these two areas of work . . . the two must go hand in hand.[5]

The length to which the CCF was given over to philosophical debate "undisciplined by an accompanying responsibility to actively build questions well above the party's political tasks. The June 1960 convention of the party devoted a considerable amount of time to discussing a critique of a spuriously "non-political", pseudo-religious, anti-Communist and at bottom anti-labour organization, the "Moral Rearmament Association", which was at that time showing modest signs of life in Alberta.[6]

It is, however, a matter of speculation as to whether the CCF won anybody closer to its point of view by opposing an organization which preached against "class conflict" and urged a "moral rearmament" on society's leaders. Nor is it clear how the concern expressed and publicity generated over MRA related to the CCF's hopes of improving its position in the party contest within the province.

One of the most remarkable of the CCF's convention resolutions, both for its political foresight and its irrelevance to what was going on in Canadian society at that time, was passed by the 1958 provincial convention, calling for government "honoraria" to be paid monthly to all mothers of children under the age of sixteen, to facilitate their remaining in the home caring for their offspring, rather than being siphoned off into the labour market for economic reasons. This resolution anticipated one of the demands to be raised by the women's liberation movement of the next generation, that of the "wages for housework" campaign, although it was motivated by some during the hour-long debate on the convention floor in terms quite out of step with the outlook which that movement adopted.

That the resolution should have come into being at all is remarkable. Its passage is testimony to the mood which the party brought to politics, which may be characterized as "utopian rationalism", and which endowed the movement which it imbued with both strengths and weaknesses.

This mood derived from the party's heritage and from the radical milieu of prairie populism, whose roots reached back to the social experimentalism of the constantly moving North American frontier culture, with its (often contradictory) vision of community-based participatory democracy and the discovery of truth by debate. Of the Canadian provinces, Alberta probably received the least-diluted injection of the populist variant of utopian rationalism, and the CCF was its ultimate Albertan receptable. The hallmark of this populism was a healthy disrespect for the heavy hand of the past and a belief that reason should be used to find better alternatives to the status quo. Reason had led these prairie radicals to reject capitalism and the market, just as open talk and free debate had won the province for the Farmers' Movement.

The strength of such an intellectual climate was that it enabled the participants in the movement to step outside of and beyond the dogmas and assumptions of the dominant ideology. Its adherents were not inclined to curl up passively in the face of the economic orthodoxies preached then (and still preached) by the *Calgary Herald* or the *Edmonton Journal*, whose message had always been that the radical movement's schemes to change the world were quite impossible.

The suppositions of the status quo, if not rebutted, can persuade the members of a society that beyond a certain point, the way things work at present, (e.g. the economic dependence of mothers on "breadwinning" fathers in the family unit, or of workers on their bosses in the factory unit, etc.) is the only way society could possibly work. This is the conservative power of ideology. Any party which is serious about constructing an alternative to capitalist society, but whose activists are unable to out-argue the media-reinforced concerns and objectives to which party members must respond from their neighbours and workmates, would be quite unable to withstand the pressure (intellectual and cultural at the very least) that defenders of capitalism would generate. In this sense, the intellectual mood sustained by the CCF was healthy and necessary. It compares favourably, one suspects, with the intellectual milieu of the NDP today.

But there is another factor in the equation: as Grant Notley warned, debate and education which are not tied into practical and *political* tasks can become substitutes for them, and become ends in themselves. This really seems to have happened in the CCF. The provincial conventions, for example, toward the end of the party's life span, became less and less the one time of the year when activists from every part of the province would come together and discuss program, strategy and the organizing of concrete measures aimed at persuading Albertans that a CCF government was in their interests. Instead, the conventions began to resemble festivals of social philosophizing, where the methodology of the "good idea" began to dominate convention activity. This methodology embodied an abstracted, historical rationalism unrelated to actual political forces. This or that "good", "rational" idea was added to the growing list of points (all of them good ideas) on the program of the CCF government-to-be, but really it could be little other than "undisciplined philosophizing", an institutionalized form of wishful thinking disguised as "socialist education". It is true that in 1958 there was a general uneasiness about the stability of the family, but there was nowhere to be seen an actual social *movement* to which one might address the call of wages for housework. One was coming, but it was over a decade away. Had there been a body of people who showed potential for being stung into action by such a political demand, it would have transcended "socialist education" and been close to socialist agitation.

The Cold War caught the whole CCF in a particularly painful vice. As a party of the left it was far less inclined than its competitors to swallow whole the American line that the post-World War II worsening of East-West relations was all the fault of the Soviet Union, or that a remedy was wholesale militarization and a bipolar division of the world. The Alberta party was even less inclined than the national wing to accommodate itself to the prevailing current of Cold War sentiment, an accommodation which manifested itself in the CCF's parliamentary contingent voting *for* Canada's entry into NATO, although criticizing the alliance as being overly military in nature. (The party's last national convention reversed this position in 1960.)

There was nothing heretical in this resistance to the national current. Indeed, the Alberta party had taken shape and undergone its most rapid growth when sympathy for the USSR, at the time a military ally of Canada, Britain and the United States, was running high. The mood of the 1945-45 Allied entente seemed to remain alive in the province's CCF membership in the post-war years, and even into the 1950s. This view was basically lenient in its assessment of the USSR, and usually held that while afflicted with the excesses of a still-developing society, it was basically a "progressive" force in the world, and just as it had been the West's ally in the collective struggle against fascism, remained a force opposed to feudal and oppressive economic conditions and for social change, in the Third World in particular, and elsewhere. This attitude, along with the observation that the USA was not always spotless on the questions of democracy and freedom, and could be considered a major threat to peace in itself, was the perspective of a substantial sector of the provincial leadership, although by no means all. The national party's position in Alberta was generally maintained by the party's provincial leader, Elmer Roper. Most important of those who held out against the national party's acquiescence in the face of the Cold War was William Irvine, who in the last decade of his life produced a stream of articles, addresses and pamphlets aimed at persuading the Canadian public of the feasibility of disarmament and an accommodation between the USA and the USSR.

In doing this, Irvine occasionally put himself and his party in the situation of leading with the chin, for he was operating (as was the whole CCF) in an environment in which the media were very hostile and eager to present the CCF in the least favourable light possible. Any deviation from Cold War orthodoxy was sure to be singled out and spotlighted, which not infrequently cost the party in terms of votes and sympathy.

Illustrative of this was an incident which occurred while Irvine was president of the Alberta party. During a group tour of the Soviet Union, investigating "the chances of war between East and west," Irvine was reported as having met Nikita Khrushchev during a visit to the Supreme Soviet. He was quoted as praising the "democratic" nature of the Soviet state. John Diefenbaker raised the matter in parliament, accusing Irvine of "eulogizing" the Soviet system and ensuring national exposure of the matter. M.J. Coldwell, CCF National Leader, responded by expressing doubts regarding the accuracy of the Tass report which Diefenbaker cited, but said that if Irvine had indeed expressed approval of "Russia's one-party dictatorship", this would be immediately repudiated by the CCF.[7] No repudiation was necessary, however. Irvine claimed that the Tass quotes had been mutilated and taken out of context.[8]

In assessing this stage of Irvine's career, Reg Whitaker argues that "Irvine's good will somewhat outran his critical faculty when confronted with the Soviet system,"[9] a point which is probably valid. In judging Irvine's analysis of the Soviet system, it must be said that he never gave much effort to the very telling criticisms which may be made of the USSR from a *socialist* standpoint (indeed, he does not seem to have specified whether he considered the Soviet Union to be a socialist society or not). This ambiguity left him in a rather weak position when attacked from the right as making apologies for the Soviets, within or outside the CCF.

The New Party Project

The impulse for the creation of the New Democratic Party is to be found almost entirely outside of Alberta. The "Diefenbaker sweep" of March 1958 underscored the marginality of the national CCF by reducing it to an eight-seat rump in parliament. The party had hitherto seemed to have at least an outside chance of rising to major party status, but the 1958 election rang the death knell of Canada's extra-ordinary four-party system. The CCF's continued existence could no longer be assumed.

The most weighty consequence of this setback was the resolution passed shortly after the election by the national convention of the newly-formed Canadian Labour Congress, which was itself without effective representation in the new parliament. This resolution was originally intended to be simply an endorsement of the CCF movement and program, but the shock of the electoral defeat altered this intent to a more bold and innovative initiative.[10]

The CLC's simple endorsement of the CCF would have been an important breakthrough for the party, but instead the Trade Union body argued that the political system effectively excluded the workers, farmers and similar groups, and proclaimed the need for "a broadly based people's political movement which embraces the CCF, the Labour movement, farm organizations, professional people and other liberally-minded persons interested in social reform and reconstruction through our parliamentary system of government". The resolution praised the CCF for its contribution to this goal, and urged that "Labour and other people's organizations . . . together with the CCF" actually create such a broader movement, the nature of which was vaguely indicated with reference to the "experience of Labour and social democratic political parties elsewhere", and the stipulation that labour had "no wish to dominate such a development". The resolution concluded by instructing the CLC executive "to give immediate and urgent attention to this matter by initiating discussions with the CCF, interested farm organizations and other like-minded individuals and groups" and to report back to the

CLC's next convention on the results of the initiative and the prospects for action.[11]

The executives of the CLC and CCF constituted a "Joint Political Committee", and began organizing support for the project. Discussion of the projected New Party was initiated at all levels of the CCF and Labour movement, in the form of conferences, seminars and forums. The same year, in July, the national convention of the CCF endorsed the CLC initiative, and hailed it as a "landmark". The "Joint Political Committee" changed its name to the "National Committee for a New Party" (NCNP), and the intended "alternative political force" became the main project of the CCF nationally and ostensibly in every province.

After the recent electoral debacle, any in the party who wanted to argue that no change was needed which might broaden the base of the party's appeal had little ground on which to stand. Nationally, the majority of the CCFers came to see the CLC's proposal as a means of overcoming the twenty-five year marginalization which had been the CCF's fate, and the threat of extinction which Canadian politics now seemed to pose.

The Alberta CCF's initial response to the New Party proposal was low-key, but generally positive. Addressing the party's 1958 convention, Elmer Roper, no longer leader but still Alberta representative on the party's National Council and now Mayor of Edmonton, called the project "a significant political event (which) . . . if it works out, would give Canadian socialists a mass movement and the framework to do more than they can by paddling around in a little pool of their own philosophical abstractions." Roper likened the project to the Commonwealth Labour parties of Great Britain, New Zealand and Australia.

As if posing an immediate alternative to any present pools of philosophical abstraction in which the party might be tempted to paddle in the interim, Roper pointed to the Manitoba CCF's recent doubling of its legislative representation in the election in that province, remarked that an election in Alberta was due in the next year and urged that "for the next twelve months we let the rest of the troubled world take care of itself and let's see if we have what it takes to do in Alberta what our colleagues in Manitoba have done. Unless we can," he added, "we'll have little to take into any new political alignment, and even less to nurture within our own little circle in the years ahead."[12]

In Roper's remarks may be clearly discerned a criticism increasingly finding expression within the Alberta CCF at this time, namely its preoccupation with ideological and philosophical questions and debates *apart* from the concrete concerns of ordinary voters, and the tendency for the party to speak its piece *outside* the perspective in which politics was seen by the mass of Albertans. An example of this is the presidential address given to the next year's convention, by William Irvine, the veteran fighter and co-founder with Woodsworth of the CCF.

Irvine spoke against the backdrop of the provincial election to which Roper had looked forward the year before having passed, with the Alberta party losing both the seats it had held when Roper spoke, and failing to retain any of its electoral deposits in the other seats contested. In the public's mind, the CCF stood on the brink of extinction. Despite the provincial focus of the convention and the party's desperate weakness in the Alberta area, Irvine refrained from discussing the situation in the province at all. The task of re-establishing the party as a relevant choice to those considering how Alberta might be governed was completely bypassed. Irvine instead addressed the international political situation, the Cold War and the arms race, genuinely important questions, thought-stimulating and unorthodox. Irvine's address was, however, concrete in his discussion of the New Party. He argued that entering politics was "the only possible course for labour" if it wished to consolidate the gains it had made in the past decades, and he argued that the world situation cried out for a "new" Canadian foreign policy, as a major priority and concern for the party project by both the national CCF and CLC.[13]

The CCF's resolution on the New Party at this 1959 convention merits note, since it suggests a reservation on the part of the Alberta CCF regarding the New Party which was to grow into some importance later. Noting that the CCF had originally been a federation of farm and labour organizations which maintained their separate identities within and outside the party, the resolution approved the New Party project and urged "that the constitution of the New Party shall be such as will establish it as a federation in which there is a place for Labour, Farmer, and CCF affiliates co-operating for the common weal".[14] In other words, the CCF was to retain its distinct identity within whatever framework the New Party was to adopt.

In spite of the CCF's 1959 approval of the idea of the New Party in principle, 1960 saw the emergence of severe objections on the part of the most influential CCF leaders in the province. These objections applied both to the project and the way it was being implemented. From what had either been a non-committal wait-and-see position, or even a cautious optimism, attitudes hardened to off-the-record opposition.

None of the Alberta leadership ever publicly opposed the New Party. Even within the movement, opposition was most often expressed by dwelling on the problems implied by the project, with the implication that it was likely to prove unworkable.

The basis for this negative turn was mainly a concern as to the political nature of the party to be created. The Alberta leadership had not been happy in the course of the last decade, as the CCF edged rightward, lessening the frequency with which it expressed an explicit commitment to socialism, substituting for it an antiseptic version of Keynesian "planning". In line with this trend, much of the mood and talk within the new elements drawn to the New Party movement gave the impression that the CCF, even after its dilution of the Regina Manifesto by the adoption of the Winnipeg Declaration of Principles in 1956, was held too old fashioned and "doctrinaire" in its criticism and rhetoric to be effective. People like Bill Irvine and provincial leader Floyd Johnson, backed by many rank-and-filers, were extremely concerned that the New Party be unequivocally socialist in its self-definition. The labour movement as a whole had only recently broken from a general posture of business unionism, and inspired little confidence as a force pushing society toward the left.

The New Party's highly visible connection with organized labour brought problems even within the CCF. In particular the past decade of anti-labour sensationalist journalism, focussing on allegedly widespread "racketeering" and corruption had promoted an atmosphere of unease and suspicion where trade unions were concerned in various rural areas of the province. Some unions *were* bureaucratized and top-heavy, particularly when compared with the standards to which people from the Alberta CCF were accustomed, and by which they judged organizations. Many farmers were half-persuaded that the rising costs of the farm industry could be laid exclusively at the door of organized labour. Sources of heated controversy in this respect were the various grain handlers' strikes at international terminals, frequently cited as proof that the unions were out to bleed the country dry, and did not mind how much they incidentally hurt the grain exporters in so doing. Even seasoned FUA leaders who were generally sympathetic to labour were inclined to be defensive and a little uneasy in differentiating themselves from a blanket condemnation of the unions, during a strike of the grain handlers.

The implementation of the New Party proposal led to a number of objections from the Alberta CCF leadership. It had quickly become clear to the NCNP that an organizational vehicle would be needed for the forces outside of the CCF and CLC if substantial numbers of "liberally minded persons" were to be brought in. The NCNP proposed the creation of "New Party Clubs", to bring together hitherto isolated individuals. This proposal met some opposition from the provincial sections of the CCF in Saskatchewan and British Columbia, a sentiment which Alberta shared. However, the NCNP's proposal was sustained with particular support from the Ontario section, and a compromise worked out.

The Alberta leadership's unhappiness centred on the fact that joining a New Party Club might mean virtually anything in terms of political persuasion, if the CLC resolution of 1958 was the only basis for the club's foundation. Membership in the CCF was contingent upon signature of a declaration of agreement with the CCF program, and agreement to abide by the party's constitution. In contrast to this, the CCF argued, membership in a New Party Club meant agreement with nothing concrete, and commitment to something as yet nonexistent. A number of objections to the vagueness of the principles of the New Party clubs were communicated to the NCNP, with very little effect.

Considerable concern was generated around the proposed basis of representation at the 1961 national founding convention, decided upon by the NCNP. CCF federal constituency associations were allowed one delegate for up to an initial fifty members, and an additional delegate for each fifty extra members (or major fraction thereof). New Party Clubs received delegates on the same basis. The problem was that the general CCF membership received representation on the basis of federal constituency association alone, which immediately generated an inequity, if the CCF and New Party clubs were seen as competitors (that they might become so was precisely what the CCF leadership feared). Calgary, for example, had two federal seats in parliament, and hence two federal constituency associations, each of which might be entitled to two delegates if their paid memberships exceeded seventy-five. But months before the founding convention there were six or seven New Party clubs in Calgary, each with an average membership of perhaps two dozen. Their representation combined would be twice the size of the CCF's, with little difference in the amount of paid membership base. Since the CCF was girding its loins for a possible fight over basic principles, that it was alarmed is hardly surprising.

The CCF also perceived itself in Alberta as in competition with the New Party clubs over membership, in part because the clubs seemed to have a disproportionately higher basis of representation to the convention, and in part because membership in the clubs cost only a dollar, as opposed to the three-dollars membership fee for the CCF. Party secretary Nellie Petersonc writing the National Office of the CCF, complained that reports from CCF constituency secretaries indicated that expired CCF memberships were not being renewed, where the members had the option of joining a New Party Club instead. She remarked that "ex-CCFers can hardly be barred from joining a New Party Club open to ex- and not-so-ex- Liberals, Tories and Social Creditors."

These perceived inequities prompted the Alberta CCF executive and Provincial Board to pass resolutions condemning the proposed basis of representation, and requesting the CCF National Committee to propose that the NCNP change it by granting the New Party clubs representation on a federal constituency basis, to eliminate the inequity described above. The Board's resolution merits quoting, since it also endeavoured to impose some philosophical criteria on membership in the New Party clubs. Besides urging that the clubs "organize themselves as Federal Constituency New Party Club Associations," the resolution also recommended that "the members of such clubs be urged to study the draft statements of program, policy and constitution and shall, to be eligible as club members, subscribe to the *basic* philosophy and goals as expressed in the draft statements".

Responding to these proposals, Stanley Knowles, chairman of the NCNP argued that "the objections raised . . . by your Provincial Executive are based on a misunderstanding of the roles to be played in the New Party by the CCF, the trade unions and 'the others' who have joined us in our efforts by forming New Party Clubs". Knowles added that "the basis of representation provides ample opportunity for the CCF to be represented in numbers far beyond those at previous CCF National Conventions."

Partly because of the disorganized state of the Provincial CCF, the New Party clubs in Alberta *did* in fact outweigh the Alberta CCF in terms of delegate to the founding convention, although on a nationwide basis CCF delegates were the largest contingent at the convention with more than double the number of club delegates.

Relations between the contending factions deteriorated in the coming months, as the New Party took on the appearance of an already accomplished fact. The debate within the CCF became acrimonious, and the partisans of the New Party were concerned at the possibility of a split, with an element of the CCF retaining the name, and possibly even running candidates for election.

Matters came to a head at the last regular convention of the provincial party, in June 1961, just over a month before the Ottawa convention to found the New Party federally. Had matters proceeded in accord with the preference of those supporting the New Party, this convention would probably have wound up the Alberta CCF's affairs in anticipation of entering the New Party *en masse*. The CCF was by no means persuaded as to the rectitude of the New Party course, however. After some debate, in which much doubt about the New Party was expressed, the Alberta convention decided to postpone a decision regarding the disposition of the CCF until *after* the federal founding convention. To this effect, another CCF convention was schedule for November 1961.

Grant Notley, who by this time was on the NCNP payroll as organizer for Alberta, recorded his feelings following the Alberta convention in a letter to his Ottawa superiors:

> Fears that some CCFers have about the New Party are only being sharpened by the growing suspicion and hostility of the Provincial Executive . . . the general tone of the convention was essentially negative . . . The calling of a one day convention next fall . . . indicates a basic lack of confidence in the whole New Party movement . . . There seems to be a growing resentment against both the labour and youth delegates. As one of the senior delegates put it "What right have you people to come into our convention and tell us what to do?" . . . After talking to some I am convinced that there was a definite campaign conducted by certain people to discredit the youth and labour delegates . . . It was a clear victory for those I have often referred to as the armchair philosophers.

At the November convention, the Alberta CCF's last convention, with the federal NDP already in existence, the CCF leadership presented the membership with two basic alternatives. One of these provided that the CCF dissolve and join the NDP. The other maintained the option of CCF affiliation and separate identity, originally enunciated at the 1959 convention. Although William Irvine and Elmer Roper both addressed the convention in support of the affiliation proposal, it failed to pass.

Rather than simply dissolving the CCF and leaving it at that, however, the convention's resolution of dissolution added the proviso that the CCF before it ceased existence would lay the basis for an organization to promote socialist research and education. The outcome of this was the Woodsworth-Irvine Socialist Fellowship, based in Edmonton, which continues functioning and giving input to the Alberta NDP, a quarter of a century after the end of the CCF.

Was the Alberta CCF Worth the Effort?

The picture presented of the Alberta CCF in 1960, that of a tired, electorally unsuccessful organization with little weight in the politics of the province, and, with some grave doubts as to the desirability of the New Party, raises the question of whether including the CCF in the founding process was actually worth the effort. Perhaps it would have been more sensible (in Alberta at least) to have bypassed the arduous process of persuading the CCF, to concentrate on New Party clubs and trade unions, letting those elements of the CCF who supported it enter it as individuals.

Such a view was not unheard of in Alberta New Party circles; indeed, elements of the CCF leadership feared it was predominant among certain New Party clubs. But to have heeded it would have been to miss a critical point: for anyone wanting to build a left wing political movement in Alberta, the CCF was the necessary point of departure.

It must be remembered that in 1960 there were very few people in Alberta who consciously inclined toward the democratic left. The CCF was certainly the largest identifiable group of people in the province who leaned in that direction at all. Membership was still in the vicinity of one thousand, and remained a living social network. People were still in contact, communicating with one another, whether membership dues were being paid or not. The organization, moreover, remained in the various localities a magnet for a certain portion of those in the province wanting to work for social change. It had recognition and a clear location on the political spectrum.

Over two generations in the making, this network had sustained and developed a social practice of open debate and philosophical radicalism in the face of the suffocating atmosphere of the 1950s. Resolutions calling for the recognition of mainland China and its admission to the United Nations were gradually becoming a part of middle of the road politics in 1960. The Alberta CCF took such a position in 1951, during the Korean war.

Not only had the CCF network promoted ideas critical and outside of the dominant business ideology, its people embodied an impressive accumulation of political experience. True, this experience was not informed by either a strategy or tactics that were effective, to which the political fortunes of the CCF as a party testify, but the membership had certainly *tasted* political work, in a variety of situations, spread geographically across the province.

The CCF's good contacts with the organized farmers' movement remained intact in 1960. Because of common experience in past struggles, and the party's programmatic commitment to the family farm, party activists still had the FUA membership's ear, if not its agreement. The CLC resolution had made explicit mention of the farmers' organizations, and this possible entry should have been one of the Alberta party's most attractive points, from the national New Party perspective.

Two other elements of the CCF membership which proved to be important in the founding process should be mentioned. These were the CCF trade unionists and the CCF youth.

There was little organizational connection between organized labour and the Alberta CCF. Some locals did affiliate with or endorse the party, but their number was few. Most of the trade unionists active in the party did so on an individual basis. They were concentrated in the cities, Edmonton and Calgary, Medicine Hat and Lethbridge, which had traditions of independent Labour politics before the CCF emerged. The mining centres of Drumheller and the Crowsnest Pass, and railroad centres like Edson spread the trade unionists' activity more widely in the party.

Their presence can be traced through newspaper reports and candidate biographies, but no estimate of the trade union element as a percentage of total membership is possible. Those whose activity brought about media attention were a mix of rank and file members, elected officers, and sometimes members of the permanent staffs of unions. It seems to have been fairly frequent for the executive members of city Labour Councils and the Alberta Federation of Labour to have held party memberships and been sporadically—sometimes quite regularly—involved in party activity.

Not surprisingly the New Party resolution of the CLC precipitated something of an upsurge in the visibility of trade unionists active in the CCF. One or two of these in Edmonton could be considered part of the CCF "old guard". Trade unionists seem as a group to have been more critical and impatient with the party's *status quo* than the membership as a whole, and became more active and involved as the New Party project evolved. As a group their experience in organizations was also greater, and they tended to bring a higher set of expectations to the organizational side of politics than did the average CCFer.

The CCF youth at the end of the fifties experienced a modest revival, spearheaded by a reactivation of the University of Alberta CCF club. The "Campus Club" (as it was known in the CCF) was given its main organizational focus by the annual Model Parliament campaign, which provided some training in debate and electoral politics. The club engaged in proselytizing and recruitment and enabled the children of the CCF-oriented families from outlying areas in the province to congregate, reinforcing their inherited politics. One of these was Grant Notley, and it was from the Campus Club that he constructed an important part of the team that he was to use in his work as Alberta New Party Organizer and later as NDP Provincial Secretary.

The U of A CCF Club converted itself to the U of A New Party club in December of 1960. This was mainly due to the fact that Notley was completely persuaded of the good prospects and viability of the New Party. Club members were persuaded that a New Party face lift for the CCF offered the chance of improving the CCF's usual meagre vote in the Model Parliament student poll. The change of image took place at a well-advertised all-day meeting attended by over fifty persons, with its emphasis on the policy and program of the projected party. A number of individuals who had been hovering on the fringes of the CCF club were persuaded to formalize their membership and commit themselves to activity on the executive or some working group.

While still the CCF Club, the U of A group had reorganized, helped educate, and provided leadership for the formerly inactive Edmonton CCF youth. This body involved perhaps twenty young people, mainly in high school, and began a slow process of recruiting high school youth, which continued for perhaps a decade. The next year the Campus Club was also involved in helping a New Party club at the U of A in Calgary get organized, which along with a Calgary city youth group would lay the basis for a much accelerated working relationship between New Party partisans in both metropolitan centres (a substantial element of which was to be drawn from the youth layers).

Organizing the New Party
The first concrete activity in Alberta concerning the New Party was taken by the trade union movement. A "Political Education Seminar" sponsored by the Alberta Federation of Labour, was held in Red Deer in early June, 1959. Its minutes report the attendance of 110 delegates from sixty-one labour organizations, plus "observers" (also called "delegates") from the CCF and the Farmers' Union of Alberta. (A "weekend school" focussing on the New Party proposal had been held previously in Medicine Hat, in which strong support for the name "Canadian Democratic Party" was registered).[22]

The main speaker, George Home, director of the CLC's Political Education Department, outline the CLC's case for a new party, stressing the basic pro-business postures of the major parties, and the CCF's superior record on a variety of issues. Anti-labour legislation in Newfoundland and British Columbia was stressed. (Indeed, Joseph Smallwood's anti-labour stance in Newfoundland, and the Federal Liberals' reluctance to dissociate themselves from it, was critical in severing the already waning ties of many trade unionists to the Liberal party all across the country).

CCF activity promoting the New Party saw the organization of a series of seminars in early 1960, aimed primarily at informing the party's membership, as well as non-affiliated members of the public about the project. In the first three months of the year, seminars were held in Lethbridge, Medicine Hat, Calgary, Red Deer and a number of small towns such as Consort, Forestburg, Wetaskiwin, and Gibbons. These rural events were more frequent in Northern Alberta where CCF organization still existed, and mainly involved the local CCF membership and periphery, plus any other individuals who could be persuaded to come along.

Press descriptions of these events suggest they differed only slightly from typical CCF events, with little effective outreach beyond the traditional audience commanded by the party. The seminars tended to be rather demanding affairs—the one in Lethbridge lasted seven hours.[23] The function organized for the Jasper Edson constituency was combined with a curling bonspiel.

Often held in austere and poorly heated local halls, so characteristic of rural CCF functions in Alberta, where political meetings assumed the form of farm socials among neighbours— neighbours tied with a bond which carried with it the feeling of a distinct, and by 1960, somewhat embattled minority. The form was directly descended from the community-based meetings of the farmers' movement. A report in the Saskatchewan *Commonwealth* reflects the flavour of these meetings:

> In most cases the meetings started in the morning, the CCF ladies served a noon meal, and the discussion carried on until 5 p.m. At others the meeting began in the afternoon, with the ladies serving supper, and the meeting continuing on in the evening. In nearly every case, the dinner or supper so generously contributed by the ladies, proved to be the social event which allowed everyone to meet together for that all-important personal exchange of greetings.[24]

The main presentation in these meetings would be a talk by Floyd Johnson, the party's provincial leader, or Williams Irvine, party president, supplemented by a trade unionist, often Roy Jamha of the Oil, Chemical and Atomic Workers' Union, or Henry Tomaschuk, president of the Alberta Council of the United Packinghouse Workers of America. The presentation would stress the economic dilemmas faced by farmers and argue that the interests of farmers and wage earners were basically compatible, in the context of a democratically planned economy.

Jamha and Tomaschuk had been active in the CCF for much of the previous decade, and had been elected as the two Alberta delegates to the CCF National Council at the November 1959 provincial convention. They were both to play major roles in the founding and development of the Alberta NDP, and their respective unions were, along with the

United Steelworkers, to be critical props on the labour side of the process. These three unions, all "industrial", CIO unions as opposed to the more conservative "craft" unions, responded positively to the turn to political involvement in Alberta. The UPWA and the OCAW both had international leaderships which looked favourably on the New Party project.[25] The UPWA, with a membership of 3,500 in Alberta, had in 1958 held a summer school with around fifty delegates, concentrating on the CLC's Political Education Program. Among other activities, it held a "mock Parliament", and the school concluded with unanimous agreement to support the New Party, including a "per capita tax" to finance the project, with the proviso that union members had the right to contract out of the financial assessment.[26]

For the first three months of 1960, the New Party movement had a federally-funded organizer in full-time operation in Alberta. A Wetaskiwin farmer, FUA activist and CCF member, (who had served in the 1940s on the UFA Board of Directors) Leslie Pritchard, was recommended by the provincial CCF executive and hired by the NCNP in January 1960 to begin organizing New Party clubs in rural Alberta. In testing the attractiveness of the New Party idea, Pritchard concentrated on the area to the north and west of Edmonton, in provincial constituencies which had shown some promise for the CCF in the late 1940s and 1950s.

Success was modest and qualified, as CCF Provincial Secretary Nellie Peterson informed Carl Hamilton, Secretary of the National CCF and also the NCNP:

> Mr. Pritchard is stirring up a good deal of interest but whether or not this will result in membership clubs it is impossible to foretell. He, along with a labour representative, will be speaking to five meetings to consider the New Party and all took quite a lot of organizing ability to achieve. CCF farmers are very sympathetic; others and that means most of them, range from interested to apathetic, with just plain apathetic remaining the best adjective to describe the majority.[27]

Pritchard, whose organizing was curtailed when he went back to work on his farm in mid-April, summarized the results of his efforts to Hamilton at the end of March as follows:

> Meetings were arranged for the following points at which no organization resulted: Boyle, Mayerthorpe, Rich Valley, Darwell, and Buck Lake. Attendance would be about a dozen, mostly persons who have supported

the CCF at some time during the past. Talking to other party supporters is slow, painful work.

Meetings at which New Party organization resulted were Dapp, Barrhead, Highridge, Sangudo and Entwhistle. I feel these groups will require "nursing" if they are not to relapse into apathy. The rest of my time was occupied in going from door to door wherever I thought my story would receive a favourable hearing.[28]

Anyone acquainted with the bleak, heavily wooded terrain of the area north of Edmonton, in February and March, with its country roads (in that period mostly dirt and gravel), snow-slicked and precarious, and its not-so-prosperous farmland will realize that the prospect of door-to-door politicking on behalf of the CCF and organized labour might have chilled the hardiest of souls. Nonetheless, the clubs organized by Pritchard and mentioned by him as possibly requiring "nursing" did in fact continue in existence, and were included in the list of "presently operating" New Party clubs two years later at the Alberta founding convention.[29]

By March of 1960, an Alberta Committee for the New Party (ACNP) was established, consisting of CCF and Alberta Federation of Labour representatives. Chaired by Ivor Dent, representing the CCF, it included Floyd Johnson, CCF leader, Andrew Borys and Earl Toane representing the CCF, both FUA activists in the region surrounding Edmonton, Arthur Thornton, the veteran Edmonton CCFer, Edmonton Trade Unionists William Grey, Henry Tomaschuk and Roy Jamha. Nellie Peterson, the CCF's Provincial Secretary served as executive secretary. Later, Pat Lenihan, a seasoned and experienced trade union organizer from Calgary, was added to the committee, the first member of this body from Southern Alberta.

It was in this period that friction between the ACNP and the NCNP first manifested itself, the record of which is revealing as to the national leadership's assessment of the Alberta CCF leadership, and also to some of the National Committee's policy regarding organization in Alberta.

Writing on behalf of the ACNP to Desmond Sparham, director of New Party Clubs for the NCNP, Nellie Peterson objected that the existence of clubs organized in Calgary by the national sponsors had gone unreported to the ACNP, which had no other way of knowing of their existence. Furthermore, it seemed the Calgary clubs had not been informed of the existence of the ACNP. The Alberta Committee requested by resolution that it be informed of all existing clubs, that the

National Director "channel all New Party Club activities through the Provincial Committee", and that it receive a portion of the dues paid by the individual club members. Concern regarding the political perspective of the clubs organized (e.g. members' awareness of CCF and CLC policy) was also expressed. Most alarming (at least to the CCF representatives) was the reported impression on the part of some Calgary club members, that the core of the New Party project was the clubs, and that the CCF and CLC roles were to be "absorbed" into the New Party.[30]

Commenting on this letter, Sparham wrote acerbically to Carl Hamilton that the Calgary clubs had indeed been informed of the existence of the ACNP and argued that the source of the friction was the Alberta CCF. Speaking of the existing CCF leadership Sparham argued that "some of the CCF leaders in Alberta . . . particularly . . . Mrs. Peterson and Mr. Irvine . . . are unnecessarily on the defensive with regards to their own role in the conduct of affairs of the CCF and see the establishment of the new party as a threat to their leadership."[31] It should be mentioned that this psychological (and none too sophisticated) interpretation of the behaviour of the CCF "old guard" (as they came to be known) was not infrequent among many Alberta protagonists of the New Party, both within and outside the CCF. The argument lacks validity, however, particularly for Irvine and Peterson, whose objections were far more likely based on matters of principle. Had either of them wanted a career with the New Party, their exceptional talents and personal dynamism would have placed them well in the running, but both of them probably had no ambition in that direction; they had been in politics for decades, and besides the factor of age, Irvine knew by this time that he was dying of cancer. A less *ad hominem* judgement would have been regardless of personal motivation, the CCF leadership didn't work as hard to create the New Party as some of the other provincial leaderships did, or as hard as some Alberta CCFers felt they should have.

Careful reading of the correspondence between the CCF and the NCNP reveals no obvious bad faith on the part of the CCF leadership. The practical advice and suggestions made (most frequently by Mrs. Peterson, as secretary) are by and large constructive, well thought out, lucidly explained, and clearly based on a wealth of practical experience in Alberta politics. Since the role of the Alberta CCF has a number of times been called into question in published histories of the NDP founding process, this point seems worth some emphasis.

The Peterson letter to Hamilton just cited also mentioned that the Calgary New Party club had agreed to work jointly on sponsoring a public function with the CCF and Calgary CLC bodies. Sparham's reaction to this further illuminates the conflict with the CCF, as well as illustrating some of the organizational concerns of the National Committee.

> I rather hoped that the initiative for the organization of this event would be left to the Calgary New Party Clubs and that they would be allowed to sponsor it. The event, after all, is intended as an appeal to the "other liberal-minded persons" to whom we are supposed to be appealing through New Party Clubs. It will be an awful pity if the conference develops instead into some kind of "negotiating conference" between the three elements of the new party movement. It seems to me that the point. . . concerning the importance of developing a publicly-demonstrable third element in the new party movement in Alberta (as elsewhere) may be prejudiced if at this early stage . . . the third and weakest element is too closely tied in with the two stronger elements.
>
> It is . . . fairly clear that some . . . of the Alberta CCF leaders do not agree with this proposition—namely that New Party Clubs should be given a fairly free run to establish themselves as separate entities . . . The Clubs cannot be separate—cannot be *shown* to be separate—if the moment they are formed they come under the domination of people who have a strong identification with one or the other two elements in the new party movement . . . if what we really want to do is to get "other liberal-minded persons" to accept present CCF leadership let us say so.[32]

Sparham's concern, of course occurs in a context of constant media implications that the New Party was destined to be nothing more than the "old" CCF in new clothing. His concern was valid: the New Party clubs' membership did consist substantially of people who had hitherto *not* chosen to join the CCF, and a good proportion of them were wary of CCF domination of the New Party.

Founding the NDP

As time for the Federal founding convention approached (it was planned for early August 1961 in Ottawa) the NCNP took steps to engage a full-time organizer on the scene in Alberta. The National Committee consulted with the ACNP, which set up a sub-committee on the selection. Five applications were submitted, among them two trade union organizers, a staffer from the co-operative movement, and Grant Notley. Notley's credentials were not unimpressive. A vice-president of the Alberta CCF (as a result of the first endeavour at self-assertion of his generation of CCF youth, which had put the senior party somewhat aback at the 1959 Convention), he had a rural background and was quite at home talking to farmers. Organizing work was not unknown to him: while on the CCF executive he had found time to accompany William Irvine and Floyd Johnson to outlying CCF meetings, observing their methods and developing his own techniques. While in Edmonton at the university, he had established contact with a layer of trade unionists, in and around the city.

The NCNP offered to hire one of the trade unionists for urban work and Notley to work primarily in rural areas. The trade union organizer declined the appointment due to union obligations, and Notley became the Alberta organizer for the New Party, starting in May 1961 at $400 per month, plus some expenses. His first action was to buy a car. He rented an office from the OCAW in the Union Hall at Jasper and 97th St. in downtown Edmonton.

Notley's task as organizer focussed on the Ottawa convention a few months hence. Of particular concern was the building up of the Alberta delegation. This involved work on the New Party clubs, CCF units and trade unions interested in the project. In the three months following his appointment, Notley travelled extensively, reliving the automobile marathon endemic to political organizing in Alberta. His stamina and persistence kept him on the highway for days at a time, and was to become legendary in the movement. Building from an initial base of just under twenty New Party clubs, including those organized by Des Sparham and Leslie Pritchard, Notley was able to organize another thirty-two clubs by the end of July, so that at the time of the federal founding of the party, fifty New Party clubs were in existence and functioning in Alberta.[33] This rate or organizing, averaging one new club every three days, was a furious pace, so the possibility that these clubs represented very little in the way of activity (other than naming delegates to Ottawa) cannot be discounted. In the best of circumstances a New Party club's program would consist of the initial public meeting which set it up, and a series of organized discussions around the proposed program and constitution of the New Party, available as pamphlets published by the NCNP and made available to club memberships, CCF groups and others interested at a nominal fee.

In August, one hundred and thirty-one delegates from Alberta made the trip to Ottawa, seventy-one from New Party clubs, thirty-eight from CCF organizations, and twenty-two trade union delegates.[34] Of the club delegates, an undetermined number were individual CCFers and trade union members, since not all of them were members of a function-ing CCF organization, or an affiliating labour body. The number travel-ling to Ottawa was in excess of the attendance at most conventions of the Alberta CCF in recent years. The new movement had been fortunate in its choice of an organizer.

After the Federal founding, organization continued. The focal con-cern was now the provincial founding convention. A federal election was known to be in the offing, and a provincial election was also due.

The Alberta founding convention of the NDP was held in January 1962 in Edmonton. One of the main concerns of the ACNP had been to make the event as large as possible, for publicity purposes. Some 379 delegates were registered, for which the credentials committee gave figures concerning geographic distribution and organizational origins. Units of the CCF sent 85 delegates, while New Party clubs sent 93. Labour delegates numbered 172 and the New Democratic Youth, 19. There were 135 delegates from Edmonton, 58 from Calgary, 18 from Medicine Hat, 13 from Lethbridge and 7 from Red Deer. Delegates from north of Red Deer outnumbered those from the south by almost three to one.[35]

Grant Notley reported that combined CCF and New Party club individual memberships stood at around 2,500, and that affiliated trade union memberships numbered around 4,000. A total of sixty-six New Party clubs had been organized and were currently functioning.[36]

The elections for the executive resulted in representation of most constituent elements. Because of the lack of available candidates, the convention chose to postpone the selection of a leader for a year. Neil Reimer (who eventually became the first provincial leader), Canadian vice-president of the Oil Chemical and Atomic Workers' union, was elected President of the party. A trade unionist, previously active in the Calgary CCF, was elected treasurer. One of the five vice-presidents was from the New Party clubs, the other four had been closely associated with the CCF, and included Nellie Peterson and two Farmers' Union activists, one of these a former provincial president of the CCF. Notley, who up to this point had been an employee of the federal NDP, was appointed Provincial Secretary by the NDP Provincial Council at its first meeting. (See Chapter One by Larry Pratt on Notley's selection).

Of the sectoral groups to which the NDP had been making an appeal, the most rewarding was the trade union movement, whose membership in the new party exceeded substantially the level of trade union membership in the CCF. The institutional form by which the New

Party organizers had anticipated an increase in trade union membership was that of affiliation, which was carried out not by individuals, but by entire union locals, through a majority vote of the membership. The fee for an affiliating local was five cents a member per month, collected by deduction from the members' payroll along with union dues. Individuals had the right to stop payment of this political levy, by so indicating to the union.

The process of affiliation had been proceeding in the year prior to the founding of the NDP, and at the provincial founding, the organizer's report indicated that locals affiliated had a combined dues paying strength of four thousand. (See note 35) Resistance to this procedure of affiliation might have been expected—it was a new phenomenon, and not recognized in the workers' political culture; certainly there were outraged comments in the press protesting the invasion of personal freedoms. But trade unionists and others active in the party do not recall much resistance to the affiliation resolutions when made. There was occasionally heated debate, but neither the media nor the employers seem to have intervened.[37] The main vectors in pushing the affiliation resolution throughout the province seem to have been union staffers and labour council leaders, although in the most pro-NDP unions (the OCAW, UPWA and the Steelworkers) leadership from above was probably less critical.

The affiliation form of membership, derived in large part from the model of the British Labour Party, presents very real problems for an organization of the left, in particular if membership involvement and participation are seen as important. Affiliation through a union branch, while it may give an affiliate member the feeling that she or he is "doing something", runs the risk of "freezing" the individual at arm's length from the party. Membership in this situation is formal and nominal, and may in the activity, education and experience of the affiliate, mean little. Indicative of this, nowhere in the minutes of the first five annual conventions of the NDP in Alberta is there any record of a resolution from an affiliated trade union local being submitted to the convention and voted on.

None of those NDP activists close to the leadership questioned on this matter recall that the inactivity of the affiliated membership was perceived by the party leadership to be a problem, nor did any recall the Executive or the Provincial Council of the party ever discussing the matter as a problem. For that matter, apart from the general hope that affiliates might in some way become active in constituency associations, individuals questioned reported that as far as they were aware, the leadership of the party never had any particular role in mind for the affiliated membership.

This category of membership did see growth in the first several years. In 1967 Ivor Dent, the party President, reported the number of affiliated members as six thousand.[38]

In later years the category of affiliated members seems to have waned in importance. This may be because a large section of the province's most militant unionists are legally barred from political affiliation—public sector workers. The Alberta Federation of Labour has established a Committee on Political Education (COPE), in which public sector workers do participate. It has as one of its tasks the publicization of the AF of L's support for the NDP.

For many trade unionists, affiliated membership was to be of minor import, and most urban constituency associations had a number of unionists as active members, participating as individuals. It is probably that trade union participation on this individual basis has in the last decade been at a higher level than ever before in the Alberta party. It does not seem that the institution of the affiliated membership, other than as a relatively small, steady source of income, had made much of an impact on party life.

The farmers' movement, politically speaking never lived up to its promise of earlier decades, in spite of the fact that the farm in Alberta has been under constant attack. Whether the CCF might have made more of it, had it adopted different tactics and strategy is an important question which socialists will hopefully pursue, but in spite of the aspirations of the New Party movement, some breakthroughs, and good friends within the movement, the NDP never realized its hopes as far as the farmers were concerned.

Formally in 1958, the FUA responded to the CLC invitation the same way as its counterparts in Manitoba and Saskatchewan: "with convention resolutions reaffirming their nonpartisan policies."[39] Probably, however, the most important factor was the all-pervasive suspicion of and hostility to the labour movement, described above. In September of 1960, Floyd Johnson was informed by Ed Nelson, president of the FUA, that (notwithstanding the 1958 FUA response) "numerous resolutions for the FUA convention have come in to the [FUA] office which urge non-participation in the New Party". Nelson also suggested there would be a better chance of moving the FUA toward the existing CCF than the projected New Party, because of fear of labour domination.[40]

At the beginning of 1961, Nellie Peterson informed Carl Hamilton of a discussion with two CCF members, "leaders of the FWUA . . . both are very disturbed at the deterioration of relations between farm and labour and by the anti-new party reactions they are meeting in their farm organization work which takes them all over the province."[41]

In spite of a complete lack of encouraging signs from the farming community as a whole, the rural CCF activists, in particular those with involvement in the FUA, responded well to the NDP. Henry Young, key figure in the founding of the FUA, and president for its five years of greatest strength, served on the party's committee on farm-labour relations, and Ed Nelson, after his term as President of the FUA expired, ran as a candidate in the Wetaskiwin riding in the 1965 federal election. Ed Nelson's son, Ken Nelson, a graduate of the CCF and New Democratic Youth, was employed for four months in 1962 as organizer for five central Alberta constituencies, mainly rural. His experiences were less than promising: he encountered "all the old CCFers who'd been around since the thirties", but found few new people who were willing to be drawn in.[42]

Conclusion

The successful founding of the Alberta NDP was of course the work of many more people than simply Grant Notley, but the role he played was quite critical, both for the party and for his future political career. It involved insight into the social forces he was dealing with, and diplomacy in reconciling seemingly irreconcilable elements. Those who worked with Notley often stress his organizing competence, even his ruthlessness. It would be wrong to give this concept too mechanical a meaning.

There is a danger in abstracting Notley's role at this time strictly to that of "organizer", a technical builder of exclusively an electoral "machine". In the founding period of the NDP, Notley often stressed that there was and had to be more to left politics than simply constructing an organization. He often repeated that the party had to be more than just a party, it had to be a social *movement* as well: this belief he got from the CCF. There is reason to believe that he never lost it completely.

The NDP was founded in the period of the first upsurge of the nuclear disarmament movement. Notley was vocal in encouraging the members of the U of A club and the youth section to become active in the Combined Universities Campaign for Nuclear Disarmament (CUCND—Canada's first "New Left" organization) and it was not uncommon in public meetings in the early sixties for time to be given over to the peace movement (specifically the Canadian Peace Research Institute) to appeal for support, including funding, from the audience.

This was not out of character. The early Notley was eager to keep the party open to social movements. In 1960, during a nation-wide strike at Dominion Bridge, Grant Notley persuaded the Edmonton CCF youth to go down to the picket line on 107th St. early in the morning, day after day, with placards proclaiming the group's support for the strikers. Eighteen years later, by now an MLA and parliamentarian *par excellence*, he agreed to the adjournment of the provincial convention to permit the delegates to join a demonstration and rally in support of a group of grossly underpaid women workers on strike against a commercially-run nursing home. When the recession's teeth began to bite deeply in Alberta, he spoke to many trade union demonstrations and mass actions, popularizing the NDP critique of the Lougheed government's pro-business policy.

Through much of his career as Provincial Secretary and later as leader, Notley was criticized from his left for a retreat into parliamentarism. The relationship between electoral politics and the creation of a mass movement committed to basic social change remains a problematic and burning issue in socialist theory, and cannot be resolved here. Suffice it to say that Notley did not display an obsessive fear of public mass action, as so many social democratic politicians have. Frequently he welcomed it, as complementary to his own parliamentary struggles.

---

[1]David Lewis, *The Good Fight: Political Memoirs 1909-1958* (Toronto: Macmillan, 1981) p. 211.

[2]Grace Skogstad, "Farmers and Farm Politics in the Society and Politics of Alberta", in Carlo Caldarola (ed.) *Society and Politics in Alberta: Research Papers* (Toronto: Methuen, 1979) p. 231.

[3]John Richards and Larry Pratt, *Prairie Capitalism: Power and Influence in the New West* (Toronto: McClelland and Stewart, 1979) pp. 107-108, p. 316.

[4]Lewis, p. 489.

[5]Public Archives of Alberta (PAA) NDP Papers (84.178, Box 5, file 5),

p. 3 emphasis added. From an untitled, unsigned, undated paper, addressed to the Provincial Council of the NDP. It is clear from the content of the paper as to its date and the authorship. A shortened version of the "four year plan", under that title was distributed to delegates at the 1964 provincial convention, see "Four Year Plan—Report to Convention", PAA 84.178.470.

[6]*Edmonton Journal*, "CCF Opposes MRA", 25 June, 1960.

[7]*Edmonton Journal*, "Alberta CCF Chief Faces Questioning", 20 July 1956.

[8]*Calgary Herald*, "Irvine Clarifies His Russian Quote", 21 August 1956, *Calgary Albertan*, "No Reprimand for Irvine Statement", 23 August 1956. See also the smug and sarcastic editorial "Yoo Hoo Mr. Irvine, Not That Tune", *Calgary Herald*, 20 August 1956 for a sense of the direction the press wished to push its audience's understanding of Irvine's position.

[9]Reg Whitaker, "Introduction to the Carleton Library Edition, p. xxxiv of William Irvine, *The Farmers in Politics* (Toronto: McClelland and Stewart, 1976) originally published in 1920.

[10]Gad Horowitz, *Canadian Labour in Politics* (Toronto: University of Toronto Press, 1968) p. 192; for a general outline of the NDP's creation, see Chapters 5 and 6 of this book.

[11]The complete resolution is quoted in Horowitz, p. 192.

[12]*Edmonton Journal*, "Roper Calls CLC Party Move 'Significant Event', 21 June 1958.

[13]William Irvine, "President's Address" in *Highlights: CCF Convention 1959* (Edmonton: Alberta CCF, undated) pp. 5-12.

[14]*Highlights: CCF Convention 1959* p. 3.

[15]See FUA President Ed Nelson's exceptionally frank and personal remarks on a current strike and his discomfort at the conflict between farmers and labour in "A Personal Dilemma: Must I Use Methods I Detest When Stating FUA Positions?" *Organized Farmer*, 17 October, 1963.

[16]The Alberta Party's qualms about the New Party clubs never became an issue of open debate. See the letter of Nellie Peterson to Carl Hamilton, 16 October, 1959, and Hamilton's reply, dated 21 October, 1959.

Public Archives of Canada (PAC) MG 28 IV 1, vol. 379.

[17]PAC MG 28 IV 1, vol. 379, N. Peterson to C. Hamilton, 15 May, 1961.

[18]PAC MG 28 IV 1, vol. 379, N. Peterson to C. Hamilton, 6 March, 1961.

[19]PAC MG 28 IV 1, vol. 379, S. Knowles to N. Peterson, 2 March, 1961.

[20]Horowitz, p. 226.

[21]PAC MG 28 IV 1, vol. 379, W.G. Notley to Desmond Sparham, 26 June 1961.

[22]PAC MG 28 IV 1, vol. 379, "Report—Political Education Seminar, Red Deer, Alberta, 3 June, 1959".

[23]*Lethbridge Herald*, 8 February, 1960.

[24]*The Commonwealth*, "Widespread CCF Activity in Alberta", 2 March, 1960.

[25]Interview with Roy Jamha, Edmonton, 15 January, 1986.

[26]"Report—Political Education Seminar, Red Deer, Alberta, 3 June, 1959", p. 11.

[27]PAC MG IV 1, vol. 379 N. Peterson to C. Hamilton, 18 February, 1960.

[28]PAC MG IV 1, vol. 379 L. Pritchard to C. Hamilton, 28 March, 1960.

[29]PAA 84.178.467, Grant Notley, "Organizer's Report", given to the Founding Convention, Alberta New Democratic Party, 20 January, 1962.

[30]PAC MG 28 IV 1, vol. 379 N. Peterson to R.D. Sparham, 6 June, 1960; N. Peterson and I. Dent to C. Hamilton, 17 June, 1960, and "Minutes, Alberta Committee for the New Party, 16 June, 1960".

[31]PAC MG 28 IV 1, vol. 379 R.D. Sparham to C. Hamilton, 22 June, 1960.

[32]*loc. cit.*

[33]PAA 84.178 Grant Notley, "Organizer's Report", undated (late July or early August, 1961).

[34]Horowitz, p. 217.

[35]PAA 84.178.467, "Minutes of the New Democratic Party Founding Convention, held January 20th and 21st at the Macdonald Hotel, Edmonton Alberta", final Credentials Committee report.

[36]PAA 84.178.467, Grant Notley, "Organizer's Report", to Founding Convention.

[37]Interviews with Roy Jamha and Ivor Dent, Edmonton, January 1986.

[38]PAA 84.178, Box 7, file 183, letter from Ivor Dent to William Grospiron, 12 June, 1967.

[39]Horowitz, p. 200.

[40]PAC MG 28 IV 1, vol. 379, letter, F. Johnson to C. Hamilton, 22 September, 1960.

[41]PAC MG 28 IV 1, vol. 379, letter, N. Peterson to C. Hamilton, 14 January, 1961.

[42]Interview with Ken Nelson by Larry Pratt and Robin Hunter, 12 June, 1985.

Chapter 4

Opportunity and Constraint:
Grant Notley and the Modern State

Allan Tupper

This essay is an inquiry into the public policy positions of the Alberta NDP under the leadership of the late Grant Notley. It first examines the core of Notley's ideas about the economic role of the modern state. Here I describe the general features of Notley's practical, agrarian socialism. I portray him as a politician more concerned with power than philosophy, but one who nevertheless maintained a commitment to several important principles. The essay then probes the problems posed for the Alberta NDP by the advent of the Lougheed Conservatives. Guided by a shrewd, competent, and powerful leader, the modern Progressive Conservative party in Alberta intervened frequently in the provincial economy. Such Tory intervention, while perhaps different from the NDP's brand, forced the NDP to the defensive and often rendered its policy indistinguishable from the governing Conservatives. For several reasons, Notley and his party were unable to devise an effective counterattack to the "strong-state" Tories.

Armed with the considerable advantages of hindsight and ample time for research and reflection, scholars often find it easy to criticize the policies of governments and oppositions. But in guiding the Alberta NDP, Notley enjoyed few of the resources available to his critics and assessors. For one thing, he was preoccupied with the task of retaining his seat in the legislature. Moreover, his political life was frequently complicated by the policy positions of the federal New Democratic party. On such key questions as constitutional reform and certain aspects of energy policy, Notley sometimes had to distinguish his position from that of his own federal party, the federal Liberal party, and the Lougheed Conservatives. A compelling example of Notley's problems with the federal NDP occurred in December 1978 when the national leader, Ed Broadbent, roundly criticized the Alberta Heritage Savings Trust Fund without first consulting Notley. Notley was particularly offended by Broadbent's reference to Alberta as a "mini Saudi Arabia" and by his apparent adoption of an "anti-Alberta" position.[1] Notley felt that Broadbent's intemperate remarks put the provincial party on the defensive and undercut the Alberta NDP's continuing efforts, described later in this essay, to discredit the Lougheed government's administration of the Trust Fund. To modify unkindly a cliché, "With friends like Broadbent, Notley needed no enemies." Finally, Alberta's economic structure, with its acute dependence on agriculture, oil, and natural gas, created serious policy dilemmas for the NDP and indeed all other political movements in the province. Can and should the economy be diversified away from its reliance on natural resources? How should the "boom and bust" problem be addressed? What sort of resource management policies can satisfy the often conflicting interests of the producing provinces, the consuming provinces, the federal government, and a heterogeneous private sector? The orthodox policies of the Canadian social democratic movement provide few answers to such vexing questions, with the result that Notley was forced to develop his own initiatives. In so doing, he was frequently portrayed by the right as doctrinaire and impractical and by the left, within and without the NDP, as timid, opportunistic, and unprincipled.

Having acknowledged several problems faced by the Alberta NDP, it must be stressed that political parties shape, not merely reflect, their environments. In its policy-making activities, the Alberta NDP, far from being the victim of complex, irreversible circumstances, is an autonomous actor capable of deciding its own fate and the content of its policies. My point is that the NDP's policy is drifting, that it must confront this problem, and that it must consider stressing its socialism. I argue that the party's desire to downplay socialism is ultimately futile and self-defeating. More speculatively, I suggest that a more clearly defined socialist alternative would serve well the Alberta political scene without radically reducing the party's electoral chances.

Grant Notley: Prairie Socialist and Democrat

At the heart of Notley's political philosophy was the conviction that political power, achieved through the electoral system, was a fundamental goal of a social democratic movement. Only through the exercise of governmental power could society be reordered and serious reforms be implemented. Neil Reimer, a former leader of the Alberta NDP, maintained that Notley believed: "It's no use having ideals if you can't practise them."[2] A corollary of Notley's commitment to the pursuit of power was his conviction that the party must make broad electoral appeals with a view to wooing various interests to the social democratic cause. Accordingly, Notley was seldom averse to modifying party policy when he sensed votes were to be won. For example, in an interesting internal party memo written in 1969 Notley fretted about the attitude of students in several Edmonton high schools toward the NDP. He warned the party that students were not interested in "left-wing dogmatic social policy," that the party must moderate its policy to appeal to youth, and that otherwise, progressive young people might fall prey to the Liberals.[3] Similarly, Notley often stressed the need to attract liberals to the NDP's ranks and to field high-profile, "superstar" candidates in urban constituencies. Later in his career, Notley became curiously convinced that owners of small businesses, if carefully cultivated, could become a bastion of NDP support. He devoted considerable effort to the pursuit of this unlikely constituency.

Notley's friends and associates are unanimous in describing his approach to public policy. They stress that he took policy questions seriously, although his primary political focus was tactical, organizational, and financial. And although he was not a bookish man, he grasped complex ideas quickly and displayed a capacity to define issues clearly. Moreover, he effectively employed advisers, learned how to tap experts, and was generally tolerant of conflicting viewpoints and advice. Notley insisted, however, on maintaining close links between party policy and electoral strategy. Many advisers recall how Notley, having listened to rambling and wide-ranging policy discussions, would summarize the matter by asking: "Now let me ask a very crass question: what does this mean in terms of votes?"[4] Several associates also lamented that Notley was impatient and unwilling to probe deeply the essence of party policy. They attribute these flaws to Notley's pragmatism, to his impatience with abstraction, and to his abiding belief that Conservative policies were so obviously bad that NDP programs, however imprecise, would stand out in contrast.

While Notley was pragmatic and electorally oriented, his politics were underpinned by a coherent set of principles. For Notley, Saskatchewan was the "promised land". The moderate, agrarian socialism of the Douglas and Blakeney governments represented for him a model of progress, tolerance, honesty, and administrative competence. Notley's speeches in the legislature were replete with almost eulogistic references to the superior public policies of successive NDP governments in Saskatchewan. Saskatchewan's pathbreaking initiatives in Crown corporations, labour relations policy, and the provincial welfare state were embraced by Notley as sensible measures that should also be implemented in Alberta.

Notley believed deeply in the capacity of the modern state to promote social justice and economic progress. Moreover, he argued that
views about the ownership of industry were now a less important criterion for distinguishing socialists from conservatives than was the concept of "active" versus "passive" government.[5] Here Notley saw a fundamental distinction between his party and the Lougheed Tories. In his
view, Conservatives viewed the state as the "repairman" for the private
sector and a vehicle to be employed only as a last resort. In contrast, the
modern socialist saw government as a benign and progressive force that
should be employed creatively in the resolution of political and
economic problems.

A related notion was Notley's idea of the "mixed economy," which
he saw as embracing co-operatives, private firms, and Crown corporations. He was adamant that a healthy balance between such undertakings
would promote a vigorous and competitive economy. Another
intertwined idea was the need for economic planning. Notley frequently
worried about the chronic "boom and bust" cycle of the Alberta resource
economy and saw the need for a planning agency capable of co-
ordinating public and private initiatives. In so arguing, he avoided references to the Soviet experience and stressed instead widespread participation in the planning process and co-operation rather than coercion. He
was wary of technocrats and saw the planners as necessarily representative of a range of political and organizational perspectives. Planning's
role was to generate a political consensus as a foundation for effective
policies.

Notley believed that government subsidization of private profit
through grants and tax expenditures should be eliminated wherever possible. His view was that government, in return for its support of private
projects, must assume an ownership stake in the resulting enterprise. In
this way, both risk and profit were at least partially socialized. Notley's
views on this topic were strongly held and moulded by several
influences. For one thing, he was appalled by the terribly poor deals
struck by several provincial governments in their negotiations with large
firms. And in the Alberta context, Notley frequently expressed shock at
the range of tax breaks and subsidies accorded to large companies by the
Lougheed government. Finally, he was impressed by the federal party's
remarkably successful attack on "corporate welfare bums" during the
1972 election campaign. In Notley's view, a suitably modified version
of this federal initiative could be effectively employed against the

Alberta Tories.

Notley's ideas about public ownership root him squarely in the mainstream of post-war social democratic thinking in Canada. For Notley, public ownership was a means to certain broader ends, but not an end in itself. It was one of several measures that social democrats might employ to offset imperfections and failures in the market economy. Neither Notley nor his party seemed inclined to specify the circumstances under which public ownership was a desirable policy. Indeed, the party's pronouncements on this question were vague. In its last comprehensive statement on the subject, the Alberta NDP saw public ownership as necessary where firms had escaped both political control and the discipline of the market, where the economy is "ill-served" by private undertakings, where there is a need for new industries or services, where a significant firm fails, and where an existing firm is operating in a manner detrimental to the environment.[6]

In practice, Notley saw three areas for public ownership—the nationalization of Alberta's private power utilities, public development of the Athabasca tar sands, and the creation, through nationalization of an integrated oil company, of a major Crown corporation in the oil and natural gas industry. Nationalization of Alberta's private power companies remains a pillar of NDP economic policy. But socialist thinking is not terribly important in the party's approach. Rather, "Public power is not a matter of 'ideology' or politics. It is just common sense and plain good business."[7] The thrust of NDP policy is that Alberta's proliferation of private utilities is wasteful and results in expensive power and significant intraprovincial price differentials. Public ownership, by eliminating duplication and profit, would deliver "power at cost" and thereby strengthen the provincial economy. Moreover, public ownership, by transferring decision-making power from boardrooms to the legislature, would be democratic. In arguing for public power, the party stresses the "practical" issues and downplays the anti-capitalist argument—that profit must necessarily be removed from certain industries and the influence of capital reduced.

Notley was also convinced that the NDP's plan to nationalize a single major oil company—Imperial Oil was a frequently-cited target—was an acceptable compromise position for a social democratic party. His view was informed by several conventional arguments, including the idea that an aggressive public enterprise in direct competition with private companies would discipline their behaviour and give the state information and bargaining power in its energy policy-making. In short, the NDP's case was not much different from that advanced by the federal Liberals when Petro-Canada was established. Notley was hostile to calls for any further expansion of public ownership in Alberta's resource industries. In 1971, for example, he actively opposed the provincial Waffle party's proposals for a wholesale nationalization of the oil and natural gas industries in Alberta.[8] And again at the party's 1974 convention, Notley worked aggressively to defeat and to limit debate on a wide-ranging nationalization proposal advanced by the Woodsworth-Irvine Socialist Fellowship. His reason for opposing nationalization was that such proposals, if endorsed or even taken seriously by the party, would scare off "moderate" voters and thus hurt the party electorally. Moreover, Notley argued that wide-ranging nationalization would be prohibitively expensive and that social democratic goals in energy policy could be realized through regulatory instruments and an aggressive public presence in the industry.

Two points about the party's public ownership policy merit attention. First, although the NDP struggled to develop a coherent position on the scope of public ownership, it was indifferent to serious thinking about how to administer Crown corporations in a mixed economy. The party's 1974 policy statement asserted that it "would not simply substitute state capitalism for private capitalism."[9] But such rhetoric was followed up only by the vacuous assertion that "a Crown corporation will not be governed by the balance sheet when that would be socially undesirable."[10] Hard questions about pricing, rates of return, and financial management are ignored, although it is probably unrealistic to expect a minor party, far from power, to unveil a blueprint for the operation of Crown corporations. A much more serious political flaw was that the NDP's public ownership policy, resting as it does upon essentially pragmatic, "market failure" grounds, is close to that of the established parties. Indeed, the Lougheed Conservatives frequently maintained that they too saw limited public ownership simply as a means to broader ends. It remained up to the NDP to distinguish between variants of intervention.

Notley's most original and principled policy positions relate to federal-provincial relations and Alberta's position in the contemporary Canadian confederation. He identified intensely with the Canadian prairies and understood the region's sense of alienation from central Canada. He often spoke of the inequities of freight rates, tariffs, and federal transportation policies. But ultimately, Notley's view of federalism was a positive one and his ideas on the topic changed and matured as his political experience broadened. Like his NDP counterparts in Saskatchewan, he saw provincial governments as potentially progressive and benign forces. And while he opposed the federal NDP's often old-fashioned "centralism," he recognized a legitimate role for a strong federal government. Indeed, he saw the need for interventionist governments at both levels and was increasingly skeptical of "zero-sum" interpretations of federalism. Moreover, Notley recognized and was prepared to defer to the national interest which he saw as legitimately overriding a single province's concern.

Such views were not always popular in modern Alberta. But Notley persevered and tried on a range of difficult constitutional and resource questions to steer a middle course between the "arid centralism" of the Trudeau Liberals and the radical provincialism of the Lougheed Conservatives. A particularly compelling example of Notley's principled stance on federal-provincial relations came in the immediate aftermath of the introduction of the National Energy Program. Backed by overwhelming public support in the province, the Alberta government initiated a series of "retaliatory" measures including proposed cutbacks in oil exports to the rest of Canada. Of the 79 members of the Alberta legislature, only Notley opposed such initiatives. And in the face of withering and insulting criticism from Tory MLAs, Notley pronounced: ". . . I'm proud to be an Albertan but I'm even more determined to be a Canadian."[11] He subsequently admitted that he felt under intense pressure to succumb to "pro-Albertan" sentiments, particularly when they were expressed by members of the working class.

Grant Notley and the Democratic State

The Alberta NDP has traditionally stressed the need for more open, more accountable, and ultimately, more democratic government in Alberta. Its early election platforms are replete with critical references to Ernest Manning's "dictatorial" government, to the weakness of the legislature, and to the advent of government by executive decree. Notley pursued this tradition with a vengeance. His political career was characterized by a continuing crusade for a stronger legislature, freedom of information, greater accountability of Crown corporations and other government agencies, and in a general sense, higher ethical standards in public life.

Notley's friends, associates, and political opponents agree that his commitment to democratic values was deep and abiding. But the roots of his ideals remain unclear. Many observers simply maintain that Notley's views were anchored in "rural populism" with its attendant emphasis on public accountability. Such views were reinforced by his admiration for such CCF-NDP parliamentarians as J.S. Woodsworth, Bill Irvine, Tommy Douglas, and Stanley Knowles. Another possible influence was Neil Reimer, the party's first president and leader. Reimer believed passionately that Manning's government was closed and dictatorial with strong fascist leanings.[12] He denounced Manning for maintaining Alberta as a closed, parochial society with more than its share of racial and religious prejudice. Reimer's influence on Notley is of course difficult to divine precisely. However, his powerful views on the weakness of Alberta's democratic traditions were frequently expressed to Notley during his very early years in active politics. At the very least Reimer's passionate ideas about the fragility of democracy in Alberta stood in stark contrast to the more benign interpretations of democratic politics to which Notley had been exposed.

For Notley, the Lougheed Conservatives' style of government raised a number of issues about democratic accountability. After its surprising 1971 victory, the government adopted a "businesslike" approach to public affairs. Secrecy was the norm, the cabinet chambers and federal-provincial conferences were preferred forums for the conduct of business, with the legislature being relegated to a minor role. But particularly problematic for Notley was the Conservatives' tendency to intervene in the economy through hybrid enterprises involving capital from both the public and private sectors.

In 1974 the Conservatives established the Alberta Energy Company (AEC), a mixed enterprise, and in a controversial move acquired the vast majority of shares in Pacific Western Airlines (PWA), Canada's third largest airline. Armed with an open-ended mandate to develop Alberta's oil and gas reserves, the AEC as established was 50 per cent owned by the provincial government. Individual and institutional investors owned the balance of shares with the proviso that no single group could own more than one per cent of the outstanding shares. Heralded by the Lougheed government as an example of "people's capitalism," the AEC was an overwhelming success. Pacific Western Airlines assumed a different, but equally controversial, form. Through secret stock market transactions, the government, as "a mystery buyer", acquired 99 per cent ownership of the profitable airline. Having done so, it revealed the nature and purpose of the transaction to Albertans. More than a month later, the deal was debated in the legislature. As well, the government steadfastly refused to designate PWA as a provincial Crown corporation. No legislation was introduced until 1983 when partial privatization occurred.

Notley was appalled by the lack of public accountability of such government enterprises. Moreover, he was frequently frustrated in his efforts to probe their activities. He learned quickly that ministers were adept at hiding behind the distinction between policy questions (which were occasionally decided by the government) and administrative matters which were routinely decided by the enterprise without political involvement. In his dealings with the AEC, Notley also learned how the government could argue that certain information must not be divulged lest it impair the corporation's profitability and harm the private investors. The need to protect the "commercial" integrity of Lougheed's enterprises vis-a-vis competitors was another commonly advanced reason for secrecy and limited accountability. In response, Notley prepared many bills proposing that both the AEC and PWA be converted into Crown corporations with greater accountability to the legislature. In advancing such measures Notley maintained: "Democratic control under a government responsible to the electors is what makes public ownership worthwhile."[13]

Notley's problems with Lougheed's quasi-public firms were modest in comparison with those relating to the accountability of the Alberta Heritage Savings Trust Fund. In introducing the Trust Fund legislation in 1976, the premier was adamant that the major investments must be decided by the cabinet without prior legislative debate. The legislature was generally relegated to a *"post facto"* audit through the Tory-dominated Select Standing Committee on the Alberta Heritage Savings Trust Fund Act. In arguing for executive control of Trust Fund investments, Lougheed maintained that an *effective* investment strategy would be impossible if the government's decisions were subject to prior debate in the legislature. He ridiculed, as naive and ignorant in business matters, Notley and a few dissenters in his own party when they maintained that wide-ranging legislative debate and a profitable investment strategy might be compatible. In short, Lougheed's view was that the entrepreneurial state that he was building in Alberta would indeed clash with such values as public scrutiny of government decisions and an active, probing legislature. And when push came to shove, democratic values and procedures were to be subordinated to the Trust Fund's bottom line.

Notley never accepted these arguments. He consistently maintained that the Trust Fund was too significant a force in Canada's political economy to be the fiefdom of an inner circle of Tory ministers and advisors. Citing Saskatchewan's much smaller Trust Fund, he argued that the legislature could be more involved in decision-making without impairing the Trust Fund's effectiveness as a policy instrument. Indeed, shortly before his death Notley publicly argued that the accountability of the Trust Fund was his first political priority.

> May I go on record now to say that the *very first thing* an elected New Democratic government would do is to bring the administration of the Heritage Fund out of the Star Chambers into the sunlight of the Assembly where it could now be administered with these facts in mind.[14]

Notley's interest in the Trust Fund was certainly not limited to rhetorical attacks on Tory policy. He was an active, aggressive, and informed member of the Select Standing Committee. He doggedly pursued ministers and the premier for details about the Trust Fund investments and his annual minority reports on the Trust Fund's administration were concise and penetrating.

Notley's continuing interest in issues of accountability and integrity in government are to a degree explained by the normal partisan drives of an opposition member in a parliamentary democracy. To the extent that Notley could strengthen the legislature vis-a-vis the cabinet and force the government to divulge more information, his position and effectiveness as a critic would be enhanced. In this quest, Notley found a natural ally in the media who were frequently frustrated by the obsessive secrecy of the Lougheed Tories. As well, Notley obviously saw partisan advantage in his ruthless pursuit of accountability. He worked hard to portray the Lougheed government as secretive, arrogant, and highly centralized. He assumed that voters would recognize and appreciate that his party stood for a different, and obviously superior, style of public administration. And in a different vein, the NDP's emphasis on accountability was a response to having been politically outflanked by the "strong state" Alberta Conservatives. Notley found himself in the awkward position of supporting the principle of such Conservative interventions as the Trust Fund and the Alberta Energy Company. But having supported Tory interventions in principle, he tried to distinguish NDP from Conservative policy by claiming that social democratic *administration* would be more open, more informed, and more humane. Hence the accountability issue simultaneously served Notley's immediate partisan goals while also reinforcing in his mind a basic distinction between the NDP and the Conservatives.

Notley's thinking about accountability transcended immediate partisan advantage. Underpinning his ideas was the view that the Lougheed government had undertaken important changes in the province's political economy. He saw the Trust Fund, the AEC, and NOVA as new, complex, but poorly understood, additions to government-business relations in modern Alberta. Notley remarked of Lougheed's interventions in 1977: ". . . the mechanisms he has chosen for this development are huge private companies backed by substantial public funds and often working in conjunction with newly created large public companies."[15] He was unsure about the precise political significance of such developments but was convinced that the new symbiosis of public and private power was potent, yet unaccountable. He sensed, and worried, that Alberta's new quasi-public enterprises had escaped both market control and the discipline of formal political accountability. The former point seems unfounded given the size of the enterprises involved, but Notley's concern with the accountability of quasi-public firms was well-placed. Under his leadership, the party grew justifiably skeptical about joint ventures and mixed enterprises.

In the final analysis, Notley's concern with accountability was related to his broader goal of strengthening democracy in Alberta. He often worried about several unsavoury features of the province's politics, notably its tradition of overwhelming governmental majorities, its tendency to equate all political life with elections and its underdeveloped sense of political debate. Notley expressed concern about such tendencies when he remarked in 1979: "It's easy enough to fall into the trap of seeing democracy as essentially no more than a plebiscite once every four years. Once every four years we allow the voters of Alberta to render a sort of yes or no verdict on the affairs of the province."[16] Similarly, in his first speech in the legislature Notley maintained that his job was to broaden the political agenda by raising alternatives and by promoting genuine debate about competing diagnoses and prescriptions. Both his supporters and his opponents are unanimous in endorsing Notley's dedication to this goal.

The Alberta NDP and the Strong State Tories

As Notley was maturing as a politician in the mid-1960s, Alberta politics were in a state of flux. Indeed, the only certainty was that three decades of Social Credit rule were ending. Under these circumstances, the opposition parties, notably the NDP and a rejuvenated Progressive Conservative party led by Peter Lougheed, trumpeted bright visions of their future. The 1967 vote saw the election of several Conservatives, but a new era in Alberta politics did not really emerge until the Tories' victory in 1971.

The Conservatives' electoral success in 1971 surprised most observers of provincial politics. But perhaps more surprising was their willingness to intervene in the economy particularly during the hectic years of the international oil crisis and the boom in Alberta's oil and natural gas industries. The Conservatives' commitment to laissez-faire was rhetorical when confronted with the need to promote and nurture an indigenous business class, to defend provincial interests against a predatory federal government, to enhance provincial revenues, and to reduce external control over Alberta's economy.[17] Important Conservative interventions were the establishment of the Alberta Energy Company in 1974, the purchase of Pacific Western Airlines in the same year, and the construction of the Syncrude plant at Fort McMurray. Royalties on Alberta's depleting oil and gas resources were also increased during this period. In 1976, the government established the Alberta Heritage Savings Trust Fund and armed it with a broad mandate. Among other things, the Trust Fund was to invest provincial resource revenues so as to strengthen and diversify the provincial economy.

Notley never developed a precise interpretation of the interests served by the reborn Alberta Conservatives. This was his gravest political weakness. His public statements during the late 1960s and early 1970s tended to portray the Lougheed Conservatives as a more modern, up-tempo version of the dying Social Credit dynasty. Notley lumped the Tories and Socreds together as the "Tory twins" and mockingly called them "Cadillac conservatives." Despite superficial differences, he argued, both governments were "right wing" instruments of Big Oil. In his view, the Tory sweeps of 1971 and 1975 represented changes in the style, but not the substance or the underlying dynamics of Alberta politics. Associates indicate that in private Notley was, like many observers of Alberta politics in the 1970s, rather puzzled by the Conservatives and their interventionist tendencies.[18]

The Conservatives' forays into the economy and their willingness to employ state powers in defence of provincial interests blurred many of the traditional distinctions between Alberta's political parties. The NDP, as a party proud of its commitment to an active public sector, was particularly troubled by Lougheed's interventions. For within a few years in the early 1970s, the Conservatives had implemented, in whole or in part, many traditional NDP policies including increased resource royalties, expanded public intervention in the oil and gas industries, and a plan for economic diversification.

NDP activists admit to the problems posed by the "strong state" Conservatives. In particular, they sensed that they were unable to develop a clear alternative to Lougheed's blueprint for the Alberta economy. Hence they were relegated to the role of proposing changes at the margin or dealing with the details rather than the general thrust of public policies. For example, in dealing with the Alberta Energy Company, the NDP supported the principle but argued that the enterprise should be a fully owned Crown corporation. Similarly, when confronting the government over its sudden acquisition of Pacific Western Airlines, Notley was forced to complain about the "undemocratic" nature of the takeover. He remarked, ". . . if the government is going to acquire businesses and as the leader of the New Democratic Party, I can hardly be critical of the principle of public investment; if we are going to acquire businesses or make public investments then we should have some kind of legislation presented to this House which allows the members of the Legislature to make the decision."[19] On the vitally important question of the Trust Fund, Notley was once again cornered. He supported the principles of the Trust Fund Legislation but argued that the investment vehicle was flawed by its lack of accountability. On perhaps the most important law passed in Alberta in the 1970s, the leader of the New Democratic Party could only remark:

> Let me say at the outset, Mr. Speaker, that I support the concept of a heritage trust fund. I think there is a great deal of merit in taking part of the revenue from declining non-renewable resources and setting that aside for future generations. That's not really the issue in this debate. I suspect that people of all political persuasions in the province of Alberta accept the concept of a heritage trust fund. But the issue . . . is this bill and many of the provisions of the bill which in my judgment have autocratic features which outweigh the merits.[20]

Did the Conservatives see the NDP as their major political threat and consciously try to rob it of its policy distinctiveness? Definitive answers to this question are difficult. Kevin Peterson, a political journalist and an experienced observer of Alberta politics, related how Lougheed shrewdly learned to employ Notley as a "bogeyman" during difficult negotiations with oil companies.[21] Lougheed frequently asserted that the emerging political opposition in the province was from the left and that for businessmen an interventionist, but pro-business, Conservative government was a much better option than the NDP. A more difficult question is whether the Conservatives actively adopted interventionist policies with a view to isolating the NDP. In any case, the early Lougheed administration, far from being a passive, "right-wing" government, was in fact an interventionist, urban-based, government of the centre.

After its important interventions in the early 1970s, the Lougheed government settled into an extended "housekeeping" period. Backed by huge electoral majorities in the mid-seventies, the government was content to administer its existing undertakings and to consolidate its electoral position. During this period, the NDP followed the government and merely criticized its secrecy, its lack of accountability, and its policy drift.

But the early 1980s witnessed a rebirth of Conservative interventionism. In 1983 the government established a new mixed enterprise, Vencap Alberta Ltd., whose role was to provide capital to high-risk, but potentially profitable, Alberta businesses. More importantly, in the late summer of 1984, the government released a "White Paper" outlining its thinking on medium term industrial policy.[22] The tone of the report was decidedly interventionist and marked a return to the heady "province-building" days of the early 1970s. The return of Tory interventionism once again forced the NDP to the defensive.

The White Paper marked a departure from the Lougheed government's commitment to the goal of economic diversification. Oil, natural gas, and agriculture were explicitly identified as the pillars of the Alberta economy. The management of such resources was the key question. But as noted earlier, the White Paper asserted an active role for the provincial government if Alberta, as a land-locked, sparsely populated hinterland, was to reach its economic potential. In outlining this philosophy, the Conservatives stressed the need for "positive," "pro-business" interventions.

> . . . positive interventions are those which are in support of the private sector and which improve, in part, the risk evaluation of a capital investment decision. In this sense, intervention by government expands economic activity and growth. Examples would include public expenditures on infrastructure . . . the development of a skilled work force through the provision of facilities for training and education; the funding

of research and development; and income tax incentives to encourage new investment.[23]

Such policies were contrasted with "negative" interventions like "burdensome regulation," "direct corporate takeovers" and "buy-in provisions." Such interventions merely redistributed assets. Among other things, the government envisioned "even bolder action" in the support of mega-projects, the identification of specific sectors requiring support, an enhanced use of tax incentives, a more active state role in determining priorities in education, and an expanded role for the public sector in the promotion of exports.

The interventionist tone of the Conservative White paper caught the NDP by surprise and once again put it on the defensive. The Lougheed government had moved to retain the political centre. It had obviously been little influenced by either the radical policies of the British Columbia government or by the milder right-wing populism of the Devine Conservatives in Saskatchewan. Observers are divided over the political motives underpinning Lougheed's return to interventionism. For example, a member of the NDP's economic policy committee interpreted the White Paper as an explicit effort to hobble the NDP:

> Alberta's new White Paper is an intensely political document. It is so because it encompasses a political strategy for addressing the concerns of both the right wing within the Conservative party and the moderate and left-wing of the population at large, represented in provincial politics by the New Democratic Party. . . . the paper seeks to maroon the New Democratic Party by advocating interventionist proposals in the ideological context of free enterprise, something the NDP cannot credibly do.[24]

Others viewed the White Paper as a more general effort by Lougheed to reinvigorate his government and to deflate the criticism that the Conservatives were tired, out of ideas, and smug.

In the period after the White Paper's release, Notley was deeply concerned about the rebirth of Tory interventionism. He was particularly exercised by an insightful article in the *Calgary Herald* by Geoff White.[25] White argued that there were few obvious differences between Conservative and NDP interventions. Indeed, the NDP's schemes for economic renewal and diversification were generally moderate enough that the Conservatives had no problem adapting them and embracing them as Tory policy. Notley's response to this reasoning was simply to worry about the "clarity" of his party's positions. To him, the NDP faced a crisis in the presentation, not the substance, of its policies. At the same time his thinking about NDP policy was influenced by Allan Blakeney's defeat in Saskatchewan in 1982. Notley saw the NDP's loss in Saskatchewan as a vote against a tired government, but also as a rejection of the NDP's excessively interventionist style. In the short term anyway, "socialism" had become a liability for the NDP.

Given such influences on Notley's thinking, the NDP's alternative economic strategy broke little new ground. The NDP denounced the Tories' indifference to the plight of the unemployed, assailed them for their neglect of the environment and the quality of life, and ridiculed their abandonment of the goal of economic diversification. More positively, the party asserted: "The NDP believes that the basis of any enlightened economic strategy must be geared to the "primacy of people over things" rather than the gain of the few at the expense of the many or the development of technology for its own sake."[26] But such thinking did not underpin the policy proposals. Rather, the main thrust was to note policy areas that the Conservatives had mismanaged (women's concerns being a noteworthy example), to stress that the Conservatives were technocrats, and to assert that the NDP's brand of planning, economic activism, and moderate nationalism would somehow yield superior results to Conservative policies. Albertans were presented with a choice between competing means rather than a choice between alternative visions of the economy.

In his penetrating analysis of the post-war British Labour party, Ralph Miliband noted several dilemmas faced by social democratic parties when they confront Conservative political opponents.[27] His insights are directly relevant to the situation faced by the NDP in contemporary Alberta. First, he observed how social democrats tend to assume romantically that their Conservative opponents will inevitably show their true colours, attack the welfare state, and advance a return to unfettered competitive capitalism. An assumption develops that the capitalist parties will eventually self-destruct and be automatically replaced by a socialist alternative. Notley's behaviour in the late 1970s supports Miliband's argument. He frequently asserted that the Lougheed Conservatives would, for unspecified reasons, abandon the centre, move to the right and thereby pave the way for an NDP government. But after fifteen years of Tory rule, no such tendencies are obvious. Miliband also noted that most social democratic parties, when facing an interventionist bourgeois party, reject a move to the left and opt instead to be "moderate" and to imitate their stronger opponents at the centre. Whether consciously or not, the Alberta NDP had adopted a strategy of down-playing its socialism and fighting the Lougheed Tories for the political centre.

Given its decision to occupy the centre, the NDP's efforts to distinguish itself from the Conservatives are almost impossible. Indeed, the party's basic distinction between NDP economic activism and Conservative passivity has become rhetorical in practice. The NDP now faces the complex task of distinguishing between *variations* of active government. And it can now only distinguish itself by advocating a larger role for government in the economy and society. Through its rejection of a class-based appeal, it foreclosed the possibility of distinguishing interventions in terms of the *interests served*. Here it could have been clearly and plausibly argued that Conservative interventions, as interventions on behalf of Alberta business, were by definition fundamentally different from those advocated by the NDP. Hence the Alberta NDP remains in a political no-man's land. It refuses to advance a clear socialist alternative, but at the same time it cannot distinguish itself from the governing Conservatives.

Economic Diversification in Alberta: The Elusive Quest

Alberta's economic and fiscal dependence on oil, natural gas, and agricultural industries is the fundamental determinant of the province's political economy. In excess of half of the province's revenues are derived from total resource revenues, a figure far greater than in any other province. Alberta's economy is thus profoundly influenced by powerful domestic and international conditions over which the provincial government exerts little influence. Moreover, the province's dependence on *depleting* non-renewable resources is a source of constant anxiety. To quote Notley: "What happens after the oil wells have been drilled, the pipelines laid, and the gas processing plants erected?"[28]

The Alberta NDP has long stressed the need to diversify the economy. As early as 1963, it emphasized the need for higher resource royalties, greater expenditures on research and development, and the need to develop indigenous petrochemical and steel industries. Neil Reimer, the party's first leader, argued that organized labour provided the original emphasis on diversification.[29] For unions, economic diversification held the obvious appeal of a broader industrial base, more industries, more workers and more members. For the NDP, a core of urban trade unionists would form a natural basis of support.

Notley's early political speeches stressed the perils of a dependent economy and extolled the virtues of an "industrial policy." He saw a need to maximize returns from royalties, and then to develop a coherent plan for the reinvestment of such rents in the provincial economy. He fretted about the lack of secondary industry, worried about the "boom and bust" cycle, and stressed the need for planning. But Notley's views were not clearly informed by any careful analysis of the economic potential of Alberta or the prairie region. He sometimes maintained that "discriminatory" federal policy accounted for the lack of secondary industry on the prairies. But later in his career, he implied that Alberta's distance from markets and small population base were the problems. Curiously, Notley simultaneously maintained that there must be economic diversification, in the form of secondary industry, the raw facts of geography and market economies notwithstanding.

Peter Lougheed also spoke frequently about Alberta's dependence on oil and natural gas. Particularly in his first term, he argued, like Notley, that Alberta's conventional reserves of oil and gas would soon be depleted and that immediate action was required if Alberta's prosperity was to be maintained. The Heritage Fund would be employed both as a source of future revenues and as a vehicle for developing, diversifying, and strengthening the economy.

However, after the oil boom of the late 1970s, the Lougheed government began to divorce itself from the concept of economic diversification. The Heritage Fund became increasingly devoted to low-risk investments and the objective of economic restructuring was seldom mentioned. Indeed, the government reduced in half the inflow of resource royalties to the Fund and began to divert its investment income to general revenues. And in mid-1984, the government's White Paper on economic strategy argued that economic diversification had never really been a basic policy goal and those who believed otherwise were confused. According to the White Paper:

> It has been the government's intention to diversify the provincial economy so as to become *less* dependent on the sale of unprocessed resources, both renewable and non-renewable. However, it was always intended and often stated that the oil and gas sector would remain a primary engine of the Alberta economy. Diversification was intended to *broaden* our base—not artificially *change* our base. Some misunderstood this intention.[30]

The rationale for the government's change of heart was never made clear. One assumes, however, that more than a decade of governing taught the Lougheed Conservatives that geography, economics, and the Canadian constitution imposed real constraints on even the most adventurous and committed provincial governments.

Notley smelled blood when he saw the Conservatives backing off their commitment to diversification. He saw an opening and a major issue whereby he could distinguish his party from the ruling Conservatives. Hence from 1980 onward he assailed the government's failure to employ Trust Fund monies for the purpose of diversification. To give the attack popular momentum the NDP held province-wide hearings on the Fund and its uses; the major finding of the inquiry was that every interest group in Alberta wanted to consume part of the Funds. Typical of Notley's own views in this period were his remarks in 1983 when the premier announced major changes in the Trust Fund's administration: ". . . an important shift is occurring. We are backing away from a fund which recognizes as one of its important mandates the strengthening and diversifying of the Alberta economy. . . . It's obvious that the government is throwing in the towel in terms of any initiatives that might be taken on the issue of diversifying the Alberta economy."[31] Rather predictably, Notley argued that the Tories' reverence for market forces and the private sector made them timid and unwilling to employ the state as an instrument of diversification.

But the NDP's thinking about economic diversification remains unclear. It has simply decided that a resource-based economy, subject as it often is to severe "booms and busts", is an inferior economy when compared to a "diversified" one. But what sort of diversification is desirable and how it can be achieved have not yet been defined.

A key NDP argument is that an interventionist government is a requisite to effective diversification. Of course, the NDP could in theory form such a government, but the Lougheed Tories with their dependence on corporate capitalism are allegedly hamstrung. Hence the NDP often advance the claim that a more "active" Trust Fund is essential to provincial economic development. Indeed, since the early 1980s the party has maintained that the Trust Fund must be converted into an "Alberta Development Fund."[32] Such a fund, untrammelled by the shackles of laissez-faire dogma, would be creatively employed by an NDP government to diversify the economy. The state would become a willing player ready and capable of restructuring the economy. Moreover, "low interest loans" to small businessmen, farmers, and homeowners would be made available and these would stimulate economic activity. In short, public monies and a government willing to distribute them are for the NDP foundations of an effective diversification policy. Another requisite is public planning. Somehow, the NDP maintained in the early 1980s that an economic plan, if formulated, would encourage diversification. The assumption was that planning, if broadly based, could generate a consensus on the future structure of the Alberta economy. A related idea, and one widely held by planners, is that if a "problem" is studied deeply and if enough information and expertise is brought to bear, a solution will ultimately appear.

But a faith in planning and active government cannot generate a practical strategy for diversification. It provides no sense of what sorts of industries are viable on the Canadian prairies, the costs of developing and maintaining them, or the necessary public policies. Illustrative of the NDP's fuzzy thinking on these questions is its argument that such sectors as aerospace, helicopter manufacturing, a centre for toxicology, "and anchors for local industry," might provide an indigenous technological base. But at the same time the party remains skeptical of any further development of Alberta's petrochemical industry which is seen as a costly, ultimately unfeasible, option for diversification. No clear economic or political criteria emerge to distinguish "desirable" avenues of diversification from unlikely ones. Nor has the party given much serious attention to the economic powers of provincial governments. In Canada's interdependent federation, major powers remain in federal hands and to be effective, intergovernmental co-operation is required. The precise limits of provincial power and the extent of requisite intergovernmental agreement need clarification in NDP policy.

I have already argued that the policy positions of an opposition party need not always be precise or fully developed. And in this sense it is perhaps unfair and probably naive to expect the Alberta NDP to unveil a detailed scheme for economic renewal. But it is not asking too much of a party to develop a coherent *political* strategy in support of its policies. In this vein, the NDP's emphasis on diversification is also lacking; its plans for economic restructuring are not rooted in a clear appeal to particular interests. Its original emphasis on diversification as a vehicle for building a larger urban working class no longer underpins party policy. Rather, diversification has simply become a convenient symbol of the failures of the Lougheed government. If the Conservatives cannot diversify the economy, then surely the NDP with its activist philosophy can do so. Economic diversification thus fills a policy vacuum. The NDP's focus on diversification also reflects a rather vague assumption that there exists in the Alberta electorate a deep anxiety about the future. Having been told by politicians for a decade that the oil is running out, Albertans now expect a solution and the NDP feels it can provide one. The truth of such an assumption is of course difficult to verify. One wonders, however, if a vague commitment to an elusive goal is really enough to spark the interest and imagination of the electorate.

Conclusions

Shortly after Notley's death, Don Braid of the *Edmonton Journal* advanced a conventional wisdom about the proper future direction of NDP policy:

> Notley kept the party on a sensible, moderate course. He alone had the stature to hold the NDP's left wing in check by convincing most New Democrats that moderation is the key to success in Alberta. The great danger now is that the party's left wing will become more vocal arguing for truly "socialist" causes. In conservative Alberta, this would be deadly.[33]

Braid's fears about a sudden, "left-wing" inspired radicalization of the Alberta NDP have not materialized and the prospects for such a revolution are indeed slim. The party seems content to remain a middle of the road party that downplays socialism and makes policy to appeal to a broad coalition of voters. Far from providing a socialist alternative, the party is now distinguishable from the governing Conservatives only by its emphasis on honest government and more caring public administration. Most apparatciks are firmly convinced that a more militant socialism would harm the party at the polls, and the left of the party is mostly dormant.

The NDP's desire to appear as a "sensible, moderate" alternative has been intensified by Peter Lougheed's resignation. For in common with other contenders for political power, the NDP believes Lougheed's departure, and his replacement by Don Getty, will seriously weaken the Conservative party which has been built and nurtured by Lougheed's dominant leadership. The operative assumption is that the Conservatives will move to the right in Lougheed's absence and thereby open the centre for the NDP. If it proceeds cautiously, if it capitalizes successfully on prevailing discontents, and if it broadens its appeal, the NDP sees itself as winning support at the expense of the Conservatives.

The view that the NDP should moderate its socialism further and become more like the other parties must be challenged on several grounds. First, the party has tried such a strategy almost since its birth with only limited results. And if nothing else, the party's weak showing in 1982 must surely raise questions about the electoral payoffs of political moderation, shallow policy analysis, and negative campaigns. More fundamentally, a social democratic party must have roots in the electorate and be more than a coalition of disparate interests that, for different reasons, oppose the government. For despite its carping to the contrary, the government of Alberta is both willing and able to buy off discontent. This is one political lesson that the NDP has surely learned since 1971. And to be quite frank, many of the NDP's "target groups"—small and medium business being a prime example—now know quite well which parties serve their interests. Finally, the advancement of a progressive alternative is the sole *raison d'etre* of the Alberta NDP. But by moderating its appeal and watering down its socialism, the party undercuts its own relevance and political significance. As Charles Taylor has asked rhetorically, the alternative to capitalism is necessarily socialism, but will the socialists offer the alternative?[34]

The Alberta NDP must reaffirm its committment to the achievement of a socialist Alberta. To this end, its policies must promote equality of condition, a greater degree of control for citizens over their conditions of life and work, and serious efforts to replace the chaos of markets with orderly planning. In this context, the real challenge for socialists is to articulate policies which are feasible in Alberta's particular social setting, to demonstrate that socialism promotes economic growth not merely a redistribution of existing assets, and to educate citizens about the virtues of a more egalitarian society.

My argument—that the Alberta NDP must strengthen, not reduce, its commitment to socialist policy—will probably not be popular among some party leaders. It implies the adoption of a risky strategy when moderation may seem more appropriate. It also challenges widely-held assumptions about the conservatism of the Alberta electorate. At the same time, however, the party prides itself as an internally democratic party and one that encourages debate about fundamental principles. Without a spirited debate about the party's direction and fundamental goals, the Alberta NDP faces, not electoral success, but a long drift into orthodoxy and perhaps political oblivion.

---

[1]Grant Notley, Letter to Ed Broadbent, 8 December 1978. NDP files, Alberta Legislature.

[2]Interview, Edmonton, 29 May 1985.

[3]*Minutes*, Executive Committee, Alberta NDP, 4 January 1969. Acc. No. 84.178/107. Alberta NDP Archive. Provincial Archives of Alberta.

[4]Larry Pratt, "Note for Notley Archive," May 1985, p. 8.

[5]Notley stressed this theme in his first speech in the Alberta Legislature. For details see Alberta, Legislative Assembly, *Hansard*, 6 March 1972, pp. 3-29-3-35. Hereafter cited as *Hansard*.

[6]Alberta NDP, "Policy and Public Ownership," 1974.

[7]Alberta NDP, "1971 Election Platform," p. 48.

[8]Bob Bell, "Waffle energy bid rejected," *Edmonton Journal*, 8 February 1971, pp. 1 and 10.

[9]"Policy on Public Ownership," p. 1.

[10]*Ibid.*

[11]*Hansard*, 31 October 1980, p. 1325.

[12]Interview, Edmonton, 29 May 1985.

[13]"Notley reveals NDP alternate Speech from the Throne for new Legislative session," *Alberta Democrat*, March 1977, p. 24.

[14]Grant Notley, "Letter to the editor," *Edmonton Magazine*, 28 March 1984.

[15]"Notley warns of government/business complex," *Alberta Democrat*, April 1977, p. 12.

[16]*Hansard*, 30 May 1979, p. 90.

[17]For a detailed analysis see Larry Pratt, "The Political Economy of Province-Building: Alberta's Development Strategy, 1971-1981" in D. Leadbeater (ed.), *Essays on the Political Economy of Alberta* (Toronto: New Hogtown Press, 1984), pp. 194-222.

[18]Interview with Kevin Peterson, Managing Editor, *The Calgary Herald*, 31 May, 1985, Edmonton.

[19]*Hansard*, 24 October 1974, p. 3182.

[20]*Hansard*, 23 April 1976, p. 837.

[21]Interview, 31 May 1985, Edmonton.

[22]Government of Alberta, *White Paper: Proposals for an Industrial and Science Strategy for Albertans, 1985 to 1990*, July 1984. Hereafter cited as *White Paper*.

[23]*White Paper*, p. 39.

[24]Gordon Fearn, "Memo on Government's White Paper on Industrial and Science Strategy," 15 August 1984, p. 6.

[25]Geoff White, "Lougheed steals Notley's Thunder," *Calgary Herald*, 14 July 1984, p. A-8.

[26]Alberta NDP, *A New Democratic Future: Proposals for an Economic Strategy, 1985-1990*, 13 October 1984, p. 6.

[27]Ralph Miliband, *Parliamentary Socialism* (London: Merlin Press, 1961).

[28]Grant Notley, "Challenge of the 70s," Provincial Leader's Address, Edmonton, 1971.

[29]Interview, 29 May 1985, Edmonton.

[30]*White Paper*, p. 29.

[31]*Hansard*, 21 March 1983, p. 187.

[32]For details see Alberta NDP Heritage Savings Trust Fund Policy Committee, *The Alberta Development Fund: An NDP Alternative*, October 1981.

[33]Don Braid, "Death posing big problems," *Edmonton Journal*, 25 October 1984, p. 7.

[34]Charles Taylor, "The Agony of Economic Man," in H.D. Forbes (ed.), *Canadian Political Thought* (Toronto: Oxford University Press, 1985), pp. 406-416.

Chapter 5

Oil, Class and Development in Alberta

Ed Shaffer

When Grant Notley took his seat in the Legislature in 1971, neither he nor the members of the newly elected Tory government were able to foresee the profound changes that were to take place in Alberta within the next few years. Decisions made in faraway places—Libya, Iran and Saudi Arabia, to name a few—gave birth to the oil boom, which ushered in a new era for Albertans, one of hope and optimism.

When, 13 years later, Notley's life came to its tragic end, the oil boom had also come to its end. As before, Albertans faced a new era, but this time one of sombreness and despair. His departure from, like his entry into, the Legislature marked the beginning of another chapter in the history of Alberta.

Unlike his Tory colleagues, Notley never viewed the boom as an unmixed blessing. He knew that it had both positive and negative aspects and he was constantly concerned about the latter. It is therefore fitting that in this volume we should examine the role of oil in Alberta's economic development, a subject to which he gave his closest attention.

Oil and Development

Among economists and other students of development, there is as yet no universal agreement on a precise definition of economic development. Some economists believe a region develops if its total income rises. Others would argue that development occurs only if income per person rises.

Others, including this author, believe that development involves much more than rises in either income or per capita income. It involves fundamental changes in the structure of the economy. Among them are: changes in the composition of the labour force; an increase in urbanization; an expansion of social services; and, most important of all, a reduction in the dependence on one or a small number of commodities.

Development therefore implies diversification. In this uncertain world, it is unwise to put "all of one's eggs in one basket". A developed, diversified economy can better withstand the loss of a specific market than one totally dependent on that market. The questions that concerned Notley, and must concern us, are: Did Alberta during the boom use its oil in such a way as to spur development, i.e. to reduce its dependence on that one commodity? In other words, did oil become an "engine of growth"?

Before answering these questions, it might be wise to examine the general question of how, if at all, the production and export of crude oil can foster development. The relationship between oil and development depends upon a number of factors, far too many to discuss adequately within the confines of this chapter. Probably the most important is the ability of an oil-producing region to capture the economic rents[1] generated by oil and to use them in a rational manner.

This ability depends on two types of power relationships: the external and the internal. In many oil regions of the capitalist world, the oil is produced by private companies. In other countries where the oil companies have been nationalized, their management remains in the hands of the former concessionaires. A substantial portion of the output of these nationalized companies is sold to the affiliates of the former private owners.

This situation engenders a conflict between the private interests, who either own or manage the companies, and the public interest. The private interests, following the logic of the market place, must attempt to maximize their profits. They will therefore try to garner for themselves as much of the economic rent as they can. The public interest, on the other hand, dictates that the entire rent remain within the domestic economy. There is thus a permanent conflict between the private and public interests over the ownership of the rent.

The outcome of this struggle depends on the bargaining power of the respective parties. In general the greater the bargaining power one has, the more economic rent he captures. If the private sector is strong in relation to the public sector, it will garner for itself the bulk of the rent. This is especially true if the output of a few, large private firms represents a significant portion of the production of the local economy. It is even more true if these private firms are either owned or controlled by citizens of the major industrialized countries, who usually receive the diplomatic backing of their governments in disputes with oil-producing nations.

Linked to, but distinct from the ability to capture rents, is the problem of using the rents in a manner to spur development. The internal disposition of the rents depends primarily on domestic power relationships, which are often themselves dependent on the external power relationships. The large oil companies, as well as their home governments, are not indifferent to the power relationships in the areas in which they have interests and they support those elements who will most likely co-operate with them. This support can influence the domestic power structure.

The dominant groups in each oil-producing area will largely determine how the rents captured by the local economy will be spent. Their power to influence the use of the rents comes either directly through ownership of the subsurface mineral rights, as in Texas and in certain parts of Canada, or indirectly through control of the State apparatus. In most parts of the world, including Alberta, the indirect control mechanism determines the uses to which the rents are put.

In these areas the subsurface mineral rights belong to the State, which as the resource owner, receives rent from the companies. The dominant groups in society, through their control of the State, gain access to these funds and determine how they will be used. In some societies these groups may view development, which carries with it the threat of substituting new social structures and power relationships for the present ones, as inimicable to their interests. In these societies the rents, instead of being used to spur development, will be used to preserve the status-quo.

Aside from these concerns, there are often legitimate questions about the economic viability of development projects. To what extent, if at all, is development feasible in sparsely populated areas, far removed from major market areas? In addition there is the problem of the reaction of the industrialized countries to the growth of new industrial areas. Will these countries impose tariffs and other import restrictions on manufactured products from the oil producing regions? How will the established multinationals act towards their new competitors? Will the multinationals engage in price wars and other predatory tactics in order to crush them? Given the problems that development might engender, the dominant groups might well use the economic rents for investment abroad or for the enhancement of their own interests at home rather than for development.

It is therefore not accidental that very little economic development has taken place in most oil exporting regions. To the extent that development has occurred, as in Texas and California, it came about as a result of a number of factors, of which oil may not have been the most important. Among them was the establishment of industries associated with the military-industrial complex in both states.

Although the exploitation of oil does not, by itself, foster diversification, it does bring economic and social changes to a region. These changes have the potential of engendering social conflicts, which could seriously undermine the position of the dominant groups. Among the changes is the creation of a small, but often significant, industrial proletariat, the oil workers. In many countries these workers have been a militant force demanding social changes.

In most areas the dominant groups have, at least up to now, succeeded in blunting this militancy through the judicious use of the economic rents. The large rents enabled them to offer these workers substantial concessions, while at the same time keeping the basic power structure intact. Rents in these countries play a role similar to that of imperialism in the developed capitalist countries: the profits earned from colonialization enabled the industrialized countries to buy labour peace at home without undermining the system.

The exploitation of oil, like imperialism, has thus bolstered the forces of conservatism. One can only speculate on the social and political changes that may have taken place in most oil areas if the ruling groups were not able to use the economic rents to strengthen their position.

Their dependence on these rents may however, in the long-run, spell their doom. If, for any reason, they are deprived of these rents, they will not be able to hold in check the social conflicts which the rents have helped paper over. The ensuing eruptions could bring about basic changes in society.

The Impact of Oil on Alberta

The impact of oil in Alberta has been similar to its impact in other areas of the world. Though oil brought important change to the province, even before the price increases of the 1970s, it failed to diversify the economy.

Alberta, unlike many other areas, was in a good position to obtain many economic benefits from oil. It had already developed a market economy long before oil was discovered. The majority of the work force was engaged in commercial agriculture producing for world markets. The population had acquired a market culture and responded quickly to changes in economic incentives. In this respect it was ripe for development.

Mitigating against development were certain severe economic handicaps, namely a sparse population and long distances from the main markets. Such economic disadvantages present formidable barriers to development. Their existence does not imply that development is impossible. Other areas of the world, like Japan, which has few mineral resources, or Sweden, which has a small population removed from the main market centres, have managed to develop.

Though important difference among Sweden, Japan and Alberta make comparison difficult, one comparison can be made. Development in Sweden and Japan did not come about through the operation of the so-called "free market" mechanism. Development in those countries was the result of deliberate government policies which interfered with the workings of the market. If these two countries had relied on the market alone, they would never have developed. Following the dictates of the so-called Law of Comparative Advantage, Sweden would have remained an exporter of raw materials and Japan, an exporter of silk.

Similarly, if Alberta is to diversify its economy, it has to interfere with the market mechanism. It has to adopt an interventionist development strategy. The real issue confronting Alberta therefore is not whether it should adopt such a strategy, but what particular strategy to adopt. The provincial government officially recognized this fact of life in 1984 when it issued a White Paper appropriately entitled, *Proposals for an Industrial and Science Strategy for Albertans*. This paper defined industrial strategy as "the sum of a government's efforts to stimulate business activity and to influence economic growth." Justifying this interference in the market, the paper noted:

> It is argued that governments should resist involvement in the market place, since a misallocation of resources results. Nonetheless, governments everywhere are in fact involved in varying degrees.[2]

Alberta, as we shall see, had a strategy for development long before the issuance of the White Paper in 1984. This strategy was born after the election of the Progressive Conservatives in 1971. No such strategy existed under the previous Social Credit government. If anything, the government had a bias against economic development.

When, in the late 1940s, the Social Credit government was faced with the bonanza of oil royalties flowing into the Treasury, it decided to use a substantial portion of these funds to expand health services and educational facilities within the province rather than to spur development. This expansion corresponded to the interests of the largely rural population.

There were a number of reasons why the province decided to expand social services rather than to use the royalties in other ways, such as distributing it as a dividend or reducing taxes or adopting a positive development policy. First, the distribution of royalties as a dividend would have created enormous administrative and political problems. Criteria would have had to be established governing the distribution. Decisions would have to be made whether each Albertan should receive an equal payment. Then an Albertan would have to be defined. Would the term Albertan be limited to current residents of the province? If so, how long would a person have to live in Alberta to be considered an Albertan? A short residency requirement would encourage migration, which the Socreds did not want. Migration furthermore would have reduce the payments going to those who lived in the province for a long time. A long residency requirement would have caused inequities and possible constitutional challenges. In addition, there was the problem of questions could open up a veritable Pandora's box.

Second, and probably more important, the payment of royalties directly to individuals breaks the link between income and work. For a market society to operate efficiently, individuals should be rewarded for their contributions to society. While there is good reason to be skeptical of how this principle is honoured in practice (one can raise serious doubts, for instance, whether the income accruing to the wealthiest families is an accurate measure of their contribution to society), it cannot be seriously breached without disrupting the whole incentive system upon which a market society is based. Unless a highly complex measure can be devised which accurately reflects each individual's contribution to society, any dispersal of royalty funds would have to be based on a principle other than work, thus eroding one of the pillars of the system.

The same reasoning applies to the complete forgiveness of taxes or forgiveness to the extent that royalties can replace taxes. While some taxes, like sales and inheritance taxes, were never introduced and other taxes lowered, tax collections were not lowered by the amount of royalties received. In addition, a drastic lowering of taxes could create political problems for any government that might feel compelled to raise taxes in the future.

The Socreds did not use the funds as a means to spur development because they did not want to change Alberta from a rural to an urban province. Their resistance to such a change stemmed partly from a desire to defend the rural way of life and partly from the fear of the

radicalism which they believed would accompany the rise of an industrial proletariat. Given these realities the Socreds opted to disburse the
royalties through the purchase of social goods and services. As in other
parts of the world, the royalties were used to buy social harmony by
papering over the conflicts in society. Initially, at least, they helped
preserve the existing social structure.

The Socred policy turned out to be self-defeating. Though it did
not encourage diversification, it spawned urbanization. Since the urban
centres received the largest proportion of the oil money, they attracted
people from the rural areas of Alberta, from the rest of Canada and from
other countries. During Social Credit's reign, employment in non-
commercial services grew far more than any other sector of the economy. Non-commercial services are mainly those services provided by
governmental agencies. Most of the employment in these services was
concentrated in agencies providing health, education and welfare. The
people providing these services had an urban outlook and rejected the
rural values of the Socreds.

In addition, the oil industry itself gave birth to employment in commercial services—legal, consulting, geophysical, etc.— trade, finance
and real estate, which were also concentrated in the urban centres. The
people employed in these private sector activities also had an urban
outlook and they too rejected the Socreds' rural values.

During the Socred years, the main linkages between the oil industry and the rest of the economy were in these sectors. The oil industry,
like any other industry in an interdependent economy, must be linked to
other industries, both industries supplying it and industries buying from
it. The industries may or may not be located in the oil-producing region.
To the extent that they are, they provide a basis for growth independent
of that of the oil industry.

In terms of development, the most important linkages should be
with manufacturing. Manufacturing industries are the only ones capable
of diversifying the economy. During the Socred years, the linkages to
manufacturing were weak. By and large, there was no significant growth
in that sector. To the extent that some enterprises were linked to the oil
industry, they became satellite firms in satellite industries. Satellite
industries are those whose livelihood depends on the fortunes of the oil
industry. Spawned by that industry, they are unable to cut the umbilical
cord tying them to oil. The growth of these satellite industries increased
the province's dependence on oil.

The strong growth in services, coupled with the weak growth in manufacturing, while consistent with the Socreds' objective of preventing the rise of an urban proletariat, nevertheless undermined that party's rural power base. The people attracted to the urban centres were not afraid of development and actually welcomed it. As they grew more numerous, they began to exert their power through a party which more closely represented their interests, the Progressive Conservatives.

The Tory Approach

In 1971, Alberta elected a Progressive Conservative government. The new Tory government instituted a different policy in the dispersal of the economic rent. It shifted the emphasis to economic development and the enhancement of Alberta's power position within Confederation.

It deliberately slowed down the growth of the public sector. Most of the growth in employment was centered in the private, non-goods producing industries. These industries prospered as long as oil prices leapt skyward. But they did not provide a basis for future expansion, as became evident during the downturn.

Despite the government's favourable attitude towards development, the links to manufacturing remained weak. Most of the development that did occur in that sector took place in satellite industries. Table 1, below, shows that in those manufacturing industries most likely to supply the oil industry with parts, the average size of the establishment in Alberta is much smaller than in the rest of Canada. After

Table 1
Average Number of Employees per Establishment
Selected Industries

1978

Industry	Alberta	Other Canada
Primary Metal	139	325
Metal Fabricating	27	35
Machinery	45	72
Electrical Products	53	121

Calculated from: Statistics Canada, Manufacturing Industries of Canada: National and Provincial Areas, 1978, Cat. No. 31-203, Dec., 1980.

three decades of oil, the industry failed to develop a large-scale, independent manufacturing base. The developments in manufacturing, as in the service sector, increased the dependence on oil. The painful effects of this increased dependence were felt during the economic downturn that started in 1981, when many of these satellite firms went out of business.

The linkages that did occur were, as has already been mentioned, mainly in the non-productive sectors,[3] i.e. services, trade, finance and real estate. In 1983 these sectors accounted for over 60 per cent of the province's non-agricultural labour force. In 1961, the first year for which comparable data is available, they accounted for approximately one-half of that force. In contrast, the portion engaged in manufacturing fell from slightly over 12 per cent to just above 9 per cent during the same period.

The non-productive sectors, while very important for the efficient functioning of the economy, cannot be, by their nature, engines for growth and development. They are basically ancillary industries which arise to service the goods-producing industries—manufacturing, mining, agriculture and construction. Without the growth of these latter industries, the non-productive industries cannot grow. They are basically satellite industries.[4]

The failure of the Conservatives, despite their development policies, to diversify requires further analysis. Led by Premier Lougheed, the Tories believed that the key to diversification lay in the private sector. It was Lougheed's belief that the profitability of the energy sector would create a positive investment climate, not only in the energy industries themselves but in those industries linked to the energy industries. Profits from oil would be invested in these latter industries. Furthermore, prosperity would attract outside investment into a whole range of industries in Alberta.

As the Government of Alberta was later forced to admit, this development did not occur. In its White Paper, it stated that during the oil boom "many entrepreneurs in Alberta who could have further contributed to diversification committed most of their cash and efforts to expansion in the energy and real estate fields".[5] Unfortunately it did not give any analysis as to why the actual investment patterns differed so markedly from the anticipated ones.

The Government of Alberta failed to recognize that private investment would flow to those industries offering the highest rate of return. Given the rapid rise in oil prices, that industry was receiving exceptionally high profits. Investors anticipating continued price increases and even greater profits flocked to the oil industry. The rapid growth of that industry triggered a migration to Alberta, which, in turn, caused real estate prices to soar. The possibilities of reaping enormous profits in real estate induced many speculators to put their money in that industry.

As the Government of Alberta correctly noted, investment in real estate does not bring about diversification. While the process of changing the ownership of property may prove highly profitable to those engaged in that trade, it does not add to the productive potential of an economy. Private investors moreover are not particularly interested in increasing this potential. They are interested solely in reaping the greatest possible gain in the shortest possible time. Given the rules of the market, they cannot be expected to act in any other fashion.

With this behaviour pattern it was unrealistic of the province to expect private investment to flow into other industries unless these industries were making equal or greater returns than oil and real estate. The probability of new industries, even those of great potential, earning such profits in Alberta in the *immediate* future is small. It is therefore quite understandable why rational investors, be they Albertans, other Canadians or non-Canadians, would shy away from them.

The belief that private enterprise alone can in today's world diversify an economy is erroneous. The only way diversification can occur is outside the market mechanism, i.e. through governmental actions. Diversification is therefore a political as well as an economic matter. The key to development revolves around the policy the government adopts toward the economic rents generated by the energy industries. If the government wants to foster development to the fullest extent possible, it must (1) maximize its collections of the economic rents and (2) use them in the most rational manner.

There is only one way any government can maximize its rent collections and that is through outright ownership of every facet of the industry. As pointed out earlier, mere ownership of subsurface mineral rights does not guarantee maximum rent collections. In order to induce private firms to develop its resources, the government usually offers them part of the rent. This is especially true if a relatively weak provincial government, like that of Alberta, must deal directly with huge multinational giants, whose annual revenues far exceed Alberta's Gross Domestic Product. (GDP)

When Alberta chose to allow private companies to develop its oil resources, it placed itself in a vulnerable position as far as the collection of economic rents was concerned. That these corporations were able to retain for themselves a significant portion of these economic rents is made clear in income estimates produced by the Alberta Bureau of Statistics and Statistics Canada. According to these estimates, the profits made in Alberta by all corporations doing business in the province, including non-energy companies, rose from 12 per cent of Alberta's GDP in 1961 to a high of 22 per cent in 1979. After falling to 16 per cent in 1980, they rose to 19 per cent in 1983, the latest year for which these statistics are available. During this entire period, the corporate share of GDP in Alberta was much higher than in the rest of Canada. In the rest of Canada, it was approximately 10 per cent in 1961 and 8.5 per cent in 1983. The differential between the provincial and national profit shares thus rose from 2 to 10.5 percentage points between 1961 and 1983.

The oil companies, who received the bulk of the profits, moreover, paid very little in taxes. According to the Auditor General of Alberta, all corporations with operations in the province paid the Alberta Treasury a little more than $800 million for the fiscal years 1979-1984. Their tax bill, before taking advantage of loopholes in the form of deductions, credits and rebates to which they were legally entitled, was $4.5 billion. These loopholes enabled the companies to reduce their taxes by 81 per cent. The loopholes were so generous that in one of the years, the fiscal year ending March 31, 1983, the corporate sector received from the province $162 million more than it paid to it.[6] During the years 1974-1984 the corporations' pre-tax profits totalled $44 billion.[7] The province's effective corporate tax rate therefore came to only two per cent.

The above does not imply that the province did not receive substantial sums in the form of royalties, lease rentals and bonus bids. These sums were large and significant. In the years 1979-1983, they amounted to approximately $34 billion.[8] What is the case is that the province, because of its lenient taxation policy, failed to maximize its collections of the industry's economic rents.

One of the consequences of this failure was the large outflow of corporate investment income abroad. In the years 1979-1983, this flow amounted to $15 billion or almost twenty times the corporate taxes paid to the province. The investment income paid to governments and to non-Canadians are summarized in Table 2, below.

Table 2
Alberta Business Sector Payments *($ Millions)*

Year	to Governments	to Non-Canadians
1979	4,695	1,902
1980	5,785	2,188
1981	6,804	3,288
1982	7,928	4,186
1983	8,465	3,853
Sum	33,677	15,417

Source: Alberta Bureau of Statistics, "Alberta
Business Sector Outlay Accounts".

Linked to the failure of the province to maximize its rent collections is its failure to make rational use of the rents that it actually collected. At the advent of the oil boom, Alberta's Tory leadership, despite their rhetoric, realized that the market, left to its own doings, would never diversify Alberta. The Government therefore established the Alberta Heritage Savings Trust Fund (AHSTF), consisting initially of 30 per cent of all non-renewable natural resource revenues, as a means to spur diversification and to protect Alberta against a "rainy day".

The Fund's establishment was, however, only a half-way measure. While it went outside the market by garnering a certain portion of the rent for the public sector, it did not take the next necessary step, the establishment of a planning agency to see that these public funds are used in a manner consistent with the objectives of the province.

One of the first tasks of any planning agency would be to set up a system of priorities, in other words to assign a time sequence to anticipated developmental projects. Another task would be to set up criteria by which any proposal could be judged. While any particular sets of priorities and criteria can be subject to criticism, they are an essential first step to a rational use of public funds. Saskatchewan's first CCF government set up a Planning Board in 1946 for the purpose of establishing a set of priorities and the criteria for investment.

If the province has established priorities and criteria, it has not publicized them. All major investment decisions are made *in camera* by the

Cabinet. Presumably the Cabinet has its own standards but they are secrets. Though there is no evidence that this has happened up to now, this secrecy nurtures a climate in which investment deals can be worked out which, while benefitting individual members of the Cabinet and the private firms involved, may be of dubious worth to the province.

There is probably a more basic reason for the refusal of the Tories to develop a comprehensive plan for diversification. Their ideology is incompatible with that of direct planning. The decisions of private firms seeking to maximize profits must inevitably run counter to dictates of a planning agency seeking to develop the province. A successful planning agency must, of necessity, curb the profit-seeking behaviour of private firms.

A planning agency might also decide that certain companies should be publicly-owned and operated. Such a concept is anathema to the Conservatives who believe that the government should not run businesses, and especially those that may compete directly with private firms. Such attitudes reduce drastically the scope for using the Fund as a means for diversification. It should, however, be pointed out that the Conservatives are not pure ideologues. They have intervened directly in the economy when they felt such intervention was in the interests of Alberta's business class. One such intervention was the purchase by the provincial government of Pacific Western Airlines (PWA). This intervention was nevertheless an exception to the Tory's overall policy and turned out to be short-lived. The airline was eventually resold to the private sector.

While outright public ownership is an anathema, joint ventures offer a more acceptable form of intervention. In such ventures the government is a partner, rather than a competitor, of a private firm. The problem with this solution is that in most industries there is more than one firm. A joint venture with one firm means that the government is a competitor with other firms, as for example the Alberta Energy Company. A possible solution is for the government to engage in joint ventures with all the firms in a given industry.

Such a solution, however, creates its own problems. From the point-of-view of diversification, it may be an unwise investment. It might mean too much money is invested in a given industry. Another solution is to use the AHSTF to help Alberta companies. This is probably the one most favoured by the local business community and many elected politicians, whose interests they represent. While some of the Fund has been used in this manner, its use has been limited. Massive help to Alberta firms would arouse the animosity of the established multinationals, who would not view favourably the use of the Fund to encourage competitors. The provincial leaders have no desire to antagonize the multinationals, whom they view as allies in their struggle with the Eastern Canadian Establishment. Given these realities, the Alberta leadership decided to use the AHSTF and the other economic rents accruing to the province as a means of enhancing their position in Confederation. They viewed the rents as a means of shifting the locus of economic and political power from the East to Alberta. Rather than use the Fund as a *direct* means of diversification, they opted to use it as an *indirect* means, believing that investment capital will start flowing into the new power centre.

Part of their strategy was to create a favourable climate for investment by reducing corporate income taxes to the lowest level of any province in Canada and offering other incentives to business. That this local version of "supply-side" economics has not worked should come as no surprise. It has not worked elsewhere either.

The NDP Approach

In sharp contrast to the attitude of the Progressive Conservatives, Grant Notley and the NDP looked upon planning as a necessity for the development of Alberta. In the election campaign of 1971 he called for the establishment of an Alberta Development Corporation, which "would be charged with the development of industries which could be publicly, privately, or co-operatively financed and which would be located in communities currently in economic decline".[9]

In his maiden speech to the Legislature, delivered on May 6, 1972, he clearly recognized the danger of overdependence and the need for planning to protect Albertans against this danger.

> As one looks at some of the rather depressing little oil towns like Lodgepole or Turner Valley or even Redwater, you find that the magic of the oil industry is rather short lived . . . We should use the present American energy crisis to drive the hardest bargain possible, and to take a substantial portion of the money that is collected in increased royalties and use that money to begin the development of prudent, well planned, carefully thought out programs to begin the development of job-producing secondary industries. That's why we need a meaningful Alberta development program.[10]

From that day until his death, Notley continued to demand that the government draw up a plan to diversify the economy. Disgusted by the failure of Lougheed's Tories to make the Heritage Trust Fund an effective instrument of diversification, he had the NDP hold province-wide hearings on the Fund. Following these hearings he proposed to replace the Heritage Fund with the Alberta Development Fund, "to turn income derived from non-renewable resource development today into a long-term economic base for tomorrow."[11]

In 1983, he introduced a bill, "The Economic Council of Alberta Act," which would have required the government to establish a Council of 40 members, representing practically all interest groups in the province (labour, agriculture, small business, Native peoples and women's groups, among others), which would be responsible for advising the Government of Alberta on economic development and diversification.

The proposed composition of the Council revealed the depth of Notley's comprehension of the Socialist planning process. He understood that planning was fundamentally a political, rather than a technical, process. Before any planning can begin, society has to answer two basic questions: for whom and for what do we plan? These are political questions which require political answers. Notley correctly felt that this Council, composed of the various interest groups, would be an effective forum in which to discuss these questions. Only after these questions were answered could the technical work of planning begin.

Because of their class interests, the Conservatives could not adopt such a view of planning. Their concept of planning, as revealed in the White Paper, is planning for the business community. Such planning, as already discussed, cannot lead to any real development.

Though the Tories failed to diversify Alberta, they nevertheless were successful in one important respect. They, like the Socreds, used oil as a means of entrenching conservatism in the province. It is today among the most, if not actually the most, conservative provinces in the country. Conservatism was however not always the prevailing ideology in the province. Before World War II Alberta was a centre of radicalism.

The radicalism stemmed from two sources: a small but militant working class, mostly coal miners, railroaders, packinghouse workers and a much larger number of small farmers. They fought for reforms in the system, including measures to reduce the dominance of the Eastern Establishment.

The election of the Aberhart government in 1935 was a manifestation of this radicalism. Though both the Socred philosophy and the Socred leadership were conservative, they were perceived by Albertans as rebels against the system. This perception was reinforced by the struggle between the Federal government and Alberta over the "funny money", the so-called basic dividends which Social Credit failed to implement.

Though initially the Socreds were not able to make good on many of their promises, they were able to retain power for a number of reasons. First, in their fight with Ottawa over monetary reform, they received widespread support, including backing from the CCF. Second, the outbreak of World War II ended the Depression and with it much of the motivation for change. The pressure on the Socreds to institute basic reforms diminished.

After the end of the War, however, dissatisfaction with the government increased. The CCF received 70,000 votes in 1944, although they elected only two members. The discovery of oil in 1947 gave the Socreds a fresh perspective. In the first election campaign following the discovery, they told their strongly religious constituents that God was on their side because He waited until Mr. Aberhart was in office before He led the oil companies to discover oil in the province. God didn't want Socialists to govern Alberta.

As already mentioned, the subsequent economic rents from oil enabled the Socreds to satisfy many of the demands of the farmers. In addition the general postwar prosperity, the Cold War and the Federal farm programs contributed to a decline in Populism. A measure of this decline may be seen in the sharp fall in CCF support, from a peak of 70,000 votes in 1944 to a mere 15,000 votes in 1959. Militancy among the working class also decreased in those years. The two main contributors to this decline were the general prosperity and the changing composition of the working class. The working class changed in two ways. The substitution of oil for coal, a process that was well underway long before the discovery of oil in Alberta, led to the closing of the coal mines at Coal Branch, Crow's Nest and Drumheller and the virtual elimination of the coal miners, the most militant members of the union movement, from the labour force.

In addition the oil industry created a new labour force, the chief components of which were skilled and white-collar workers. Most of those directly employed in the oil patch were relatively skilled. Another skilled group directly benefitting from the activities of the oil industry were the construction workers. While most of the latter were unionized, they have been among the most conservative elements within the labour movement. Their conservatism was reinforced by their ability to obtain extremely favourable contracts during the oil boom.

A great many blue-collar workers were not organized. This was especially true of those employed in the small satellite establishments which had mushroomed during the boom. These workers often sought to improve their positions by changing jobs rather than by organizing unions. Because they perceived they had limitless opportunities under the system, they too became a force for conservatism.

As already mentioned, most of the new jobs created by oil were white-collar jobs in services, distribution and finance. Workers in these groups have traditionally shunned unions and have been forces for conservatism. Benefitting directly from the oil boom, these workers generally supported the system until the bust.

Thus, the post-war working class accepted conservative ideology. Their perceptions of society were reinforced by the reality that they did make substantial gains in their living standards, a large part of which were made possible by the huge economic rents generated by oil.

To the extent that there was dissatisfaction among the workers, the provincial government leaders were able to focus this dissatisfaction on Ottawa's policies. Taking full advantage of the traditional animosity towards the "Feds", they were able to shift the blame to Ottawa. Albertan "provincialism" became a substitute for Canadian nationalism.

During most of the oil boom of the 1970s, Alberta's leaders were eminently successful in sapping the militancy of earlier periods. Their success however was never complete. Even in the best of times, when they were most able to deliver the goods, they encountered some opposition. Grant Notley's small electoral successes are a testimony to this.

The Future

With the collapse of the oil boom, this opposition has risen. Interestingly enough, among the most militant sections of the union movement today are white-collar workers, especially those employed by the provincial government. Faced with cutbacks as the provincial government is shifting its declining economic rents from the public to the private sector, these workers are waging a fight to preserve their jobs and their working conditions.

Another group that has become militant are the farmers. Confronted by a succession of droughts, falling food prices, high interest rates, and rising fuel and other input prices, they are demanding that the province take action to relieve their plight. Militant farmers have, in several instances, blocked sheriff's sales in order to help a farmer save his property.

Construction workers, hard-hit by unemployment, have also become quite militant, engaging in demonstrations and confrontations with Tory politicians. Instead of offering them "goodies", as in the past, the politicians tell them that they have to accept lower living standards. Both ideology and finances dictate the officials' stand. Ideologically they are committed to keeping Alberta attractive and safe for investments. They view low wages as an inducement to investment. In addition, faced with the prospects of declining oil revenues, they are less able to buy support.

The prosperity created by oil was only able to paper over the basic divisions in Alberta society but not to eliminate them. With the end of the oil boom, these divisions are beginning to resurface. The emerging struggles will bring changes to Alberta; the real question is what type of changes will occur.

Fortunately for Alberta, Grant Notley kept a democratic Socialist perspective alive during the oil boom. He knew that the future prosperity of Alberta lay in the rational use of its resources and that only intelligent planning can guarantee such a rational use. Notley left a legacy that can guide Albertans to a better future. Let us hope that his successors will nurture this legacy and bring it to fruition.

---

[1]Economic rent is the difference between the price received for a commodity and the cost of producing it. A normal or average profit is included in the cost of production. Traditionally the economic rent earned by oil production has been very high.

[2]Government of Alberta, *White Paper: Proposals for an Industrial and Science Strategy for Albertans, 1985 to 1990,* Edmonton 1984, p. 39.

[3]The non-productive sectors are those employing white collar workers. The terms "productive" and "non-productive" are based on the labour theory of value, which stipulates that only productive workers, who directly change the form of matter, create value. Most blue collar workers are considered to be productive labourers because they are the workers who change the form of matter. Non-productive, it must be pointed out, is *not* synonomous with uselessness. Though non-productive workers do not directly change the form of matter, they may perform highly useful tasks, like the clerical work so essential for the efficient

functioning of the economy. Because they, like the productive workers, must live by selling their labour power, they can be considered as members of the working class.

[4]Construction, though a goods producing activity, might also be considered a satellite industry. Without growth in the other sectors, construction cannot grow. The economic downturn of the early 1980s dealt a severe blow to construction. It was one of the industries most severely affected by the recession.

[5]Government of Alberta, *White Paper: Proposals for an Industrial and Science Strategy for Albertans, 1985 to 1990*, Edmonton: 1984, p. 30.

[6]Auditor General of Alberta, *Report of the Auditor General for the Year Ended March 31, 1983*, p. 74 and *Report of the Auditor General for the Year Ended March 31, 1984*, p. 69.

[7]Calculated from: Alberta Bureau of Statistics, "Alberta Business Sector Income Accounts".

[8]This sum includes all "investment income" paid by all corporations, both private and Crown, to all levels of government—federal, provincial, municipal—in Canada. It consists of royalties, lease rentals, bonuses, interest and profits of Crown corporations paid to governments. Though the bulk of this sum was paid by the oil companies to Alberta, some of it was paid by other types and some of it went to other governments.

[9]Press Release, New Democratic Party, August 5, 1971.

[10]*Alberta Hansard*, March 6, 1972, p. 3-34.

[11]Alberta NDP Heritage Savings Trust Fund Policy Committee, "The Alberta Development Fund, An NDP Alternative", October, 1981, p. 14.

Chapter 6

Insults to Democracy During the Lougheed Era

Ron Chalmers

Introduction

The Government of Alberta, since Premier Peter Lougheed's Progressive Conservative party came to power in 1971, has undermined the principle and spirit of democracy while retaining its symbols and exploiting electoral success.

Criticism of the Lougheed government from outside the Legislature has mainly focused on substantive policies. But opposition within the Legislature has often concentrated on issues of democratic process. The late Grant Notley, from his election as an MLA in 1971 until his death in 1984, and Robert Clark, Social Credit Leader from 1975 until his retirement in 1982, were perhaps the strongest voices for democracy within the Legislature.

In Alberta, Lougheed's government has not been unique in perpetuating and exploiting a narrow form of democracy. Nor has Alberta been unique in Canada. But the focus of this paper is limited to Alberta in the 1970s and early 1980s. The criticism flows from the first principles of democracy: that people participate actively and directly in their own governance; that effective participation is both a means toward better laws and an enriching activity in itself; that the legitimacy of indirect democracy depends upon its representativeness and accountability.

While political criticism need not shrink from such ideal criteria for judgement, neither should it rush to a moralistic or partisan interpretation of the evidence. It shows that Notley, as NDP leader, was an effective spokesman for the democratic cause and also reveals the same cause espoused by Clark as leader of the Social Credit Party. With these two leaders and parties so divided on major substantive issues but united against the Conservatives on procedural issues, one might suspect that a clamor for more democracy is simply a predictable complaint of opposition politicians—of the "outs" against the "ins".

Perhaps so. This paper is intended to help document the insults to democracy during the Lougheed era but it stops short of explaining them, of tracing them to anything unique in Conservatism, or of assuring that the prospect for democracy in Alberta would automatically improve under a different government. For now, suffice to show that such insults have occurred under the Lougheed government.

Direct participation between elections was a fashionable concept during the populist and progressive eras from the 1890s through the 1930s. The most popular ideas were the initiative, which would allow people outside the legislature to draft a bill and, with sufficient support, to force the legislature to vote on it, and the referendum, which would enable the government to refer any piece of its legislation to a binding, province-wide vote.

Alberta's contribution to direct democracy was the recall, which would allow the electors of any constituency, with sufficient signatures, to recall and dismiss from office their elected member of the legislature. Notoriously, the Social Credit Government's Recall Act of 1936 was itself repealed in 1937, to stymie a recall petition circulating in the constituency of Premier William Aberhart.[1]

However short-lived that experiment, it was more promising than anything since.

Centralization of Power

Premier Lougheed's Conservative government has consistently moved power in the opposite direction: from Legislature to Government; Government to Cabinet; and Cabinet to Premier.

For instance, Lougheed in 1976 introduced legislation to create the Alberta Heritage Savings Trust Fund. Opposition members, while agreeing with the principle, wanted public hearings to help determine just how the fund should be structured, controlled, and used.

Provincial Treasurer Lou Hyndman dismissed that as unnecessary, insisting:

> There was an election campaign [in 1975], in effect a provincial referendum where every voter—the entire population of the province—had a period of weeks to reflect upon and make a decision upon the heritage fund. ... That was the public hearing where there was an endorsement of this fund.[2]

Elections, while essential to democracy, cannot fairly be read as blanket approvals of all government actions before or after the election. But this speech was typical: the Conservatives have consistently cited electoral results as categorical approvals of their every policy and practice, including some that were demonstrably unpopular, such as their opposition to a Charter of Rights and Freedoms in the Canadian Constitution, and their opposition to mandatory seat belt legislation.

Elections are not designed to involve people in policy-making. They serve the exactly opposite function of removing the great mass of people from policy-making, leaving it to the elected few. In that role, elections do a particular disservice to democracy in Alberta. In 1982, for instance, an election converted 63 per cent popular support for the Conservatives into 95 per cent of the legislative seats. That is too much distortion already, without a further far-fetched claim that the result implies anything more than a vague and general support for Conservatism.

Mr. Hyndman went on to argue that the proposal for a Heritage Fund hearing "reflects adversely on every one of the members of this Legislative Assembly" who had talked to their constituents in the election campaign and didn't need any hearings.[3]

Years later, the economy declined, public criticism of the Heritage Fund rose, and Premier Lougheed reversed that reasoning, now saying the Fund would be more popular if only the government had communicated its nature more effectively. But he still didn't hold public hearings. Instead, he used slick advertising and glossy brochures to tell the public why they should appreciate the fund—as he created it.

Use of the Mass Media

This advertising mentality dates back to the 1971 election, when Lougheed's party spent 85 per cent of its campaign budget on television advertising.[4] Television then was a perfect medium for the Conservative message because there really was no message—only an image. In 1971, Peter Lougheed did not campaign against the record of an incumbent Social Credit Government, nor on the promises of a new Conservative Government, but only on a fresh face and an impatient, one-word slogan: NOW!

If you saw that slogan on a wall today, you might think it a piece of punk graffiti. But in 1971 it summarized the opportunist philosophy of the Conservative Party. Lougheed's winning insight was, in the words of Meir Saferty, his "ability to convince the electorate it needed a change, not of policies, but of style."[5] In 1971, Peter Lougheed saw that times had changed since Social Credit was elected in 1935, that television had replaced radio as the persuasive medium, that image was replacing oration as the persuasive technique, and that television image depended less on substance than on such studio techniques as rehearsal, make-up, multiple takes, careful camera angles and creative editing.

Today, every party relies heavily on television advertising. There's nothing unique about the Alberta Conservatives' use of television as a means for displacing issues with images. But it was Lougheed who pioneered this particular insult to democracy in Alberta, and who since has proven his preference for rehearsal over spontaneity, monologue over dialogue, and mediation—via the mass media—over direct encounter, all to the detriment of the public thought, discussion and debate which are the vital processes of democracy.

The Evolution of Ideology

This is not to lament the passing of Social Credit nor even to say that politics took a turn for the worse with the Conservatives' election. Democracy in Alberta already was sick; it just hasn't got any better. And remember, the 1960s had been a decade when so many political activists and observers hoped, with seeming realism, for a revival of public participation.

I don't refer only to the vision of the radical left. For instance, American sociologist Daniel Bell, a decade before Social Credit finally fell, announced "the end of ideology" in American politics. Ideology, in Bell's terms, was in many ways typified by Social Credit. As that party first came to power in 1935, it typified Bell's three criteria for an ideological movement by simplifying ideas, establishing a claim to truth, and demanding a commitment to action.

Indeed, it was just such preposterous and simplistic ideas as those of Social Credit, with an all-embracing claim to economic and historical truth and a religiously fervent demand for action, that led Bell both to condemn ideology and, perhaps wishfully, to envision democracy moving beyond ideology.

Bell was criticised, especially from the left, for seeming to urge a middle-of-the-road liberalism and seeming to suggest that strong beliefs and principles had no place in modern democracy. In fact, he said "Men need—as they have always needed—some vision of their potential, some manner of fusing passion with intelligence."[6] We're still waiting for that. We went from the passionate stupidity of early Social Credit, to the dispassionate intelligence of later Social Credit, to the contrived and calculating style of the Lougheed Conservatives.

The Subordination of Local Governments

The downgrading of democracy may be most quantifiable in terms of the Lougheed Government's treatment of municipalities.

Municipal governments are closest to the people and often in the best position to decide among competing claims for localized public services. Yet constitutional, economic and practical reasons preclude municipalities ever attaining sufficient local taxing powers and tax base to fund needed local programs. So they depend upon provincial grants.

The insult to democracy emerges in a Conservative pattern, since 1971, of shifting away from unconditional grants toward conditional grants, thereby shifting decision-making power, over the use of grants, away from municipal governments toward the Provincial Government.

In 1972, 61 per cent of grant money to municipalities was unconditional.[7] By 1978, that figure had dropped to 34 per cent,[8] and by 1985 to approximately 13 per cent.[9] Unconditional grants were about four per cent of the provincial budget when Peter Lougheed became Premier, and are about one per cent as he leaves.[10]

Another abandoned opportunity for delegated democracy was the Environment Conservation Authority, or ECA. It was created by the Social Credit Government in 1970, with statutory power to "inquire into any matter pertaining to environment conservation."[11] In 1975, the ECA held public hearings on the issue of a dam on the Red Deer River, and produced two major reports recommending, on environmental and social grounds, that the government abandon its preferred site.

Instead, the Lougheed Government kept its dam site and abolished the ECA.

It then created a new body, the Environment Council of Alberta, with no power to investigate anything, except as directed by the Environment Minister. That body gives well-respected advice but remains, politically, a counterfeit of the ECA. Ever mindful of image, the Government even gave it the initials of the more democratic instrument it replaced.

While the Lougheed Government has reduced the delegation of power to public authorities, it has increased its delegation of power to private corporations, including Syncrude and the Alberta Energy Company, through investment of public money.

Such investments have been criticized from the right as "socialist," and from the left, by Larry Pratt, "as a form of public works undertaken for the benefit of the province's business community and urban class."[12] These ventures remain in private control despite investments of public money. They reduce democracy by removing control of public funds from the elected Legislature to a private executive.

In 1976, Robert Clark asked Energy Minister Don Getty "what instruction were given to the president of the Alberta Energy Company along with the proxy right for the Province of Alberta's majority voting position?"[13]

Getty's bland answer was: "Just that the proxy be handled in the best interests of the shareholder."[14]

But Albertans had elected the Government, not the AEC President, to interpret their best interests. The following month, Mr. Clark moved a resolution requiring the Energy Minister, each year, to obtain legislative direction in voting the province's 50 per cent shareholding in AEC— worth $75 million.

Notley supported Clark, saying "the issue here is really how we . . . are in fact going to hold the government accountable for the $75 million in shares which this government holds in trust for the people of Alberta."[15]

Getty's argument was rather muddled. But a clear statement of the apparent Conservative position which, the following speaker said, also had been the Social Credit position, was expressed by Gordon Taylor, then independent MLA for Drumheller, previously a Social Credit cabinet minister and later a Conservative MP.

He argued that the AEC is responsible to the Government, which is responsible to the Legislature and to the public: "I don't know how much clearer we want the line of responsibility drawn."[16]

This exaggerates the distinction between Government and Legislature; and misinterprets the lines of responsibility among the AEC, Government, Legislature, and the public. Of course there is a difference between the roles of Legislature and Government—also between those of Government, Cabinet, Inner Cabinet, and Premier. They all are differences of power and proximity to policy making. But that hierarchy has evolved—and could devolve. Every essential principle of parliamentary government could be respected within a practice of widely expanded public involvement and legislative activity—either in committee of the whole or in smaller committees, to debate more actively and openly and develop policies that now emerge from the secrecy of caucus, cabinet, or the Premier's office. The lines of responsibility cited by Mr. Taylor apply only after the fact and are no substitute for initiatory, pro-active public participation and parliamentary democracy.

The lines of responsibility are indeed as defined by Taylor. But the actual working of responsibility is not a matter of definition but rather an open question of facts. No body can effectively exercise responsibility over another body without the commensurate authority and resources. The Legislature of Alberta lacks this authority, controls no such resources.

The Right to Information

A key resource is information. In that same year, 1976, Notley introduced a "right to information" bill similar to a bill sponsored in Ottawa by Conservative MP Ged Baldwin. Notley's bill was talked out of the legislature by Government backbenchers. The cabinet Ministers never entered the debate, the Bill never came to a vote and Alberta never got free information.

The continuing struggle of the opposition members to preserve the role of the Legislature vis-a-vis the Government has been played out, year after year, in debates over the Heritage Fund which, whatever its social and economic purposes, serves a political purpose of letting Cabinet avoid the Legislature in allocating public funds.

After the opposition members failed, in 1976, to involve the public in formative decisions about the fund, their next effort was to preserve at least a role for the Legislature.

Premier Lougheed had said the fund would begin with a transfer of $1.5 billion worth of cash or other assets from Treasury. So Walt Buck, Social Credit MLA for Clover Bar, moved an amendment to the Heritage Fund Act, requiring the Government to obtain Legislative approval for such a transfer. Notley supported the amendment, observing that "if we're not going to determine what money is transferred to the fund and what assets are transferred to the fund . . . the question of accountability becomes very real."[17]

The Government defeated that amendment, denying the Legislature control over which assets would enter the fund.

Having lost the fight for democracy at the input side of the political system, Clark then turned to the output side. He moved another amendment, requiring Legislative approval in the choosing of particular Heritage Fund investments. Lougheed replied that that possibility had been discussed with members of the financial and investment community (though not with the Legislature), and "generally speaking the advice . . . was that they hoped we would be wise enough not to put ourselves in [that] strait jacket."[18] Democracy as a strait jacket!

Notley, insisting that government spending must require legislative assent, correctly replied that "there is no historical basis at all for a distinction between an investment and an expenditure."[19] In this, he was echoing the surprising position of a Conservative member, Ron Ghitter of Calgary Buffalo, who, debating the bill at second reading, had cited authorities all the way from Lord Durham back to Aristotle, in support of "the fundamental premise that expenditures and, for that matter, investments must be designated and not delegated by the elected body."[20]

Ghitter also assisted the democratic cause, in the same speech, by refuting the Premier's paternalistic claim regarding legislative approval for investment, that, in Lougheed's words, "anybody with just a modicum . . . of business experience would recognize how impractical and ridiculous such an approach is."[21] Ghitter, a successful corporate lawyer, cited his own ample experience and said: "I do not believe that the condition of prior legislative approval would be that encumbering."[22]

The opposition scored a minor moral victory when Ghitter abstained from the vote on Clark's amendment. Of course, his Conservative colleagues defeated the amendment and the principled argument against making investment decisions outside the Legislature was never answered.

As a last measure, Clark moved an amendment requiring the Government, after investments, to explain how it made its decisions. Notley supported that, saying "if we are going to have intelligent after-the-fact accountability, we have to have access to information."[23]

Lougheed replied that his Government would report the nature, terms and conditions of investments—but not the reasons, process or advice received—a token gesture which, Notley said, reduced the legislative watchdog to a snapping Pekingese. But the amendment lost, the bill won and the Government gained control of a Heritage Fund, today worth over $14 billion, with no direct public involvement in its design, no legislative approval of the assets initially placed in it, no legislative approval needed for investments of it and little legislative accounting of its investment strategy.

This Government's tendency to spend public money without assent from the public's elected representatives appears also in its use of special warrants. The Financial Administration Act allows the Government to spend money this way, with legislative approval coming months later, if the legislature is not sitting. As this is being written, the 1985 fall sitting has been displaced by the Conservative leadership convention. The new Premier, Don Getty, has suggested that fall sittings should be permanently abandoned.

Yet the Financial Administration Act only authorizes a special warrant if "an expenditure of money is urgently required."

This past spring, the Legislature rubber-stamped special warrants for $287.1 million, including one "urgent" expenditure of $112,000 to assist staging of the Edmonton Breeders' Crown Horse Race.

The depth of any government's commitment to Parliamentary democracy can perhaps be measured by the urgency of the expenditure it considers sufficient to skirt the Legislature. The Alberta Government will do it for a horse race.

Conflicts of Interest

The aim of democracy, of course, is to serve broad public interests through broad public involvement. Representative democracy always is problematic because, by directly involving only a few individuals in government, it creates the possibility of conflict between their narrow private interests and the wider public interest.

A government's claim to democracy depends in part on the way it protects against that possibility. Lougheed, in 1973, announced a policy requiring all cabinet ministers publicly to disclose their private interests and to place any holdings of publicly-traded companies into a blind trust which they would not manage or influence.

While this formality went beyond any of his predecessors', Lougheed's subsequent behavior suggests it was more a token gesture than any indication of a deep commitment against conflicts of interest.

The absence of any statutory requirement for compliance with Lougheed's policy has been a continual cause of opposition criticism. In April, 1985, Ray Martin, leader of the NDP Official Opposition, asked Government House Leader Neil Crawford, in the absence of the Premier, how the policy was enforced. Crawford replied that "the system in all respects . . . is functioning and adequate to the purposes for which it was designed,"—although Martin had discovered that one cabinet minister had never filed a statement of disclosure and the Premier had done nothing to ensure that such statements were filed.[24]

The previous day, Martin had exposed an equal neglect when, quizzing Lougheed and Public Works Minister Tom Chambers about Municipal Affairs Minister Julian Koziak's interest in two businesses that had made over $10 million off the government, it became obvious that the Government had neither a general standard as to the propriety of such a potential conflict nor a procedure for considering specific cases.

In 1976, Walter Buck had asked Lougheed whether he would follow the Federal Government's example with legislation controlling the activities of senior civil servants who leave the government, then work as professional lobbyists.

Lougheed replied: "There should not be restrictions of any significant nature placed upon such activity," and "there should be a greater degree of movement from the private sector into the public sector and back into the private sector."[25]

Subsequent events proved Lougheed sincere on this point. After Attorney General Jim Foster left the Government in 1979, he soon returned to lobby his former cabinet colleagues on behalf of his new business clients.

And the born-again lobbyist is only one of several incarnations in which Conservatives return to the scene of their mischief. The history of the Lougheed Government is replete with well-paid political appointments of former Cabinet Ministers, MLAs and party activists.

One recent case of exceptional career mobility is George de Rappard, former executive director and campaign manager of the Conservative Party, and chief executive of Dial Mortgage Co., until it went broke. Following that failure, de Rappard entered the public service at the entry level of Deputy Minister to the Cabinet. In June 1984, he was charged, under the Alberta Securities Act, with filing a false and misleading prospectus, while raising capital for Dial in 1979. Awaiting trial, he took a leave of absence from his job. Six months later, the case still had not come to trial so Lougheed took him back. This appeared exceptional, but the man was suffering the loss of an exceptionally large salary of $95,000 per year. And the Premier had already told reporters he believed de Rappard was innocent. That a knowledgeable lawyer and public figure like Lougheed would make such a comment on a case before the courts shocked some people—including John Faulkner, who had been fired from his job as Special Prosecutor in the Dial case simply for confirming to a reporter that de Rappard was under investigation.

The trial started in February 1985 and the case was promptly dismissed on technical grounds that the Alberta Securities Commission had exceeded the one year allowed to file charges, from the time of their staff first learning of an alleged offence.

Either the judge had erred in law, as the Attorney General's staff did suggest, or the Securities Commission had bungled their prosecution. But Attorney General Neil Crawford would not appeal the dismissal. And Consumer and Corporate Affairs Minister Connie Osterman, who was responsible for the Commission, would not order an inquiry into the Commission's workings, as urged by the Legislative Opposition.

Lougheed complacently told the media, in this case, with the factual guilt or innocence of his chief public servant still unresolved, that the statute of limitations was "as good a defence as any."[26] He later accused his critics of a "witch hunt."[27]

Notley, in 1975, had proposed a motion merely to establish a legislative committee to consider conflict of interest legislation in Alberta. The Government defeated that motion. Notley introduced a Conflict of Interest Bill, and the Government defeated that too.

In 1979, Clark followed Notley with a bill that asked the Government to make explicit what conflict-laden situations were unacceptable, and to outlaw them. Greg Stevens, the minister responsible for personnel administration, argued against the bill on the single ground that his Government, including senior public servants, did not in practice act against the public interest and so did not need such a control.

Clark then reminded him that, in the recent history of the Lougheed Government, the former Attorney General, at the request of a cabinet colleague, had directed the R.C.M.P. to investigate an individual against whom the R.C.M.P. were contemplating no criminal charges; that the former Deputy Minister of Agriculture had used his official position to arrange the sale of his own agricultural products; that executives of two crown corporations had solicited funds for the Conservative Party; and that funds were solicited for the Minister of Housing from businesses to which his department let contracts.[28]

Perhaps the most notorious conflict Clark cited was Lougheed himself accepting free airline flights for personal vacations, from CP Air, a major airline operating in Alberta, subject to some provincial regulations and, at that time, competing with the Alberta Government-owned PWA.

When Lougheed was questioned in the Legislature about that scandal, which he had never disclosed, but the media had discovered, he fell back on his familiar recourse to the results of the last election. "That was a matter I presented to the people of Alberta," he said, adding, "I'm prepared to rest my answer with the decision the people made on March 14 [1979]."[29]

Although Lougheed repaid the value of those tickets, he never introduced a policy on ministerial acceptance of gifts generally—insisting only that he was upheld by his election victory. Again, the premier's interpretation of election results had been selective and self-serving. Only a few days later, during the throne speech debate, he cited his position on six major issues, not including ministerial gifts, as all being mandated by those same election results.[30]

Conclusion

This brings the argument full-circle, starting and ending with the observation that the Lougheed Conservatives' election campaigns are insults to participatory democracy, just as their subsequent invocations of electoral results are insults to Parliamentary democracy.

Yet they keep winning elections—open elections—so what is the value of such criticism?

John Stuart Mill noted that the value of anything appears only in people actually valuing it and choosing it.[31] That's the utilitarian position. It applies perfectly to the value of democracy; if people value it, they will act politically to enhance democracy in Alberta.

The same point emerges from the writings of Karl Marx: Theory becomes practical when it moves people to action.[32]

The Lougheed Government's ongoing insult to democracy will not correct itself, as witness the recent comment of Lougheed's successor, Don Getty, who warned, shortly after announcing his leadership candidacy, that a competitive race could be expensive, divisive, and dangerous to party health. Democracy, remember, is a strait jacket.

It's not the Conservatives' job to enhance democracy. It's the job of those who would replace them by persuading Alberta voters to value and choose democracy. This defines one task for a democratic party in opposition: finding the arguments to convince the public that their best interests are not served by a suppression of democracy.

This essay has reviewed the Lougheed record from a singular, democratic perspective which perhaps implies that a broad "public interest" can be defined in purely procedural terms. Against that, one can argue that an enhancement of democracy would serve particular class interests—while existing restraints on democracy serve opposed class interests. Indeed, Pratt and Tupper have argued, with particular reference to the Heritage Fund, that "the relative strength of executive discretion and weakness of legislative accountability cannot be understood outside the context of Alberta's overall strategy of development."[33] And Pratt has argued elsewhere that Alberta's development strategy particularly favors the urban business class.[34]

The present paper does not extend to a political analysis of the historical, ideological or material reasons for the poor state of democracy in Alberta. While the Pratt and Tupper argument has some explanatory power, it appears not to account for: the Ghitter argument (cited earlier) that wider democracy is consistent with businesslike government; the Lougheed argument (which Pratt and Tupper cite) that cabinet control of Heritage Fund investments is needed for loans to other provinces—an activity unrelated to Alberta's development strategy; and the ubiquitous argument of the New Democratic Party that a province-building strategy could be undertaken consistent with greater democracy.

Of course, any opposition party—including the Alberta Conservatives in the late 1960s—naturally campaigns for more democracy. And no incumbent government campaigns against democracy. The further task for a democratic party, therefore, is to strengthen the ideological commitment to democracy once in office and to identify and overcome those organizational factors that may tend to push any Government toward expansion of executive privilege and insults to democracy.

Likewise, a task of political criticism is to advance the understanding of modern democracy beyond the dated and incomplete—but unrefuted—pessimism of Michels, Mosca and Pareto, by helping to blueprint a re-invention of democracy that would realistically recognize those factors which tend to obstruct it and by proposing reforms whose realistic prospects for improvement will help persuade the electorate to demand a democratic government.

---

[1]C.B. Macpherson, *Democracy in Alberta: Social Credit and the Party System*, 2nd ed. (Toronto: University of Toronto Press, 1953, 1962), p. 153.

[2]*Alberta Hansard*, April 23, 1976, p. 845.

[3]*Ibid.*

[4]Walter Stewart, "The Upwardly Mobile Mr. Lougheed," *Maclean's*, January, 1972.

[5]Meir Saferty, "The Rise of the Conservative Party under Lougheed, 1965-71," paper presented to the Canadian Political Science Association

meeting, Saskatoon, June 30, 1979, p. 24.

[6]Daniel Bell, "The End of Ideology in the West," in Chaim I. Waxman, ed., *The End of Ideology Debate* (New York: Simon and Schuster, 1968), pp. 87-105, at 102, reprinted from Bell, *The End of Ideology* (New York: The Free Press, 1960).

[7]Alberta Provincial-Municipal Finance Council, *Report on the Responsibilities and Financing of Local Government in Alberta* (Edmonton: Government of Alberta, 1979), p. 214.

[8]*Ibid.*

[9]Joan Bryden and Portia Priegert, "Revenue Share Rejected Again," *Calgary Herald*, Sept. 27, 1984, and Government of Alberta, *Budget Estimates*, 1985.

[10]Government of Alberta, *Budget Estimates*, 1971, 1972, 1985.

[11]"Environment Conservation Act," S. 7 (1) (b), *Revised Statutes of Alberta*, 1970.

[12]Larry Pratt, "The State and Province-building: Alberta's Development Strategy," in Leo Panitch, ed., *The Canadian State: Political Economy and Political Power* (Toronto: University of Toronto Press, 133-164), p. 155.

[13]*Alberta Hansard*, April 22, 1976, p. 780.

[14]*Ibid.*

[15]*Ibid.*, May 12, 1976, p. 1274.

[16]*Ibid.*, p. 1275.

[17]*Ibid.*, May 17, 1976, p. 1363.

[18]*Ibid.*, p. 1366.

[19]*Ibid.*

[20]*Ibid.*, April 26, 1976, p. 868.

[21]*Ibid.*, April 23, 1976, p. 833.

[22]*Ibid.*, April 26, 1976, p. 868.

[23]*Ibid.*, May 17, 1976, p. 1370.

[24]*Alberta Hansard*, April 18, 1985, pp. 454-455.

[25]*Ibid.*, March 29, 1976, p. 433.

[26]Kevin Stevenson, "Premier hails Dial decision", *Edmonton Sun*, Feb. 27, 1985.

[27]Wayne Kondro, "Premier decries Dial 'witch hunt'", *Edmonton Journal*, March 8, 1985.

[28]*Alberta Hansard*, June 7, 1979, p. 243.

[29]*Ibid.*, May 25, 1979, p. 12.

[30]*Ibid.*, June 4, 1979, p. 159.

[31]". . . the sole evidence it is possible to produce that anything is desirable, is that people do actually desire it." John Stuart Mill, "Utilitarianism", in Mill, *Utilitarianism, Liberty, Representative Government* (London: Everyman's Library, 1910), 1-64, p. 32.

[32]"In practice man must prove the truth, that is, the reality and power, the this-sidedness of his thinking." Karl Marx, "Theses on Feuerbach," *Selected Works* (New York: International Publishers, 1968), 28-30, p. 28.

[33]L.R. Pratt and A. Tupper, "The Politics of Accountability: Executive Discretion and Democratic Control," *Canadian Public Policy*, VI, 1980, pp. 254-264.

[34]Pratt, *Op. Cit.*

Chapter 7

Intraparty Democracy and the Alberta NDP

T.C. Pocklington

The New Democratic Party, in Alberta as elsewhere, prides itself on its internally democratic character, contrasting its practices favourably with the elite domination characteristic of the "old-line" parties. This self-congratulatory outlook in regard to intraparty democracy is shared by other social democratic and labour parties in the liberal countries. These democratic parties of the left, unlike their liberal, conservative, and Communist opponents, are internally democratic, it is maintained, in that their rank-and-file members participate in the making of party policy and ultimately control it. Most members of these parties have tended to accept without much reflection the idea that intraparty democracy is both possible and unquestionably a Good Thing. This faith in the viability and desirability of intraparty democracy has remained largely intact in spite of the contention of a number of thoughtful students of political parties that it is chimerical. The most famous of these students was the Swiss sociologist, Robert Michels. In his renowned book, *Political Parties: A Sociological Study of the Oligarchical Tendencies of Modern Democracy*[1], first published in 1911, Michels examined the workings of a number of political parties of the left, paying particular attention to the German Social Democratic Party. Although these parties professed a commitment to govern themselves democratically, Michels found that none of them did so. A combination of psychological factors (which induce party officials to try to dominate and rank-and-file members to comply) and "technical" factors (which necessitate the concentration of information and authority in the hands of leaders) ordains an Iron Law of Oligarchy:

> Reduced to its most concise expression, the fundamental sociological law of political parties . . . may be formulated in the following terms: "It is organization which gives birth to the domination of the elected over the electors, of the mandatories over the mandators, of the delegates over the delegators. Who says organization says oligarchy."[2]

According to Michels, the main psychological factors which predispose political parties to oligarchy are the needs of the followers rather than the leaders. Most people have neither the inclination nor the energy to acquire even an elementary understanding of public affairs, let alone a capacity and commitment for the sustained, difficult and time-consuming (as well as often tedious and discouraging) work that is required to maintain and advance the vitality of a voluntary organization. To begin with, then, the ascendancy of the few stems from the frailties of the many. Before long, recognition of the efforts (and sometimes major sacrifices) made by the leaders on behalf of the followers becomes overlaid with powerful sentiments of gratitude. Criticism of leaders then becomes castigated as evidence of ingratitude, thereby deepening the gulf between followers (those who owe gratitude) and leaders (those who deserve it). Finally, there develops an attitude of followers to leaders that goes beyond gratitude, which Michels calls a "cult of veneration." "The masses," Michels writes, "experience a profound need to prostrate themselves, not simply before great ideals, but also before the individuals who in their eyes incorporate such ideals." Although Michels finds the main psychological causes of oligarchy in the character of the masses, he sees these qualities as being buttressed by the dispositions of the leaders. "The apathy of the masses and their need for guidance," he says, "has as its counterpart in the leaders a natural greed for power." Leaders may come to office with the loftiest ideals and the purest motives of service. But the experience of respect, if not adulation, soon persuades them that they are worthy of deference, cut from finer cloth than their followers. Before long they become more strongly committed to the retention of their positions of eminence than to the advancement of their ideals. Party leaders of working-class origin don't want to return to the obscurity of the shop floor, and leaders drawn from the middle class find increasingly unattractive such humdrum careers as teaching, journalism, and petty posts in the civil service. This induces leaders to distance themselves from the rank-and-file and to resist measures of democratic accountability. In short, Michels maintains that the psychology of the mass membership and the leadership of a party combine and reinforce each other in creating and sustaining oligarchical rule.

Although he regarded psychological factors as significant contributors to the oligarchical character of political parties, Michels attached even greater importance to what he called "technical" factors. The basic technical factor is that such a large group of people as constitutes the membership of a mass political party is incapable of working effectively towards the achievement of its goals unless it is organized. But organization does not occur through spontaneous generation. In the very process of organization there arises inescapably a differentiation between those who organize and those who are organized. But this initial differentiation is only the first of several technical factors that promote and sustain oligarchy. Organization breeds specialization. As political parties achieve some success, especially in expanding membership and attracting support in elections, they require people with exceptional political and bureaucratic aptitudes and skills, who are elevated above rank-and-file party members both by acknowledged competence and by official position. Finally (and more likely sooner than later), the party evolves a sizeable group of more or less full-time politicians and functionaries whose skills, familiarity with parliamentary practices, political savvy, contacts with important groups both inside and outside the party, and access to information are so much greater than those of rank-and-file members that they are able to direct the party pretty much as they see fit. The forms of internal party democracy may remain, but the reality is government by an elite.

Most subsequent commentators have had serious misgivings about Michels' psychological theories. And they have found that his sociological generalizations fail to make proper allowance for degrees of oligarchy (and thereby democracy) in voluntary organizations.[3] Nevertheless, the predominant view among students of political parties is that intraparty democracy in anything like the sense in which that term is understood by members of political parties which, like the NDP, purport to be internally democratic, is impossible. In this connection it is interesting to note that Walter Young, in his meticulous and perceptive study of the national CCF, relied on Michels' analysis not only to explain but also to defend the ascendancy of a small group of oligarchs (notably David Lewis, F.R. Scott, Tommy Douglas, and M.J. Coldwell).[4]

The thesis of the present essay is that the prospects for intraparty democracy are both better and worse than Michels and his intellectual successors have supposed. These "realists," it is maintained here, have based their arguments on a conception of intraparty democracy which, though it gives the appearance of being hospitable to the conclusion that intraparty democracy is both possible and desirable, is in fact quite impracticable. On the other hand, however, I argue that a less imposing sort of intraparty democracy is both possible and desirable, that once this is acknowledged some steps can be taken to strengthen the reality rather than the rhetoric of intraparty democracy, and that the Alberta NDP is well placed to take those steps.

It has been remarked frequently that Michels' study covered only political parties that professed to be both democratic and socialist. This limitation has commonly been supposed to be reasonable, and even meritorious. And so it is, in a way. After all, only parties of this kind professed to be internally democratic. A finding that parties which strived for intraparty democracy failed to achieve it would obviously carry infinitely more weight than the "discovery" that conservative parties, which made no pretense of being internally democratic, fell short of a standard they did not accept. But a careful reading of *Political Parties* reveals that Michels did not confine his attention to parties of the left for "scientific" reasons alone.[5] He assumed (and many have assumed after him) that only in such parties is there a case for internal democracy. The reasoning is crisply stated by Leon D. Epstein:

> Because the working-class party, labor or social democratic, viewed itself as the representative (and the only true representative) of a presumed majority of the population, its organization of that majority seemed to provide the legitimate policy-making agency. The important thing was to maintain democracy in intra-party deliberations. A conference or congress fairly elected by party members could be the policy-maker for the working class. The party's parliamentary delegation, on the other hand, was merely to carry out the policy.[6]

Michels, himself a socialist when he wrote *Political Parties*, assumed that the case for intraparty democracy applied to, and only to, socialist parties. The case is that the point of intraparty democracy is to implement the will (or advance the interests) of a majority of the electorate. The majority of the electorate is the working class. Socialist parties, and only socialist parties, aspire to speak for the working class. Therefore, the case for intraparty democracy applies to, and only to, socialist parties.

The fact that Michels found that socialist parties are not internally democratic appears to have inhibited the recognition that his assumptions seem to be remarkably congenial to the conclusion that intraparty democracy within socialist parties is both possible and desirable. It seems desirable because, given a clear-cut choice, the interests of the majority are to be given preference over those of a minority. And it seems possible because the interests of the working class are taken to be homogeneous, so that the socialist party can easily be microcosm of the working class and need make little, if any provision for accommodating intraparty conflict. I argue, first, that crucial assumptions embedded in this view are now false, and second, that even if they were true they would not yield the conclusions they are supposed to yield.

No doubt some electorally significant non-Communist parties of the left once regarded themselves as *the* voice of the working class. But none of them does so now. Moreover, neither the NDP nor its predecessor the CCF, with its dual constituency of workers and farmers, has seen itself as speaking for a homogeneous working class. Nowadays such parties present themselves, not as the voice of a class, but as advocates for the "have-nots," a somewhat vaguely defined sector of the population of which it can be said for certain only that its members have less—less income, wealth, status and power—than the "haves." The have-not sector may be regarded, as the working class once was, as the majority, but its members cannot plausibly be regarded as homogeneous in their interests. Moreover, those designated as have-nots clearly do not see their interests as identical, and they are far from unanimous—this puts it mildly for Canada—in accepting the pro-have-not party as their voice.

The strength of the support which seems to accrue to the defence of intraparty democracy when it is assumed to apply to a party which is, or aspires to be, the voice of a homogeneous working class can be judged best when that prop is removed. When we consider the situation of a party which makes no pretense of being the voice of a homogeneous constituency and whose chosen constituency gives it far from unanimous support, we see that serious problems arise in regard to intraparty democracy. In the first place, the question now presents itself whether the members of the party are representative of a majority of the electorate as a whole. They can no longer be assumed to be so. On the contrary, political sociologists assure us that those who have more will tend to participate more fully and effectively than those who have less. This does not mean that the interests of the worst off must be ignored or discounted, for the party members could be altruistic advocates of this dispossessed. The problem is that they could be unrepresentatively altruistic. For example, they might differ from the majority by being exceptionally sympathetic to unwed mothers, indigenous peoples, and homosexuals. This problem may be magnified in the process of making policy within the party. Policies are not adopted by all members of the party in huge assemblies but by representatives meeting in party conventions. The members who bestir themselves to participate in the selection of these representatives may be unrepresentative of the members of the party as a whole, and those who are chosen as representatives may be unrepresentative of those who select them.[7] Under these conditions, there is a very real possibility—might one not say a high probability?—that party policies will sometimes not be those that would have been favoured by a majority of the party's rank-and-file members, let alone a majority of the electorate.

Still another difficulty arises for intraparty democracy when the party does not aspire to be the voice of a homogeneous majority of the electorate. In these circumstances those who are called upon to speak for the party cannot assume that official party policy is automatically the policy preferred by a majority of the votes. That being the case, the party's parliamentarians, especially when they form a government, can be faced with the choice whether to enact party policies which they believe not to be supported by an electoral majority or to defy the party. Defiance of party policy is of course a departure from intraparty democracy, but it need not be a violation of—indeed, it may be required by—the view that the justification of intraparty democracy lies in its efficacy as a means of implementing the will of the majority. In any case, the crucial point is the practical one that a parliamentarian who is committed to implement the will of the majority must exercise his best judgement to do so, and his best judgement may diverge from party policy.

It may be objected that the problems about intraparty democracy discussed above are illusory because the analysis within which they were identified failed to recognize the phenomenon of "false consciousness." Just as Marxists maintain that proletarians have certain definite interests which can be satisfied only through a revolutionary transformation of society, whether they realize it or not (and indeed if, possessing only trade union consciousness, they deny it), so it may be maintained that have-nots have basic common interests, even if they regard themselves as members of a vaguely defined middle class and give their allegiance to liberal and conservative political parties. The idea here, of course, is that have-nots constitute a majority of the populace even if they are unaware of this fact and that a pro-have-not political party may justify its practice of intraparty democracy on the ground that it is the voice of the majority. This objection does not hold water. The idea that the have-nots have common interests which many or most of them cannot (yet) discern presupposes that some people can discern them. Either those who can discern them are equally adept at doing so or they are not. If they are equally adept, there is no argument to intraparty democracy, for then every adept Tom, Dick and Harriet will agree, so that there is no case for debate and voting. If they are not equally adept, the more adept should lead and the less adept should follow. A quasi-Leninist problem admits only of a quasi-Leninist solution.

Lest anyone should suppose that a compelling case for intraparty democracy would come into play if only social democratic and labour parties would transform themselves into "genuinely socialist" organizations, aspiring to speak for, and only for, the working-class majority, note that the argument stated in the previous paragraph, slightly modified, blocks that avenue. Either the working class majority is virtually unanimous in its assessment of the means required to advance its interests or it is not. If it is virtually unanimous, it has no need of an internally democratic political arm, for the members of the political party that speaks for it will be likewise unanimous. They will require no procedures and practices for airing and resolving differences, for they will have no differences. If the members of the working class are not virtually unanimous, this must be for one or the other of two reasons. The one possibility is that, although the objective interests of the proletariat are homogeneous, some members of the class suffer from false consciousness. But if this is so, the appropriate vehicle is surely a Leninist vanguard party, practicing, at most, "democratic centralism," not an internally democratic party. The other possibility is that the lack of unanimity is attributable not to illusion but to the fact that there are grounds for reasonable people to disagree as to how best to pursue the interests of the working class. But this depiction of the situation yields no automatic justification of intraparty democracy. It appears to be quite compatible with two or more internally oligarchical parties bidding for the workers' votes. In any case, it does not yield a justification of intraparty democracy that rests on the proposition that the working class constitutes a majority of the population. It was in anticipation of these considerations that I was careful to say that Michels' assumptions *seem to be* remarkably congenial to the assumption that intraparty democracy within socialist parties is both possible and desirable. As it turns out, the claim that a social class or other segment of the population constitutes a majority does not by itself yield a justification of intraparty democracy either in the full-blooded socialist version of it assumed by Michels or in the limper versions which are more appropriate to contemporary social democratic and labour parties.

Michels makes a second assumption which is congenial to the conclusion that intraparty democracy is both possible and desirable. Like the assumption we have just considered, this one is still widely accepted.[8] Like it, too, it turns out to be indefensible. As one follows Michels' presentation of the evidence and argument which culminate in the formulation of the Iron Law of Oligarchy, one becomes aware that two quite different sets of considerations are taken as indicative of the absence of intraparty democracy. One set of considerations has to do with impediments to the setting of policy by rank-and-file members of the party. The other set has to do with incongruities between the policy views of the rank-and-file and those of official party spokesmen and, more generally, obstacles to control of the latter by the former. Thus, on the one hand, Michels frequently argues, in the manner of Mosca,[9] that democracy is impossible in any large group because sheer numbers create a need for organization, organization implies leadership, and leadership is incompatible with untrammelled rule by the rank-and-file. In short, one line of argument Michels uses to support the Iron Law of Oligarchy is that the very fact that a large political party must be organized means that direct democracy within the party is impossible. On the other hand, however, Michels sometimes accepts the need for organization and hence leadership as given, and finds evidence for the Iron Law of Oligarchy to consist in psychological and sociological factors which distance the party leaders from the rank-and-file and promote the ascendancy of the former over the latter. For example, at one point he remarks that "the leaders, who were at first no more than executive organs of the collective will, soon emancipate themselves from the mass and become independent of its control," and attributes this to "the technical specialization that inevitably results from extensive organization."[10] When he argues in this way, Michels does not decry the absence of direct democracy; he laments the emasculation of representative democracy.[11]

The foregoing may leave the mistaken impression that Michels provides separate and distinct analyses of the factors which militate against direct democracy and those which militate against representative democracy. This is by no means the case. On the contrary they are so thoroughly unsegregated that they eventually merge into the notion that the representative role appropriate to intraparty democracy is that of delegate.[12] The attractiveness of the delegate notion of representation to partisans of intraparty democracy is transparent. Their paramount interest, after all, is in party policy, so it is not surprising that they should be drawn to the notion of representation which is, so to speak, "nearest" to direct democracy. This nearness stems from the fact that the delegate is entirely subordinate to the group he or she represents. The delegate operates under comprehensive instructions from the group, and is given no discretionary authority whatsoever. The delegate carries out the wishes of the members of the group as *they* understand them, not as he or she interprets them. So near is this notion of representation to direct democracy that it has been suggested that the delegate does not "represent" at all but merely "presents."[13]

To give credence to the delegate notion of representation is to extend hospitality to intraparty democracy. For according to that notion it is possible for spokespersons for a party to act as comprehensively instructed ambassadors in the broader political arena. And this means that the main impediment to intraparty democracy, the exercise of excessive or inappropriate discretion by party spokespersons, is eliminated. Michels does treat the delegate notion of representation as credible, for it is that notion—or, rather, the actualization of that notion—which he finds to be thwarted by the actual practices of professedly internally democratic political parties. Thus, in the very activity of arguing that intraparty democracy is impossible Michels assumes that the notion of representation most congenial to intraparty democracy is sound. I argue that the delegate notion of representation is inadequate, and hence that the prospects for intraparty democracy are (in one important respect) worse than Michels believed.

At least five sorts of instances can be identified in which party spokespersons could not act as delegates even if they wished to do so. First, delegate representation presupposes that the representative has received instructions from the party. But it is impossible for a party to have a handbook of policies to meet every eventuality. When in government a party may be faced with an emergency, such as the devastation of some citizens by fire, flood, tornado, or drought. The government must decide whether or not to compensate the victims and, if so, to what extent and in what manner. It is a safe bet that the party will have no policy on such matters. In opposition the party has little control over the legislative agenda, and there is no guarantee that the government will not introduce bills on matters not covered by party policy. And sometimes parties simply refrain from taking a position on very divisive issues. For example, the Australian Labor Party's current "position" on abortion is that "the matter of abortion can be freely debated at any State or Federal Forum of the Australian Labor Party, but any decision reached is not binding on any member of the party."[14] In these instances the delegate notion of representation simply has no purchase. Second, given that experienced legislative draftsmen cannot word legislation in such a way that it stand in no need of interpretation, it is reasonable to assume that the mainly amateur participants in party conventions will do no better. Moreover, anyone who has participated in a party policy convention will be aware that resolutions are sometimes deliberately formulated in a vague or equivocal fashion so as to avoid or terminate acrimonious debate. Obviously, when interpretation of party policy is required it is impossible for representatives to act as mere delegates. Third, parliamentarians not uncommonly find themselves in a position in which strict adherence to party policy would mean total rejection of the policy, whereas willingness to compromise would result in partial implementation. For example, when the Australian Labor Party forms a government, it must cope with a very powerful upper house in which it is almost invariably outnumbered. If it attempted to implement party policy fully in a number of areas, such as tax reform, its measures would be rejected; only diluted policy stands a chance of enactment. Similarly, when the NDP holds the balance of power in a minority government situation, its parliamentarians must choose whether to adhere to party policy with the stringency of a monastic vow or to extract limited concessions in return for continued support. And this choice is even starker in countries in which coalition rather than minority governments are prevalent. In these sorts of cases, where the question is whether part of a loaf is better than none (or, more realistically, how much of a loaf is better than none) the notion of the representative as mere delegate is again inapplicable. Fourth, party representatives may be persuaded during the period between conventions that the implementation of a particular party policy would be unlikely to achieve the objective(s) it was designed to achieve or that it would be likely to subvert other party policies or principles. For example, whatever becomes of tuition—free post-secondary education under NDP governments? It goes without saying that party representatives are not *delegated* to give sober second thoughts to party policies. Finally, parties which profess a commitment to internal democracy have never evolved procedures to enable ordinary party members to participate in the ranking of party policies in order of priority. Party conventions adopt or reject resolutions, but they are given (or have taken) no opportunity to declare officially that some of them are more important than others. Party officials therefore may (or, rather, must) decide without instruction which policies to emphasize, which to give lip service and which to disremember. Granting party notables the authority to decide such weighty matters is of course incompatible with their being mere delegates.

In summary, the delegate notion of representation is inadequate and therefore a deceptive friend of intraparty democracy. It has been argued so far that Robert Michels' thesis that intraparty democracy is impossible incorporates assumptions which are at once congenial and uncongenial to the conclusion that it is both possible and desirable. It has also been argued that these assumptions, though still widely accepted by proponents of intraparty democracy are mistaken. The question naturally arises whether a case can be made for a form of intraparty democracy less imposing than the one intimated by Michels but robust enough to be worth defending. I believe that it can.

Both in its etymological derivation and in its current usage the term "democracy" and its cognates refer to government by the people. "The people" in a political party are, of course, its members. There is a good deal to be said about qualifications for membership in an internally democratic political party. Fortunately, it is sufficient for present purposes to say no more than that membership should be denied or rescinded only very reluctantly.

An internally democratic party, then, is one that is governed by its members. But what is government by the members? Democratic government has two essential features: a decision rule and a set of specifically democratic rights. The decision rule is simple majority rule. According to this rule fifty per cent plus one of the members is sufficient to decide any and every issue. The democratic warrant for this rule is that, first, unanimity is generally unattainable in a large organization, and second, the requirement of an extraordinary majority (two-thirds, for example) gives a veto to a minority (one-third plus one), which is intuitively antithetical to government by the people.

The term "specifically democratic right" is meant to emphasize, what is too often ignored, that not all rights are essential to the working of a democracy. The right to be tried by a jury of one's peers, to engage in homosexual practices, and to hold potlaches may be important, even precious rights, but they are not essential to democratic government. But if an association is to be governed by its members, each of them must have the following specifically democratic rights:

(1) The right to an equal formal voice[15] on all issues that are decided by the association. Obviously the government of an association cannot be a government by its members unless *all* of them have a voice in decision making. And unless they have a formally *equal* voice, the members whose wishes are given special weight constitute at least the embryo of an oligarchy.

(2) The right to advance proposals for decision by the association. If the

right to place items on the agenda for decision is limited, the agenda makers are in a position to ignore proposals not to their liking. And this, too, is a step in the direction of oligarchy.

(3) The rights to freedom of speech and assembly.

For purposes of the present analysis, these rights are not crucial on the *liberal* ground that people should be permitted, within broad limits, to do what they want, and lots of them want to air their views and engage in debate. They are crucial rather on the *democratic* ground that people cannot decide whether or not they support proposals unless they are informed about the nature and probable consequences of accepting or rejecting them. Perfect knowledge being unattainable, informed decision making is guaranteed, to the extent that it can be guaranteed, by the rights identified above.

For reasons sufficiently discussed earlier, the democratic decision rule and the specifically democratic rights must be exercised within a political party largely within a context of representative democracy. The sole exception to this requirement of democracy through representation is that internally democratic parties must maintain reasonably small forums in which rank-and-file members may advance, debate, and endorse or reject policy resolutions. With this notable exception, the democratic credentials of a political party have to do with its success in establishing and sustaining an internally democratic system of representation. There are three main requirements for the maintenance of an internally democratic system of representation. First, rank-and-file members must participate directly in the nomination of party candidates and in the selection of representatives to party conventions. Second, all members of the party executive must be elected by the party convention. And third, resolutions endorsed by party conventions must be recognized as official party policy.

This last requirement, which is absolutely crucial, may be thought to contradict our earlier observations about the unsoundness of the delegate notion of representation. But it does not. We saw earlier that the exercise of discretion by party representatives—impermissible under the delegate notion—is unavoidable in five sorts of circumstances: when the party has no policy on a matter which its representatives must address; when party policy resolutions are vague or ambiguous and so require interpretations; when the objectives of party policy can be achieved in part only through compromise; when new evidence or argument suggests that the implementation of party policy would frustrate ends it was designed to achieve; and when representatives are forced to attach higher or lower priorities to party policies. But it is not always permissible for the representatives of an internally democratic party to exercise broad discretion. On some matters the party will have no policy, but in many if not most areas it will, and in an internally democratic party, these policies will be the official policies of the party, binding on its representatives.

It is no doubt impossible to formulate policy resolutions so clearly that they do not require (or are unamenable to) interpretation. But many resolutions are clear enough that their import is unmistakable. Moreover, even when resolutions are vague or ambiguous, party representatives who have attended the party conventions at which the resolutions were formulated and who keep in touch with their party constituents must recognize that the range of interpretative discretion open to them is far from indefinitely elastic. To deny party representatives the authority to achieve successes by way of compromise is to reject politics in favour of abstract moralism. But it will be clear to any representative that some compromises would be regarded by a sizeable majority of fellow party members as treasonable rather than reasonable. All authority, prominently including the authority to compromise, is limited by its own justification. Similarly, the authority of representatives to alter or ignore declared party policy on the ground that implementation would undermine overriding party objectives must come into play quite infrequently. Moreover, there is always a fairly early opportunity to handle situations of this kind—consistently with intraparty democracy: representatives can state their case for deviation from party policy at the next party convention for endorsement or repudiation. Finally, the right of party representatives to rank party policies in order of priority—or, rather, the requirement that they do so—does not give them *carte blanche* (probably it would be more accurate to say "should not") to produce whatever ranking seems to them desirable or expedient. Exposure to debate at party conventions and regular contact with party members must impress on representatives that some party policies are considered by the bulk of the rank-and-file to be far more important than others. In summary, the notion "official party policy" is by no means empty. Even though representatives of an internally democratic political party cannot be mere delegates, there are definite limits on their authority to exercise discretion.

The requirements for intraparty democracy stated above are demanding but not very demanding. It needs to be emphasized that even the strictest adherence to them would not produce the imposingly democratic sort of political party envisaged by Michels and some current proponents of intraparty democracy. In the first place, these requirements carry no guarantee that party members will speak for a majority or even a very large minority of the electorate. On the contrary, both academic studies and participant observation indicate that only a tiny minority of any electorate is so highly politicized as to join a political party, let alone participate in it actively. And party members tend to be, among other things, much better educated and better off financially than the average citizen. Since it is now beyond dispute that social background tends to affect political attitudes and opinions, the fact that party members are typically atypical must have a bearing on the defence of intraparty democracy. Second, there is also no guarantee that those selected to attend party conventions will be typical of the party rank-and-file. No doubt there has always been a considerable element of self-selection in the choice of delegate to party conventions, with some members eagerly seeking credentials and others deferring. But as the cost of travel and accommodation increases a growing proportion of party members is being excluded from seeking credentials for want of the wherewithal to attend conventions. Third, it must be conceded that some of the requirements for intraparty democracy stated in the previous paragraph are in the nature of toothless precepts. It is, for example, mildly illuminating to point out that party representatives can, but only psychically gratifying to say that they should, restrict their exercise of discretion in light of the expressed wishes of party members and not just the actual wording of policy resolutions. For leaders are often subject to powerful temptations to maximize the scope of their discretion, and there is no institutional machinery for preventing this, so that the precept in question is something of a paper tiger. Fourth, there is, ironically, an irremovable impediment to control over party policy by the rank-and-file members in the very requisites of intraparty democracy. An internally democratic party must select two sets of representatives who are called upon to adhere to, and, when necessary, interpret, establish priorities among, compromise, and revise party policies. On the one hand, the party must choose an executive to perform the tasks of the party convention when the latter is not in session. And on the other hand, it must choose candidates for public office. There is no guarantee that these two sets of representatives will agree as to what the party's policy is or should be on a particular matter. Indeed, even if this were not the lesson of experience, there would be good reasons to expect them occasionally to disagree, not the least of which is the fact that they are invariably chosen by different party constituencies. When such disagreement occurs, there is no canon of intraparty democracy and no institution of intraparty democracy to resolve it. This suggests a final and particularly important barrier to any very imposing form of intraparty democracy. The only institutional means available to the rank-and-file members of a party which aspires to be internally democratic to induce party representatives to adhere to the policy preferences of the former are electoral. Of course rank-and-file members may *urge* their leaders to comply with party policy as the former understand it, employing whatever modes of influence they can command. But recalcitrant leaders can be disciplined only by being denied reselection at the next party convention or nominating meeting. In this respect there is a discomforting similarity between parties, such as the NDP, which aspire to be internally democratic and those, such as the Canadian Liberals and Conservatives, which have no interest in intraparty democracy. For in the latter, as in the former, members can and sometimes do attempt to influence party representatives to pursue some policies rather than others, and occasionally use nomination meetings for this purpose. Finally, there is a constraint that is so important that it deserves somewhat more extended treatment.

We have concentrated so far only on the various party representatives, including both extra-parliamentary representatives (delegates to party conventions, those who are elected to party councils and executives, and party leaders) and parliamentary representatives (successful and unsuccessful candidates for public office under the party banner), who are subject to some measure of institutionalized accountability to the rank-and-file. But it needs to be kept in mind that some of the most influential people within a political party are not subject to such accountability. In social democratic and labour parties, party secretaries invariably occupy positions of strategic importance. In addition there are commonly party organizers, policy advisors, editors of party publications and, for those who have been elected to public office, legislative assistants. These people are not accountable to the rank-and-file (except in the unlikely event that they become so intolerable to so many party members that the pressure to fire them becomes irresistible). They are by no means mere functionaries who simply carry out orders. Partly because they are chosen, at least in part, on the basis of ability, partly because for them politics is a full-time or near full-time vocation, partly because the very nature of their duties gives them access to valuable personal contacts and tidbits of information, and partly because a condition of their employment is that they be attuned to the wishes of the party's parliamentary and extra-parliamentary leaders, they are in a position to exercise very considerable influence on party policy and practices.

A small sample of the important matters on which these party bureaucrats typically have considerable influence would include the following:

(1) *Setting the preliminary agendas of party conventions.* (These agendas are sometimes altered, but never drastically.) This power is far more significant than it may appear on first consideration. Since conventions never have time to consider all the resolutions before them, placing items towards the end of the agenda effectively kills them. Moreover, those who set the agendas for party conventions can fill them so full of functions designed to applaud the achievements of present and past party dignitaries that the time available for consideration of policy is severely curtailed.

(2) *Setting the themes of election campaigns.* During election campaigns party appeals, even in parties of the left, do not consist simply of lists of proposed policies. The appeals are centred around a theme or set of themes. Those who determine these themes are in a position to decide whether (or to what extent) to concentrate on immediate electoral gains as opposed to longer-term objectives. Since the central policy orientations of social democratic and labour parties usually develop gradually rather than through abrupt shifts, this is no paltry power.

(3) *Allocating scarce resources among various party activities.* No organization has enough money and other resources to do all the things it wishes to do, and social democratic parties characteristically face very tight constraints, especially in regard to finances. It is therefore necessary to decide whether (or to what extent) to concentrate, for example, on making a good showing in the legislature, on developing new initiatives in policy, on strengthening the party organization in winnable constituencies, on nurturing party organization in relatively weak constituencies, or on engaging in extra-parliamentary activities the electoral returns from which will be distant and possibly negligible. Although the influence of the party bureaucracy can be limited to some extent, it cannot be eliminated. One of the important strengths of Michels' analysis is that it explains and illustrates this point clearly and vividly.

In light of the foregoing analysis, is there anything left of intraparty democracy? Of course there is. Internally democratic parties provide, as part of their official institutional apparatus, local forums in which rank-and-file members can advance policy proposals for discussion under the protection of the specifically democratic rights, and in which both policy proposals and aspiring delegates to party conventions are selected or rejected according to the majority principle. They hold party conventions, also governed by the majority principle and the specifically democratic rights, at which policy resolutions are endorsed as party policy. As a result party representatives are accountable to the rank-and-file, at least indirectly, for adhering to party policy (or for interpreting it, modifying it, or ignoring it for acceptable reasons). This is a far cry from the situation in parties which eschew intraparty democracy, in which the influence of members on party policy cannot take the form of holding representatives accountable for pursuing policies formally endorsed by the members.

So modest a conception is practically immune to the standard objection to intraparty democracy, namely, that it is wildly utopian. But it is not immune to a similar objection favoured by political scientists of a "realist"[16] bent. This objection stems from the facts, which were acknowledged as sticking points earlier in this essay, that intraparty democracy is in practice government of the party by those who choose to become members—or, worse, the active minority of such members—and that party members are unlikely to be typical of a large segment of the electorate. The trouble with these members, it is argued, is that they are inclined to be preoccupied with matters other than electoral success. James Q. Wilson, a vociferous critic of intraparty democracy, put it this way:

> The party is an agent of conflict, an instrument of political warfare, for which internal democracy is about as useful as it would be for an army. The ultimate decision of the voter is the test, and it is folly to give the advantage to the enemy by being preoccupied with the votes necessary to settle who shall be officers and what shall be the strategy.[17]

One might well ask how Professor Wilson discerned the Real Essence of the Political Party. Did he intuit that parties are instruments of political warfare rather than testaments to the infinite mercy of God or agents of the Cunning of Reason? Was it through divine revelation that he found that THE test is the ultimate decision of the voters rather than the opportunity afforded to party members to get in touch with their own feelings or avoid the temptation to split infinitives?

But this sort of mockery is a bit unfair to Wilson, for he prefaces the passage quoted above with a condition, "If the party is to be a competitor for votes," he writes, "then the requirement of that competition will be, in most cases, the opposite of party democracy."[18] Let us not engage in pedantry by noting that Wilson immediately forgets that he is talking about "most cases" and ignores those (few? quite a few? lots?) in which the requirements of party competition would not be "the opposite of party democracy." What is more important is the fact that Wilson, like many "realist" critics of intraparty democracy, *invents* an absolutely clear-cut choice between serious electoral activity and quasi-political evangelism.[19] It would be disingenuous to deny that there is some basis for this parody. Every political party that prides itself in its internally democratic character has some members who would rather be doctrinally pure than electorally successful, and even some who regard the pursuit of electoral success as conclusive evidence of heresy. But this sort of purism is neither logically nor in practice a necessary concomitant of intraparty democracy. Logically, there is nothing to prevent party conventions from endorsing policies that have broad electoral appeal. And in practice the policy conventions of social democratic and labour parties do not have the tone of gatherings of anti-vivisectionists or Marxists who are more interested in piety than praxis. But it is true, of course, that internally democratic political parties often subscribe to policies which they would reject if their sole object were to maximize immediate electoral advantage. To the "realist" such conduct deserves the harshest criticism of all, to wit, that it is unrealistic. However, leaving aside any moral criticism of the credo of the hard-nosed that "Winning is not the main thing, it is the only thing" (for, after all, moralizing is unrealistic), it is surely pertinent to observe that the self-professed realists' conception of realism is remarkably myopic. Every competent strategist knows that those who attempt to win a battle at every opportunity often lose the war. If the goal of a political party is to see its policies enacted as public policy, and if the electorate is not yet willing to endorse those policies, it would surely be most unrealistic for that party to concentrate its efforts entirely on immediate electoral success. On the contrary, realism clearly dictates that such a party should devote a good part of its electoral energies to converting voters to its way of thinking. To act otherwise would be not only unrealistic but also—no less a sin in the eyes of "realists"—irrational, for it would involve the adoption of means which are not instrumental to the goal they were supposed to achieve. "Realists" can reject this line of reasoning, it would seem, only by appealing to some overriding argument according to which it is wrong for political parties to seek objectives other than immediate electoral success. To my knowledge, "realists" have yet to present such an argument, and it is difficult to see what such an argument might be. I conclude that the possibility of making a case for intraparty democracy is not precluded by the fact that party members, being atypical of the electorate, are not disposed to concentrate single-mindedly on electoral success.

Defending intraparty democracy against criticism is not unimportant, but no amount of it adds up to a positive case for the internally democratic party. An argument in favour of intraparty democracy may be either general or particular. A general argument is one according to which all parties in liberal democratic countries should be internally democratic, including those which exhibit no current or prospective interest in intraparty democracy. A particular argument is one according to which there are special reasons why the social democratic and labour parties which are already committed to intraparty democracy should maintain and even deepen that commitment. I shall say very little about the general arguments, even though I regard them as the stronger of the two types. Space is limited here, and the general arguments require lengthy exposition. In any case it seems most inappropriate to devote much space in a book about the Alberta NDP to arguing the massively impractical case that the Progressive Conservative Party should head for higher ground.

However, it will not be amiss to sketch briefly one general argument for intraparty democracy, since there is a lesson to be learned from it. In his *Considerations on Representative Government*, John Stuart Mill argues that political participation improves people. He does not speak about intraparty democracy but about participation in local government; however, the argument he makes about the latter is clearly applicable to the former. Mill maintains that the principal criterion of a good form of government is its capacity "to promote the virtue and intelligence of the people themselves.[20] He goes on to identify three paramount types of human excellence, the intellectual, the practical, and the moral, and maintains that democracy promotes these excellences far better than any other form of government, "any participation, even in the smallest public function," being conducive to this end.[21] I believe that Mill is right, but to show that this belief is well founded would require a very extended argument. In the first place, it would require a moral argument, thoroughly contrary to the leading brand of contemporary liberalism, that it is part of the role of politics to improve people, rather than simply to give them what they want, employing means best devised by experts. And in the second place, it would require a complex empirical argument to the effect not only that political participation does improve people but also that it does so more effectively or more fully than alternative possibilities. For reasons already mentioned, this is no place to attempt to supply the required arguments. Nevertheless, even this very synoptic sketch of a general argument provides a valuable lesson. It is apparent that there is no prospect of producing a persuasive argument for intraparty democracy (or for democracy in any association whatsoever, for that matter) which presupposes that democracy is simply a Good Thing, that is, something that is good in itself. If democracy is desirable, it is desirable on account of its effects. Accordingly, a plausible defence of intraparty democracy must show, first, that it has certain effects and, second, that these effects are on balance good.

In my judgement, it is possible to construct a persuasive defence of intraparty democracy which is specific to social democratic and labour parties. The basis of this argument is the fact, noted earlier, that such parties nowadays present themselves as advocates for a somewhat ill-defined but not entirely shapeless sector of the populace labelled the "have-nots." It takes no great powers of insight to observe that representatives of non-Communist parties of the left are less than militant in advocating policies designed to benefit the worst-off of the have-nots, such as the poor. (Such policies rarely surface during election campaigns.) And, at the same time, they eagerly seek to expand the category of have-nots. (It should be obvious that standard NDP rhetoric increasingly finds small businessmen in the ranks of the downtrodden.) Nor is it difficult to explain these phenomena. Although they often also have loftier motives, professional politicians and those who aspire to join them are typically concerned to enhance their income, job security, prestige, and power. And the surest means to these ends is public office. The bulk of the electorate does not believe that political parties should appeal exclusively, or even primarily, to one sector of the populace. Moreover, the "have-not" category is very heterogeneous, and its better-off members, such as skilled workers, are not typically galvanized by appeals to share the wealth. In any case, the worst-off groups, with their very high rates of non-voting, are feeble electoral allies. It is not surprising that ambitious leftish politicians are keen to avoid—or, at least, mute—electoral appeals that can be portrayed by their opponents as fomenting class antagonism.

The pressures on elected representatives of social democratic and parties to pursue policies which are "moderate," "responsible," which "avoid extremes" (the euphemisms are legion) are even greater in the period between elections, especially when such parties form governments. Among the things that the haves have in far great measure than the have-nots are resources for influencing governments and skill in deploying those resources. Invariably, then, leftish governments are under strong and persistent pressure to temper even mild policy commitments which the haves see as inimical to their interests. To state the point bluntly, representatives of social democratic and labour parties face strong inducements to sell out.[22]

A persuasive argument in favour of intraparty democracy within such parties is that it provides an inducement not to sell out. The presence of official party policies endorsed by representatives of the party rank-and-file and machinery to hold party representatives accountable for pursuing those policies (or providing good reasons for failure to do so) function as an obstacle to opportunism. If it is desirable that there should be political parties which act as advocates for the have-nots, then these parties should be internally democratic. Since it is clearly desirable, if only on the grounds of fairness in competitive party systems, the have-nots should have party advocates, and since liberal and conservative parties are generally uninterested in performing this role and "genuine socialist" parties generally incapable of performing it, we have a compelling case in favour of social democratic and labour parties which practice intraparty democracy.

It follows from what has been said above that the NDP should practice intraparty democracy. But it also follows that many enthusiasts for intraparty democracy should develop a lively appreciation of its limits. Intraparty democracy cannot be direct democracy. Nor can party representatives be mere delegates of their party constituents. Representatives must have the authority to exercise a considerable measure of discretion and, in the final analysis, they can be held accountable for adhering to party policy (or departing from it only on reasonable grounds) only by electoral sanctions. Having thrown cold water on some unrealistic expectations for intraparty democracy, I want to conclude this essay by suggesting that the Alberta NDP is currently well placed to take some practical steps to enhance intraparty democracy—steps which, if successful, would be worthy of emulation by other social democratic and labour parties. The steps I propose are meant to increase the control of the party rank-and-file over party representatives (both parliamentary and extra-parliamentary) without undermining the discretionary authority required by the latter. And I see the Alberta NDP as well placed to take these steps because it is neither so weak that a successful experiment could be dismissed as lacking broad implications nor so strong that the prospect of an unsuccessful experiment could be deemed too risky.

I begin with a proposal which, because it is merely exhortatory, is the weakest of the lot. If party activists are seriously concerned that party representatives should adhere (within the limitations already noted) to party policy, they would do well to remind the representatives at the most appropriate times—that is, when the latter stand for selection and especially, re-selection—that such fidelity is a condition of party endorsement. It is ironical that the parties that pride themselves on their internally democratic character are notoriously reluctant to use the archetypical democratic instrument, the ballot, to encourage democratic accountability.

Second, it is clearly desirable on democratic grounds that the opportunity to seek election as a delegate to a party convention should not be confined to those—increasingly few—who are sufficiently affluent to attend. The currently modest assistance of delegates should be increased substantially.

Third, the discretionary authority of party representatives, and thereby the likelihood that their policy positions will differ from those of rank-and-file members, is directly related to the vagueness of the policy resolutions endorsed at party conventions. And the vagueness of those resolutions is, in turn, directly related to the number of them taken up at each convention. The larger the number of resolutions considered, the greater the probability that some or all of them will be unclear (or, hardly less repugnant, referred to a committee for clarification). The obvious solution is to reduce the number of resolutions considered at each convention. Of course problems would arise in the implementation of this reform. It is a matter of judgement—and therefore a matter that would engender controversy—how many resolutions can be addressed with reasonable care at a party convention. And it is predictable that some cogs would grind in any machinery devised to decide which resolutions, or policy areas, would be taken up at any particular convention. But these are relatively minor problems compared to the far more contentious ones regularly tackled by internally democratic parties.

Finally, by far the most important obstacle to rank-and-file control of party policy is the absence of any procedure whereby members can establish priorities among party policies. As matters stand now, party policy consists of all the resolutions that have been endorsed, and never rescinded, by party conventions. Many of these resolutions, as already mentioned, are very vague, and some require no more than that party representatives take steps to right loosely described wrongs. As a result, party representatives are virtually unconstrained in deciding which policies to emphasize, which to "put on the back burner," and which to ignore. And their political ambitions are likely to attract their attention to policies which have a high potential for short-run electoral advantage but lower priority for party members. It is far easier to decry this situation as inimical to intraparty democracy than to propose a practicable remedy for it. It would be manifestly impossible to rank all policy resolutions in order of importance at regular intervals. The only body which would appropriately formulate the ranking would be the party convention. And in order to have any point the ranking would have to be carried out at every convention. But that task would take up the whole time of the convention(at least), leaving no time for the consideration of new resolutions. Moreover, even if a reasonably thorough ranking could be accomplished without taking up too much of the time of party conventions, a reasonable concern for rank-and-file participation in the setting of priorities could easily become a debilitating preoccupation, subverting the indispensable representational role of party representatives. It needs to be kept in mind that representatives of even the most internally democratic party are very public participants in a competitive party system. That being so, they cannot set the terms of political debate unilaterally, especially when they are in opposition. They are forced to confront their opponents on grounds which are often not of their own choosing, not by crass political opportunism, but by the stark realities of competitive party politics, which provide an arena for conflict rather than a stage for soliloquy. The obvious conclusion is that intraparty democracy in the Alberta NDP could be, and therefore should be, enhanced without undue cost if ordinary members demanded some voice in the setting of priorities among policies. One way in which this could be done would be by setting aside a time period at the party convention in which the delegates could designate a small number of policies (let us suggest three as a suitably odd and mystical number) as paramount in importance. This reform would increase the control of the rank-and-file over party policy without dangerously eroding the discretionary authority of party representatives.

There is a powerful case for intraparty democracy, at least within social democratic and labour parties. And intraparty democracy can be strengthened and extended. But those who would strengthen and extend it should not underestimate the magnitude of their task. It goes without saying that party leaders will resist even the modest sorts of reforms suggested in this essay. The observation that the powerful do not relinquish power without a struggle is a truism because it is true.

---

[1]New York: The Free Press, 1962.

[2]*Ibid.*, p. 418.

[3]See, e.g., S.M. Lipset, M.A. Trow, and J.S. Coleman, *Union Democracy: The Internal Politics of the International Typographical Union* (Glencoe: The Free Press, 1956), Ch. 1.

[4]Walter D. Young, *The Anatomy of a Party: The National CCF 1932-61* (Toronto: University of Toronto Press, 1969), pp. 167-68, 174.

[5]Michels was certainly a seminal thinker, but at crucial points his work is slipshod and anecdotal, and therefore open to conflicting plausible interpretations. By far the best effort to make sense of it is Gordon Hands, "Robert Michels and the Study of Political Parties," *British Journal of Political Science*, I (April, 1971), pp. 155-72. Also helpful are Juan Linz, "Robert Michels," *International Encyclopedia of the Social Sciences*, Vol. 10 (New York: Macmillan, 1968), pp. 265-71; and John D. May, "Democracy, Organization and Michels," *American Political Science Review*, X (June, 1965), pp. 417-29.

[6]Leon D. Epstein, *Political Parties in Western Democracies* (New York: Praeger, 1967), p. 314.

[7]Some evidence that party activists are atypical may be found in Maurice Duverger, *Political Parties: Their Organization and Activity in Modern State*, 2nd ed. rev. (London: Methuen, 1959), pp. 109-16; James Q. Wilson, *The Amateur Democrat* (Chicago: University of Chicago Press, 1966), pp. 156-63 and ch. 9; and Andrew Parkin, "Party Organization and Machine Politics: The A.L.P. in Perspective", in Andrew Parkin and John Warhust, ed., *Machine Politics in the Australian Labor Party* (Sydney: George Allen and Unwin, 1983), pp. 20f.

[8]In this essay I frequently attribute views to rank-and-file members of political parties without documenting the attributions. I am confident that readers will find them confirmed on their own experience.

[9]Gaetano Mosca, *The Ruling Class* (New York: McGraw-Hill, 1939), esp. ch. 2.

[10]Michels, *op. cit.*, p. 70.

[11]The terms "decry" and "lament" are not inapt. As the following passage indicates, Michels did not see scientific inquiry (he often remarked that his study was "scientific") as incompatible with strong commitment: "Democracy is a treasure which no one will ever discover by deliberate search. But in continuing our search, in labouring indefatigably to discover the indiscoverable, we shall perform a work which will have fertile results in the democratic sense." (Michels, *op. cit.*, p. 423).

[12]This meshing (and partial confusion) of the two lines of analysis is particularly evident in Part I, chapter 2 "Mechanical and Technical Impossibility of Direct Government by the Masses."

[13]J. Paul Johnston, "Representation," in T.C. Pocklington, ed., *Liberal Democracy in Canada and the United States* (Toronto: Holt, Rinehart and Winston, 1985), p. 110.

[14]Australian Labor Party, *Platform Constitution and Rules as Approved by the 36th National Conference* (Canberra: 1984), p. 250.

[15]The term "equal *formal* voice" is meant to exclude the requirement that party members must have an equal (actual) voice. The latter would require that members be equally influential, which is impossible.

[16]The label "realist" is commonly applied to political scientists who, following J.A. Schumpeter [*Capitalism, Socialism and Democracy* (4th ed., London: Unwin, 1954), ch. 22], identify democracy with competition among elites for people's votes rather than widespread popular participation in politics.

[17]Wilson, *op. cit.*, p. 347.

[18]*Ibid.*

[19]It is true, of course, that some realists do not place such a heavy emphasis as Wilson on immediate electoral advantage and do not draw such a sharp distinction between electoral success and intraparty democracy. But the view that electoral success is the principal consideration and that democracy arises mainly from competition among political parties rather than from activities that occur within them is very widely accepted. Consider the words of a prominent student of Canadian political parties who was a strong supporter of the CCF/NDP: "As one element in a national polity, democratically organized political parties

contribute significantly to the maintenance of democracy in that polity. The pluralist democracy requires not only a variety of associations, but a certainty of effective influence in the final decision-making process. Democratic political parties are an important channel for this influence. . . . The inevitability of oligarchy under the circumstances described above is not an inherently evil condition; like the law of gravity it is easy to live with as long as we keep our awareness of it. . . . Winning elections is still the prime function of the political party." (Walter D. Young, *op. cit.*, pp. 174-75).

[20]John Stuart Mill, *Considerations on Representative Government* (New York: The Liberal Arts Press, 1958), p. 25.

[21]*Ibid.*, p. 55.

[22]"Parties whose purpose is to hasten social change must, by definition, pursue policies which are unpopular in the sense of differing from what would occur in the existing state of public opinion. Since the professional skill of members of parliament largely consists in the ability to bring themselves and public opinion into as close a relation as possible, members of parliament tend to be the section of such a party which is least inclined to see the early and rapid application of its policy." [D.W. Lawson, *Labor in Vain?* (Croydon, Victoria: Longmans, 1966), p. 32.]

Chapter 8

Grant Notley and Democracy in Alberta

Frederick C. Engelmann

Introduction

More than one third of Grant Notley's tragically foreshortened life was spent as leader of the Alberta New Democratic Party. For all but three of these years, he represented his party in the Alberta Legislative Assembly. Born in the typically Albertan rural town of Didsbury, Notley, no matter how studious and eloquent, always appeared as the typical Albertan—typical of this Western breed of farmers and small entrepreneurs which, certainly through the sixties, dominated the politics of the province. His intelligence and studies made him feel equally at home in urban Alberta, which came to the fore in the energy-blessed seventies. Grant Notley, thus, was a son of C.B. Macpherson's dominant petite bourgeoisie and moved easily among at least some segments of Larry Pratt's new middle class.

While this sounds like a winning combination, it is only fair to say that political success eluded Grant Notley. He took over a party with no seats and sixteen per cent of the vote (1967). The election of 1971, which gave him his seat for Spirit River-Fairview, saw the party badly squeezed between the ascending Progressive Conservatives and the descending Social Credit. In his final election, 1982, Notley managed to double the party's seats to two and to raise its vote percentage to nineteen per cent. Yet a shift of only a few hundred votes in 1982 would have deprived the NDP of both seats.

We will never know whether Grant Notley would have been able to succeed in Macpherson's rustic Alberta. We know that he was unable to translate his image of the petit bourgeois rural social democrat into political success in the urbanized oil-heady Lougheed period. The thesis of this chapter is that this charismatic man with his human message failed to capture both of Alberta's crucial groups—the remnants of the petite bourgeoisie and the rising new middle class.

Democracy in Alberta: Macpherson vs. Richards and Pratt
There is overwhelming evidence that politics in Alberta have differed sharply from politics in other provinces. Scholars, observers and those just applying simple arithmetic agree that ever since confederation in 1905 Alberta has been governed by parties with overwhelming majorities. What is more, each governing party has formed an era during which it has not faced serious competition from any other party. Macpherson's quasi-party system, a concept with which Richards and Pratt do not disagree, has been a reality all along. *One* party has mattered at any one time, and as soon as it faced real opposition it was removed from office and from serious contention.

Before going into a brief discussion of Macpherson's and Richards' and Pratt's theories, I should like to offer my interpretation of Alberta's governing parties. The Liberal regime was not unusual for a fledgling province. Alberta shared it with Saskatchewan where, with one minor interruption, it lasted till 1944. After this pro-federal regime, installed by the party that wrested the embryo province from the solid Calgary Tories and represented the Central Albertan forces in line with the Laurier Government, Alberta has so far had three regimes which have one thing in common: they represent(ed) a force of Western alienation: a force determined to solve Alberta's problems on Alberta's terms and to do so essentially in opposition to Ottawa. I would submit therefore that, since 1921, Alberta has been ruled by one and the same force—the Provincial Liberation Front. I am making this claim realizing fully that we are dealing with three different parties and by no means identical circumstances. The United Farmers of Alberta was a British-American version of the Progressive movement, with origins not totally dissimilar from that part of the CCF that was later launched by M.J. Coldwell in Saskatchewan. Social Credit was something new, farther to the right, and originating with the economics of Major C.H. Douglas and the evangelism of William Aberhart. Lougheed's Progressive Conservatives are urban, business oriented, representatives of Pratt's new middle class and again, farther to the right. If it had not been for the fact that Peter Lougheed's grandfather, Sir James Lougheed, had been a notable Conservative and the great loser to the Liberals, in the struggle for the about-to-be-born Alberta, the party might well have assumed a different name. While Peter Lougheed took over the tiny party, the federal Progressive Conservatives, though in opposition, dominated (as they do now) Western Canada. But not only did Lougheed insist on a thoroughly separate provincial organization—the Diefenbaker Progressive

Conservatives had more in common with Social Credit than with the young Lougheed party. There is indeed no good reason to assert that, in 1971, Alberta politics returned to a more traditional Canadian pattern. The Provincial Liberation Front remains in office.

Let us now look at the two theories of Alberta politics. C.B. Macpherson's theory is based on the fact that Alberta was—until 1941 at least—a society of small independent community producers. Writing in 1953 in *Democracy in Alberta*, he concludes about Alberta's class composition:

> [I]n the whole economy of Alberta, independent commodity producers (farmers and others) have, until 1941, outnumbered industrial employees, the former being about 45 per cent, the latter 41 per cent, of the gainfully occupied population in 1941. This is sufficiently different from the prevalent proportion in Canada as a whole, where independent producers were less than 30 per cent and industrial employees some 60 per cent, that we should not be surprised to find some difference in political behaviour.

These independent commodity producers have an ambivalent orientation toward property. They firmly believe in the property they own, primarily their land. On the other hand, they show considerable hostility against the propertied interests they depend on, located outside of Alberta, in the East. These interests are the Eastern-based banks and railways and, to a lesser extent, the grain exchange and private elevator companies.

This ambivalent attitude toward property is of course related to the split political position of the independent commodity producers in their provincial society, which they dominate and where there is a virtual absence of classes, and in the wider Canadian society, where they face the Eastern interests, especially banks and railways. This split position did not fit into the Canadian two-party system, which Alberta entered with confederation in 1905. While the two-party system was introduced to the new province, Macpherson emphasizes that "it did not take firm root or become fully operative." The tradition born of the homogeneous class competition and the dependence on the East, leading to a quasi-colonial status, was rather a non-party tradition. Beginning with the Non-Partisan League in 1916, Alberta began to extricate itself from the Eastern-imposed two-party system. The outcome was the United Farmers of Alberta, which swept the province in 1921 and governed for fourteen years. The United Farmers of Alberta thrived on the absence of classes in Alberta and the dependence of the East. In this position, there was no ground on which it could be seriously opposed. With political opposition essentially unnecessary, the system became a plebiscitary system in which, during normal times, the governing party convincingly wins plebiscites. The non-party tradition thus leads, in Macpherson's phrase, to a quasi-party system.

During the UFA period, Alberta clearly was such a quasi-party system. But with the UFA discredited, primarily under the impact of the Great Depression, it was followed by William Aberhart's Social Credit, born of Mayor C.H. Douglas' abstruse economics and Aberhart's radio-transmitted evangelism. Facing a dying UFA, Social Credit swept Alberta in 1935 and won every one of the single-member constituencies (there was proportional representation in Edmonton and Calgary). Thus, one dominant party simply followed another. There was no real party competition: the dominant party, representative of the independent commodity producers, changed; the quasi-party system survived. It is of interest to the present work that the United Farmers were initially more friendly to social democracy than Social Credit. Yet it is of overriding importance that during both regimes Alberta could easily be governed without much regard to urban workers.

Macpherson looked at Alberta in 1953, Richards and Pratt in 1979. This generation spans the social changes following Leduc (1947) and the major oil crises of 1973-74 and 1978-79. It also spans massive in-migration to Alberta and the change from a rural to, not only an urban, but a metropolitan, majority. Richards and Pratt see flaws in Macpherson's class analysis of Alberta, which includes radical workers (to be discussed briefly below) and the Calgary bourgeoisie from which, not unimportantly, the Lougheeds stem. This bourgeoisie, also, was less dependent on Central Canada than Macpherson's theory would indicate. Yet, no matter how valid Richards' and Pratt's criticism, Macpherson describes correctly the bulk of Alberta's society from the First World War to 1947.

Richards and Pratt point in *Prairie Capitalism* to the crucial social development in post-Leduc Alberta: "Oil brought prosperity, urbanization, and the rise of a new middle class which lacked attachments or loyalties to populist concerns." Thus, the first of Macpherson's points, the essentially classless society dominated by independent community producers, gradually lost validity. Yet, it took twenty-four years after Leduc for the independent-commodity-producer-based Social Credit to be defeated. In 1971, the urban new middle class, based on the new energy wealth, voted Lougheed and his Progressive Conservatives into office—with 90% of the metropolitan seats, but not a single one south of Calgary, and the new government established a new Alberta, complete with large bureaucracy, public enterprise and urban culture (strangely unaccompanied by a concomitant rise of higher education). Macpherson's second point, the dependence on Central Canada, became the subject of an epic Edmonton-Ottawa struggle over the pricing and use of energy resources, which reached its height with the last Trudeau government, but continues to the present. Prairie capital swelled rapidly to the end of the oil boom (1981), only to slump into a more doubtful situation marked by the collapse of the Continental and Northland banks. Meanwhile, the seventies, and the eighties so far, show a solid social base for the Progressive Conservative government made up of the independent and—to a slightly lesser extent—the dependent sectors of the new middle class; so far at least, the government is supported by a majority of the remaining independent commodity producers.

Thus, while 1971, unlike 1935, marked a social shift, there was nothing internal or external to stimulate markedly political competition. Once again, there was dominant party. The quasi-party system survived.

The Left in Alberta 1905—1971

Most families that came to Alberta since the oil find of 1947 know little about Alberta's radical past, but there is such a past, involving not only farmers but also workers. In fact, important radical labour activity has older origins. By confederation in 1905, Alberta had unionized workers in the transportation and mining sectors, and the latter already had a brief history of violent confrontation with owners and management.

During the Liberal era, the miners were very active politically. There was competition between the more conservative United Mine Workers and the radical International Workers of the World and its Canadian successor, One Big Union. Just before the end of the Liberal era, in 1920, the moderates prevailed.

The first ten years of the UFA period was an era of good feeling between farmers and workers. According to Henry Wise Wood, farmers and workers were separate, but not antagonistic, interests. Electoral cooperation gave labour six legislative seats in 1926, and four each in 1921 and 1930. At the onset of the Great Depression, Premier Brownlee did, however, refuse to accede to labour demands.

When the CCF was launched at the Calgary meeting of 1932,

Alberta labour found itself torn between the new socialist party and old allegiance to the UFA. While there were not enough organized workers in the seriously to affect seriously the outcome of the 1935 election, this old allegiance to a dying party, rather than full support for the young CCF, contributed to the huge landslide in which Social Credit took every one of the single-member seats (there was proportional representation in Edmonton and Calgary, and the only opposition seats came from the two large cities).

There was, of course, another aspect of Alberta's Left before 1935: the farmers. The main manifestations of early farm radicalism were the cooperative movement and a general, anti-eastern populism. While the UFA was founded in 1909, Henry Wise Wood was persuaded to enter politics only after the Non-Partisan League, in which William J. Irvine was particularly active, established itself in 1916 and merged with the UFA in 1919. While political action continued throughout the UFA period and the cooperative movement flourished, farm radicalism declined sharply by 1922, once the worst of the agricultural depression was over.

In the Social Credit years, farmers' political action was given up for pressure group activity. The Alberta Farmers Union, in existence until 1949, was the only farm group with a radical tinge. The occasionally radical, though non-partisan, National Farmers Union was founded in 1969 and thus belongs in the Notley (and Lougheed) era.

The rural domination of the Alberta Legislature under Social Credit, enforced by gerrymandering, no doubt contributed to the political weakness of Alberta labour during the Social Credit era. Though the labour movement united into the Alberta Federation of Labour in 1956, as a consequence of the American AFL-CIO merger, labour continued to be weak politically. The by-election victory of Garth Turcott (NDP) in the mining riding of Pincher Creek-Crowsnest in 1966 was reversed in 1967. At the time, the NDP was led by Neil Reimer of the oil workers. While the NDP went without a single seat in the 1967 election, it did manage to raise its vote to an appreciable sixteen per cent. It did reasonably well in such labour ridings as Pincher Creek-Crowsnest, Edmonton-Norwood (then Notley's riding) and Edmonton-North-East (now Beverly).

The Left and the Quasi-Party System

Before we can hope to evaluate Grant Notley's impact on Alberta's quasi-party system, we must assess the left's place in the quasi-party system before him. Here, our orientation will be the Macpherson theory up to 1947 and the shift to the Richards-Pratt theory in the years after Leduc.

The argument over the leftness of the UFA may well be interminable, but hardly anyone will doubt that the UFA, along with other United Farmers and Progressive parties, was firmly to the left of Liberals and Conservatives. Assuming this last point, we arrive at the following table (Table 1), giving the left vote per province during the decade (1921-30) in which the UFA won elections in Alberta.

Table 1
Left Vote in Provinces 1921-1930 *(per cent)*

	PEI	NS	NB	QUE	ONT	MAN	SK	AB	BC
1921							15	43	
1922						49			
1923	3			3	27				
1924									26
1925		3	2				23	49	
1926					9				
1927	0			2		44			
1928		1							5
1929					6		7		
1930			0					47	
AV.	2	2	1	3	14	47	15	46	16

Table 1 shows Alberta just barely behind Manitoba in the top cluster. BC, Saskatchewan and Ontario are far behind, while the left vote in the remaining provinces never reached five per cent. We can therefore say flatly that Alberta, from 1921 to 1935, not only had a left-of-centre government, but that this left-of-centre dominated quasi-party system was based on a popular vote averaging close to fifty per cent.

Once the Social Credit regime took over the quasi-party system, the left vote (for the CCF) reached 30% in 1944, but dropped to 21% in 1948. In all other elections, including 1967, the left vote stayed well below 20%.

We can thus conclude that the left's hold on the quasi-party system, before Notley's leadership, was tenuous throughout. It was tenuous in the elections of 1921, 1926 and 1930 not because the left vote was insufficiently ample, but because the leftness of the UFA, of which labour groups were at best junior partners, was always tenuous. From 1935 on, there were only two elections in which the left vote was above 20%, while Social Credit —with its initial right-wing populism and later alliance between Main Street, Alberta, and the oil industry—was firmly in control of the quasi-party system.

When Grant Notley became leader of the NDP in 1968, he took over virtually the entire left in Alberta: with a respectable vote of 16%, to be sure, but in an unpromising position vis-a-vis the quasi-party system. The balance of the chapter will assess how Grant Notley coped with this principal feature of democracy in Alberta.

The NDP's Support under Notley

In 1971, when Grant Notley first led the NDP in an Alberta election, and when he captured the seat representing Spirit River-Fairview which he was to hold for the rest of his short life, he did not achieve Neil Reimer's sixteen per cent of 1967. Rather, the NDP vote in 1971 was 11.4%. The reason for this slump can hardly be ascribed to Notley. 1971 was not a typical Alberta election. Peter Lougheed's Progressive Conservatives, holding ten seats at dissolution (after having obtained 6 seats with a 26% vote in 1967) were clearly knocking on the door of Social Credit's new premier Harry Strom. While a PC victory was not generally expected, the outcome of the election was in some doubt. To a number of potential NDP voters, an NDP vote must have seemed a wasted vote in a real contest. The vote declined almost everywhere. If anything, there was a sharper drop in labour constituencies, possibly because Neil Reimer was no longer the leader. However, a post-election survey showed Notley to be more popular than either the NDP as a party or its candidates.

This same post-election survey clearly shows the extent to which trade union members were caught in the squeeze between the Progressive Conservatives and Social Credit. While 66% of trade union members designated the NDP as the party which represents trade union people, only 15% of trade unionists stated that they voted NDP!

In the 1975 election, the question "who governs?" was no longer a question and the Progressive Conservatives drove all but four of the Social Crediters out of the legislature. Notley managed to get only an additional 1.5 percentage points for the NDP, just about 13 per cent of the vote. The already small Calgary vote declined, while the Edmonton vote rose significantly, also in middle-class constituencies. There was also a sharp rise in votes in the Ukrainian East of the province.

The 1979 election brought the NDP vote back up to the 1967 level of 16%. Most of the gains came from Edmonton. With 54% of the vote in Spirit River-Fairview, Notley won his biggest personal victory.

More than three years later, in 1982, the NDP raised its vote to 19%, its then highest percentage, tying the second best showing of the CCF. Calgary returns inched upward. The Edmonton advance continued, but it was effectively capped by a pinpointed PC effort to get rid of the pesky one-man opposition. While Ray Martin squeaked through in Edmonton-Norwood to become the second NDP member, the shift of a few hundred votes would have defeated Martin *and* Notley.

These are observations based on raw data. A grouping of constituencies gives us a better idea of what happened to NDP support from 1967 to 1982, from the last Reimer to the last Notley election. We already know that the total vote went up from 16% to 19%. We can learn more by grouping the constituencies into six clusters: Calgary, Edmonton, Other Urban, Suburban, Rural North, Rural South. Table 2 reports the vote change for each grouping from 1967 to 1982, expressed in percentage points:

Table 2
Percentage Point Change in NDP Vote
in Groupings of Constituencies 1967-1982

Constituency Grouping	Number of Constituencies		Percentage Point Change for Grouping
	1967	1982	
Calgary	9	16	+1.7
Edmonton	11	17	+14.2
Other Urban	3	4	-1.4
Suburban	3	4	-2.1
Rural North	25	25	-1.2
Rural South	14	14	-3.5

The table shows that, under Notley, the NDP has become an Edmonton party. Nothing much else has changed. Because of low vote levels, the

Calgary gains and Rural South losses are unimportant. The Rural North change, however slight, belies the often-heard contention that the NDP has become a Northern Alberta Party.

The NDP's Appeal Under Notley

The support picture just shown gives us hints about the social groups that supported the NDP under Notley. I say "hints" because election data do not tell us "who" votes which way but only "how many" do in a constituency. We can, however, venture an educated guess about the new people Notley attracted to the NDP. We know that most of them live in Edmonton, where the party previously had a rather narrow labour base. Because Edmonton is the home of myriads of white collar workers, much of the new support probably comes from this quarter. Yet there are also myriads of white collar workers in Calgary, where NDP support remains slight. The difference between the two cities is that in Calgary the private sector predominates, in Edmonton the public sector. My guess, therefore, is that the NDP attracts thousands of Alberta government workers and their families. If this is so, was it the consequence of an active or a passive appeal of Notley's NDP? That is, if white collar employees from the public sector are attracted to the NDP—and circumstantial evidence makes it appear so—is this because they are attracted *by* the NDP or just because they find the NDP more acceptable than other parties?

The CCF, the NDP's predecessor, was a party of farmers and workers, while the NDP has been directing its active appeal much more to blue collar workers. The Alberta NDP, like its Saskatchewan counterpart, has always raised issues of interest to farmers as well as issues pertaining to workers. Added to these were social issues of interest to the population at large. The target group who received additional attention by Notley was small business. While this was no doubt helpful in Spirit River-Fairview, there is little evidence, tangible or otherwise, that small business required Notley's attention, nor was it likely to do so. Comparative politics teaches us that the small businessman in free enterprise countries, while skeptical of large monopolies, has a firm belief in the capitalist system and is suspicious of social democratic advances. A group which is much freer of such suspicion are middle and small salary earners, especially in the public sector. While Notley appeared to succeed with many such people in Edmonton, it was not because of any special appeal he directed at them.

I would hypothesize, from what again must be emphasized is partial and unreliable evidence, that Notley would have enhanced the electoral success of the NDP if he had openly appealed to small and middle employees for support. It would have been awkward to restrict this appeal to public (including educational) employees, but a general white collar appeal might have been made. Appealing to profit-sector employees and their familes might not have brought in myriads of votes, but probably thousands, and the Calgary vote might have risen also. In Edmonton, a targeted white collar appeal might have raised the NDP voting average (32.3% in 1982!) up to the Progressive Conservative level, with a good chance of capturing half of the city's seats. This recipe is of course available to Notley's successor also. I can see nothing incompatible or contradictory between it and the appeal for votes the NDP made under Notley's leadership.

In Chapter 10 of this book, Garth Stevenson makes a similar observation, but in different terms. He suggests that the Alberta New Democrats consider themselves primarily a party of the working class. His target for the party is the same as mine: clerical, sales and service workers. He especially includes, and here I could not agree more, women in these categories. Stevenson then points to practical difficulties with his approach, dismissing them in the end without ever really putting them out of the way: (1) immigration, (2) in-migration to Alberta, (3) migration from farm to city, (4) upward mobility, (5) diversity of geographic and cultural origins, (6) Western alienation, (7) NDP middle class leadership, and (8) such liberal policies as opposition to NATO and freedom of choice (the abortion issue). There is little anyone can do about the first six difficulties except to raise social and tax equity issues which may have a tendency to overcome them. The seventh, middle-class leadership, has been with us since Marx and is shared by all Western Socialist and Social Democratic movements known to me. It is of course true that candidates for the Legislative Assembly should be less homogeneous than Alberta New Democratic candidates in fact are—an aim that could be achieved best by having good old-fashioned schools for candidates (unions and the party would still have to overcome financial hurdles). The last point, that liberal issues are not supported by the working class, strikes at the heart of Socialist and Social Democratic politics. Second International parties have always resorted to political education to liberalize workers. If this effort is abandoned and reversed, the supporters could easily turn these parties into parties of militarism, of forcing women to bear children, of the death penalty, not to continue the parade of horribles.

My final disagreement with Stevenson is the class appeal he suggests. The reason why I have not emphasized a stronger NDP appeal to those who, even today, earn their bread by the sweat of their brow, is that even in their case there is no evidence that, in Alberta, they would want to be addressed as working class. To address clerical, sales and service workers as working class would be, I submit, as effective as addressing a Ukrainian picnic in French.

Notley and the Quasi-Party System

Was Alberta's Quasi-Party System Grant Notley's nemesis? My answer is a qualified "yes." Need it have been his nemesis? My answer here is a qualified "no."

To begin, let me answer the first question. Grant Notley stemmed from independent commodity producers. If he had become a political leader half a century earlier, his talents might well have allowed him to govern the province. Even thirty years after that, he might have made a strong opponent to a faltering Aberhart government. In 1968, while Notley appreciated the new urban interests, his background was no longer in great demand. After an unsuccessful attempt at election in Edmonton-Norwood, Notley secured about as rural a seat as there was in the province, but his appeal fell on deaf ears in rural Southern Alberta and remained muted in other rural areas. He was listened to with interest in Edmonton, and sometimes politely in Calgary, but it was clear that he did not represent the dominant strain of the quasi-party system of the seventies. In Lougheed's world, he remained an outsider, and not only because he was a social democrat. He succeeded neither in representing the urban middle class nor in leading an opposition stemming from important elements of that class. A Notley who might have coped reasonably well with the Macpherson version of the quasi-party system never quite came to grips with Pratt's version which remained so firmly in Lougheed's hand.

On the second question, all I can do is speculate. Maybe the best answer here is that Notley's untimely death kept him from having a glimmer of a chance. The two oil booms of the seventies made it practically impossible to mobilize disaffected elements of the urban middle class. From 1973 to 1981, probably the majority of the new middle class were actually or potentially wealthy people. Relatively few, and few of the politically active, felt that their life was sufficiently stationary for them to cast their lot with a social democratic party. For many who were hurt by paying high rents, home ownership—if not real estate speculation—was or seemed to be only a few years away. Many who would normally think in terms of social services or a stationary existence were actual or potential investors or speculators in the economy. Notley's social concerns were not a high priority with them.

The political genius of Lougheed and George de Rappard temporarily obliterated the recession with the "quick kick" of the November, 1982 election, in which anyone with a realistic assessment of the economy was decried a "knocker." It was not even easy—nor was much hard attempt made—to persuade a large minority of Albertans that their government, since 1979, had put all its eggs in the province-building basket and had begun a severe neglect of people's programmes. We will never know how successful Notley would have been in mobilizing the disaffected parts of the urban middle (and lower-middle) class for the election expected for 1986. Disappointments in investments in ventures and real estate, losses of well-paying jobs, bank failures, and falling oil prices might have enabled Notley to forge an alliance of the disaffected with farmers and workers that could, over ensuing years, have spread from North to South.

The most important thing Notley would have needed to do in 1986 would have been to follow Stevenson's and my advice to solicit the support of Alberta's clerical, sales and service workers. Subject to refutation, I still believe that the New Democrats are fairly successful with the non-profit, especially governmental, part of white collar workers. But I would give higher priority to private white collar than to blue collar workers, believing, again subject to refutation, that the majority of the latter want to have little or nothing to do with their Alberta tradition of the first decades of this century.

Outlook

It may seem strange to close a chapter of a memorial volume with a section called "outlook." My excuse for this closing is that Grant Notley was not given the opportunity to live out a full life and that his life's work was brought to an abrupt halt in his prime. His work is thus before us, to be completed, if at all, by others.

Does the NDP have any chance at all to make the breakthrough to become the dominant party in a quasi-party system, or can it become a party competing for provincial office, as it has in British Columbia,

Saskatchewan and Manitoba? The first scenario is not easy to imagine in what surely is Canada's most capitalist province. In Alberta, either Liberals or a wild-eyed movement on the libertarian right seem to have more of a chance for political dominance than a social democratic party. But, in early 1986, Alberta's future is in some doubt. Peter Lougheed's strong hand no longer guides Alberta's political destiny, and the uncertain economic future, as well as the not wholly known leadership abilities of Don Getty, may bring about a political turnover, around 1990, for which the NDP is, in 1985, readier than others as an organization. If these uncertainties are accompanied by a loss of faith in Alberta's buccaneering capitalism, a moderate social democracy based on rural independents and urban wage and salary workers of all stripes might just make it to the fore. It is difficult to see how the NDP's now extremely small leadership group would pull this off, but an enlarged caucus in 1986 could just possibly give the party something like the credibility of the Lougheed opposition in 1967.

This scenario is not probable as of early 1986, but Alberta society could become more settled and more typically Canadian than it has ever been, even before 1921. Should this occur, Alberta politics could become more settled also. The quasi-party system could disappear, and the NDP could become part of a two-, three- or even four-party system. In such a case, Grant Notley, were he alive, could lead a social democratic party to importance and occasional success. If another leader succeeds in this, he will owe much to the man from Didsbury who understood the whole range of problems of the province but evoked the following of relatively few during his short life.

Epilogue

The 1986 election showed indeed that the NDP is now the Edmonton party. With 43% of the city's vote (the Tories pulled 38%), it captured eleven of the fifteen Edmonton seats. All else remains uncertain, but the growing militancy of organized labour could help bring about Garth Stevenson's class-politics scenario.

Chapter 9

From Consensus to Competition:
Social Democracy and Political Culture in Alberta

Gurston Dacks

The political culture of Alberta is entering a period of fundamental change. The unity and certainty of conviction which underlay the single party dominance for which Alberta has been renowned are now threatened. Challenging them are the politics of fragmentation and fear, fear of economic decline which will shatter the historic Alberta consensus. While this change has improved the competitive position of social democrats in the province, over the long run it equally may impose upon them an even more marginal existence than they have historically endured in the province's politics. This essay will identify the basic elements of the political culture of Alberta which denied significant success to the CCF and thereafter to the NDP. It will review the volatile condition of Albertan political culture at present and suggest how the culture which congeals out of this fluid period will condition political competition within the province for the foreseeable future.

This task requires an appreciation of political culture. Political culture is the pattern of fundamental ideas, of basic beliefs and values, by which a group of people interpret politics and decide how they will behave when faced with political choices. People respond to the world subjectively. They interpret it, not as some detached observer would, but as they personally believe it to be. A sensitivity to the political culture of a society can help explain the political behaviour of large numbers of its members because their beliefs usually assume patterns which are widely shared for at least three reasons. First, they may share ideas because they have been exposed to the same agencies of mass socialization, such as formal schooling and the media. Second, the similar personal experiences they have encountered, for example, the Great Depression or powerlessness in the marketplace, tend to lead people to similar conclusions. This is especially true if the existing political culture of their society provides clues which encourage a particular interpretation and if prominent members of the society, those with privileged access to the means of disseminating ideas—the media, school curricula, pulpits—find it in their interest to promote a particular interpretation. Third, newcomers to a society, wishing to be accepted into it and to rationalize their decision to migrate to it, often adopt the society's ideas with a fervour far surpassing that of their more established neighbours. A further factor which makes political culture useful in illuminating political behaviour is that political culture is relatively enduring. For reasons which will be discussed below, people resist changing their basic ideas. Their opinions may shift, and public opinion is notoriously unstable, but their underlying systems of belief are quite fixed. This durability allows political scientists to explain specific political phenomena as reflecting the application of the general patterns of political culture to particular circumstances. They may seek to explain the sources of political culture by examining objective factors, such as economic structures, or the manipulation of popular thinking by elites, but they recognize that a more immediate cause of patterns of behaviour in a society is the set of basic ideas widely shared by its members.

For politicians, the significance of political culture is that it sets the stage on which they must play out their roles. However, the setting is not the script. While political culture does close some options and constrain strategic choices somewhat, it also provides opportunities for strategists who can identify elements of the culture which their party can relate to the circumstances of the moment to produce an electorally persuasive formula. Political culture need not make passive victims of politicians. To the contrary, it offers them materials with which to work. The difficult challenge facing social democrats in Alberta is to mould the raw material which Alberta's political culture offers into an electorally successful strategy. To meet the challenge, they must first identify the relevant elements of Alberta's political culture.

Since the turn of the century, this political culture has rested on twin pillars. The first of these has been the alienation Albertans have felt towards national political institutions; these they have viewed as the means by which central Canada has effected its domination over the West. The second has been the inclination of Albertans to relate to provincial politics in terms of the interest they have believed they share in a single dominant commodity rather than in terms of social class or some other form of consciousness. These two orientations have reinforced each other to produce the Alberta consensus. A perceived homogeneity of interest has permitted Albertans to view the dominant issue in provincial politics as an external one—the need to give the provincial government the strongest possible mandate with which to represent Alberta in negotiations with Ottawa. This over-riding concern has enabled successive provincial governments to avoid being called to account for inadequate policies regarding such "domestic" issues as labour relations and social conditions within the province. In turn, the absence of real debate, that is a debate whose outcome might affect the tenure of government, has reduced the prominence and legitimacy of these issues in the political consciousness of most Albertans.

The history of Alberta's alienation in Confederation is well documented[1]. Ottawa's delay in granting responsible government[2] and provincehood and its retention for a quarter century after 1905 of control over land and resources laid the foundation for this alienation. The quasi-colonial political economy which Albertans endured heightened their sense of grievance against central Canada. Because they could not match the political power of central Canadian interests[3], they laboured under tariffs, the depredations of railroads, banks and grain companies controlled in the East and markets whose terms they could not set. In addition, the lack of military spending in the West during the First World War[4], Ottawa's indifference to the needs of the fledgling oil industry in the fifties and the more recent struggles for control over and revenues from the oil and gas industry, culminating in the conflict over the National Energy Program, have heaped additional layers of intensity onto their alienation.

As an inevitable consequence of this alienation, winning political parties have included in their appeals to the Alberta electorate the claim that they, of all the contenders, will prove most effective in confronting Ottawa. They have further argued that their effectiveness will be all the greater if they receive an overwhelming mandate. The mandate has usually been forthcoming, particularly during periods of intense Ottawa-Alberta conflict.

That this mandate has been obtained reflects the second basic feature of Alberta political culture, namely that, more than any other factor, a few dominant industries have defined Alberta political thinking. These dominant industries, first grain and more recently oil and gas, have served as political benchmarks because very large proportions of Alberta's electorate have identified as their primary political interest the promotion of these industries. In other words, the primary organizing principle of Albertan political thought has not been social class, but rather the belief on the part of large numbers of voters that they share an interest, transcending class differences, in the dominant commodity. So important has this interest been for them that they have equated promotion of it with loyalty to the province itself. These electors have included not only those engaged in the act of producing itself but in addition the many others in the commercial, service, transportation and governmental sectors of the economy who have recognized primary production as the source of their personal well-being.

In the sense in which the term is used in this paper, the dominance of a commodity rests more on political perceptions than on economics. After all, if a commodity such as oil and gas declines, it might still be the dominant, that is, the largest, economic sector, particularly if its decline undercuts other sectors of the provincial economy. However, it might lose its political dominance if people lose faith in it as a secure base for their future prosperity. Thus, the political dominance of a commodity is subjective. Many voters who equate their interests with those of the commodity will respond in one of two ways. They may define the basic purpose of politics as promoting and protecting the commodity. Alternatively, they may defer to the elite which has been recognized as representing the commodity. If enough voters respond in these ways, then the commodity is dominant in the political sense. In the case of Alberta, differences have certainly existed over the division of the income derived from the dominant commodity and over myriad other issues. However, because conflict has always been more intense between Alberta interests and outsiders than among Albertans themselves, the internal divisions which shape the politics of other provinces have been submerged.

Three explanations for this pattern may be offered. The first, noted above, is that the dominant commodities in Alberta's history have been vulnerable. Albertans have often felt that market terms dictated elsewhere have given them a distressingly low share of the final price charged for the commodities which they produced. Because so many Albertans have felt that this injustice has touched their lives, it has unified the province. To fight among themselves for the income which they received after railroad companies, the grain exchange, eastern banks, pipeline companies and Ottawa have commanded their shares—and, in the case of energy, after it has been reduced by subsidies enjoyed by eastern Canadian consumers in the form of artificially low prices—has appeared to Albertans much less rewarding than attempting to seek a larger overall share. Rather than fight over the crumbs, they have preferred to seek a larger pie.

The second explanation is that during most of Alberta's history, the class distinctions which existed were blurred by a persistent belief in social mobility[5]. Many farmers toiled on in difficult circumstances, believing that, despite the hardships they might have to endure, they could make a go of their farms, expand their holdings and prosper. Workers in many industries have enjoyed sufficiently high wages as to view themselves as beneficiaries of the economic system built upon the dominant commodity, rather than to identify with any notion of the working class. Their anger has tended to be reserved for eastern Canadian forces which they believe thwart the potential of the western oil industry.

The third explanation is the role of Alberta's elite in transforming important commodities into articles of political faith. Elite members have conditioned Albertans to equate elite interests with the general interest of Alberta or at least as so crucial to the general wellbeing as to invalidate concerns over the uneven distribution of the benefits and burdens associated with the commodity.

The idea of dominant commodity interest should not be interpreted as a denial of the reality of class structure and class conflict in Alberta. The history of the province refutes any such denial. In the early decades of the century, the conditions of workers in such industries as coal mining and meat packing were appalling and they responded by creating militant unions and attempting to confront their employees over a long period of time[6]. Labour mayors were elected in both Calgary and Edmonton and socialists were also elected as MLAs. The social conditions existed for a substantial CCF showing in the formative provincial election of 1935, but because of its links with the United Farmers of Alberta, the CCF was unable to contest that election. Alberta radicalism committed itself to Social Credit. By the time the doctrinal attraction of Social Credit waned, prosperity arrived and discouraged Albertans from attempting further political experiments. Thus circumstances, as much as political culture, explain the hard fate of the Alberta CCF[7], and that fate cannot be taken to prove the absence of class conflict during the Socreds' long term of office. More recently the bitter struggle between unions and employers in the construction industry, the activities of the dandelion movement on behalf of the unemployed, and the farm survivalists have in their own ways drawn attention to basic economic conflicts within Alberta which can be interpreted in terms of social class. The efforts of the Government of Alberta to place the burdens of the post 1982 recession primarily upon workers and recipients of social services also reflect the relevance of a dominant social class in public policy.

Class has been important as a social phenomenon and as a focus of public policy and conflict throughout the history of Alberta. This cannot be denied. What can be denied, however, is that social class has been the crucial political dimension in terms of which Albertans have divided. Elections in Alberta simply have not turned on issues of class within the context of Alberta society. Of course, it might be argued that Albertans have constituted a "class" in the context of the Canadian metropolis-hinterland relationship. This interpretation places questions of social class at the centre of Alberta electoral politics over the decades. However, it also confuses the nature of issues within the province and obscures the ways in which social change in Alberta may in turn change the terms of electoral competition within it. In the past, social issues within the province have been raised at election time, but not by parties which have come close to winning. Instead, from the UFA on, electorally successful parties have emphasized the unity of Albertan society and its interest in promoting the commodity which has sustained it.

To explain this pattern, it must be noted that many of those who feel that they have not shared this interest have been politically insignificant. They have simply figured among the politically invisible. Many native, poor, elderly and other Albertans who lack resources, contacts and confidence have abstained from participating in a system which they believe they cannot influence. As has been noted above, of those who are marginal to the majority interest in the commodity, many have retained a faith in their eventual upward mobility in the system sustained by the commodity. Other Albertans have recognized the reality of social class and objected to the approach to issues of class, or other questions, taken by the provincial government, but have not expressed their objection with their vote. For them, their identification as Albertans has taken priority. This is enough to disguise their concern because elections based on a single member constituency plurality system tend to channel conflict along a single dimension. In the United Kingdom, this dimension is social class. In Canadian national politics, it is regionalism. In Alberta, it is the struggle with the East. A great many Albertans believe that the status quo in the province benefits them. In contrast, relatively few Albertans believe that the status quo in the province does not serve them, and place this realization first on their political agenda and combine with it the vigour to challenge the system politically. Compared to the number of such people, the mass of Albertans who either have benefitted from primary production or who believed that they have or that they could reasonably expect to in the future, has been so large as to make electoral politics directed at any subsector of

Albertan society, such as a particular social class, completely unviable.

Politics in Contemporary Alberta

The conjunction of this perceived community of interest with the alienation Albertans have felt against central Canada has produced decades of single party dominance in Alberta. That it will continue to do so is now far less certain. The alienation can be expected to persist as long as the Alberta energy industry produces large economic rents. Alberta and Ottawa can be expected to continue their struggle over their respective shares of this revenue. Albertans will also find themselves resisting efforts by consumers, clustered in central Canada, to reduce the cost of the energy they use from what it would otherwise be. Albertans' view of their oil and gas resources both as finite and as a form of patrimony, a provincial inheritance, can be predicted to compound their resentment at the energy policy challenges emanating from central Canada. Similarly, the issue of free trade promises to pit the two regions of Canada against each other so long as both assume that free trade benefits resource producers and threatens manufacturers. Thus, the cut and thrust of practical politics can be counted on not to refute, but rather to reinforce, Alberta's alienation toward central Canada.

Where the change will come in Albertan political culture is that the unity and confidence which have produced such great political cohesion in the province can be expected to break down in the next several decades. What distinguishes the present and future of Alberta from the past is the loss of confidence in one or two commodities which integrated Alberta society for so many decades. Agriculture certainly cannot stand as the integrating commodity it once was. Whereas in the late 1930s, agriculture accounted for two thirds of the province's economic output, it now produces only 4% of the total[6], well behind the mining, finance, service, trade, construction and transportation sectors. In human terms, only 8.7% of Alberta's population lives on farms[7]. While agriculture will always play a major role in the province, high capital costs and unfavourable prices for the commodities it produces are shrinking its profitability. Indeed, it may decline even more if free trade compels Canada to accept alterations to the agricultural marketplace which further undermine the competitive position of Alberta farmers. Even without such a future decline, the farming community has diminished to the point where it constitutes only one of several important interest groups in Alberta politics. Gone are the days when agriculture represented an economic sector to which parties such as the Liberals and the UFA would cater in order to ensure both their own re-election and the wellbeing of the province.

Similarly, though not so drastically, oil and gas may well be in the process of losing their constituency. They still dominate the provincial economy, but they no longer offer the future of boundless promise which they once held out to Albertans. All who look to the future recognize that oil is a depleting resource[10] and that the Government of Alberta has been unable to translate the income generated during its depletion into the type of diversification which will assure future economic health. Nonconventional forms of hydrocarbon energy abound, but the lesson of the past decade has been that these may not prove sufficiently profitable to interest private-sector developers. Indeed, the vagaries of the international energy market make even conventional energy a commodity upon which it is dangerous to count for one's wellbeing. Gas appears to be in plentiful supply, but deregulation and unfavourable market conditions, at least in the short and medium range future, suggest that prices and production may not return to the levels which contributed so much to Albertans' confidence in the seventies. Indeed, the historic political economy of East-West relations in Canada is already responding to the present oversupply situation in that political decisions, which reflect the nation's centre of political gravity in Ontario and Quebec, are allowing the market to set lower prices for Alberta's natural gas. Albertans may well blame the East, but their anger may be diffused by the complexity of the mechanisms which determine gas pricing and the number of interests—producers, pipeline companies, distributors, consumers and, of course, governments—which must be sorted out in order to understand gas pricing issues. What they may be left with is even less confidence in the oil and gas industry because, whatever the source of its problems, it appears less and less likely to accomplish the dreams which its boom inspired a decade ago. It may be better to have oil and gas than not to have them, but they are clearly not secure bases for economic stability and growth.

It might be argued that there have been times in Alberta's past when the dominant commodity failed to finance the needs of its population or at least disappointed its adherents. The thirties challenged the faith of farmers, while energy developers experienced frustrations in the fifties. However, in both instances, those involved could view their difficulties as temporary and have faith that they would be able to produce their commodities in abundance and find favourable markets for them. This is now less the case regarding oil and gas than it has ever been for a dominant commodity in Alberta's history as a province. A succession of lean years and the uncertainties of a future marked by resource depletion, vulnerability to unstable world markets and the domination of Canada's political economy by Ontario and Quebec mean that Alberta has entered into a period of diminished self-confidence. As a result, Albertans who used to do so will find it increasingly difficult to interpret their self-interest in terms of the single industry or commodity which has defined the Alberta consensus. Increasingly, they may come to define their political interest in terms of the category within Albertan society to which they belong. If they do take the intellectual leap of reorienting their thinking in this way, they will discover that Albertan society contains all of the dimensions of social differentiation found in the other provinces and resembles them in terms of the political relevance of these social differences[11]. While attitudes are slow to change, their recent experiences cannot help but encourage particular groups of Albertans to reconsider their economic and social interests. Prolonged unemployment cannot help but raise questions in the minds of workers, both about the industry which they assumed would provide for them and about the government which seems unable to respond to their situation. Similarly, those who have suffered business failure will assess the impact of government policy on the fate which has befallen them, as will farmers who have experienced or who are anticipating the loss of their farms.

To the results of this process of reflection must be added the contribution to Alberta's political culture of recent immigrants to the province. Understanding this contribution is, however, a complicated matter. It has been argued that the immigrants to Alberta who have been drawn by the oil boom have reinforced the conservative bias of the province both directly and indirectly. In the direct sense, the oil industry has held free enterprise to be an article of faith, except when seeking government assistance, and those who came to Alberta's oil patch with such ideas added to the conservative flavour of the province's politics. Indirectly, the immigration which oil spawned included individuals from a variety of countries who for various reasons looked with suspicion upon left-wing ideas[12]. However, the influx into Alberta undoubtedly brought many workers and others who had lived in provinces, and elsewhere, where social democracy was and remains a viable political force, hence a model to be considered when the conventional wisdom comes into question, as it will increasingly in Alberta. The resultant of these conflicting forces cannot be established with any confidence. All that can be suggested is that immigration has brought to Alberta a group of people most of whom did not grow up thinking in terms of their relationship to a single commodity and entrusting their future to it. It is precisely these people who may be willing to consider innovative responses to problems which the tradition of provincial unity has failed to address. At the very least, the presence of these people in Alberta has contributed to making the province's social structure more closely resemble the general Canadian milieu, thus creating at least the potential for great electoral success for the NDP.

The realization of this potential will be very difficult because political culture is so durable. People become intensely committed to what they have learned from the school of daily experience and the opinions of others they respect—teachers, parents, peers and the media, for example. Putting aside these ideas, revising one's world view, is for most people a psychologically threatening experience. To pursue it is to accept at least as an hypothesis the possibility that one might have made mistakes in the past. Questioning one's analysis inevitably leads to questioning the judgement of the sources of one's information. Evaluations of friends and those one trusts may have to be revised. Such a reassessment could lead to altering relationships which have proven gratifying in the past. Most people find all of this prospect of change distressing and would rather avoid it if at all possible. Hence the stability of political culture.

For this stability to be upset, reality must intrude upon people's thinking in such a compelling and undeniable fashion that they simply cannot square their ideas with what is happening to them. The relevance of this feature of political culture for the future of the NDP is that Albertans have recently received in the school of hard experience some very painful lessons which have shaken their complacency. The 1986 provincial general election suggests that these lessons have been forceful enough to deflect many Albertans from their conventional voting patterns. An increase in its share of the popular vote from 19% to 29% enabled the New Democrats to elect sixteen members to the legislature as contrasted to only two who had represented the party previously. However, the triumph of May 8 does not prove that hard times have led enough Albertans to re-examine their social and political beliefs to form the kind of enduring New Democratic voting bloc to enable the party to repeat or even to build on its 1986 success.

New Democrats must never forget that this success was due not so much to an enlarged New Democratic vote, as to the abstention of many former Conservative voters. It might be argued that the Tory vote fell from 588,000 in 1982 to 365,000 in 1986 because complacency kept its voters at home and party activists from working to get them out to vote. However, there is no evident reason why the Tories should be more complacent in 1986 than in 1982. The suggestion of complacency is even harder to sustain in the face of the fact that, even in ridings in which the Conservatives knew they had a fight on their hands, such as Edmonton-Strathcona, their vote totals were down substantially. The voter turnout of 47.5%, the lowest in the province's history, suggests that many former Tory voters were sufficiently displeased with the Conservatives and the provincial economy not to vote for them, yet could not bring themselves to vote for the New Democrats, who only gained 30,000 over their 1982 total. This figure might have been even lower if the right had managed to present itself more credibly. As it was, the Liberals, running on a free enterprise platform, multiplied their vote fivefold. All of this testifies to the continuing strength of the crucial political orientation of so many Albertans—their identification with a dominant commodity and the elite which speaks for it. At the same time, the disillusionment which the low turnout reflects could represent the first stage of a profound cultural evolution in Alberta. What remains to be seen is where the process will lead. In looking to the future, two patterns appear possible.

The first possibility is that while oil and gas will falter, they will still generate sufficient economic activity as to discourage most people from reconsidering the political thinking which leads them to shun a social democratic electoral option. In this scenario, even if the provincial economy only manages to maintain its 1985 level of performance, or if the government can convince Albertans that a further decline will prove short-lived, it could probably preserve the Alberta consensus. After all, it could point to statistics which indicate that the level of unemployment in the province until recently has been less than the national average[13]. It could argue, particularly to an electorate made credulous by both economics and culture, that fuller employment will return once aberrant market forces correct themselves. It could also draw to the attention of disgruntled workers the fact that their average weekly earnings are well above the national figure[14]. This would enable it to continue its successful strategy of dividing the labour force and encouraging those who are employed to distinguish their interests from those of the marginal work force. Such an outcome would continue the phenomenon that Alberta ". . . union members are no more liberal than the general population . . . "[15], a generalization which probably holds true for Albertan workers in general. This outcome would mean business as usual in conservative Alberta, with the only major question being the identity of the party which would express the dominant ideology of the province.

Is this a likely pattern for the future? The international factors which will seal the fate of Alberta's energy industry have proven to be quite unpredictable. However, a variety of factors, in addition to the general durability of political culture, would reinforce any tendency to continued political quiescence. The first of these is the enduring cushion or anchor which conservative thinking enjoys in the rural parts of the province south of Edmonton. In 1986, the tide of New Democratic success in the North produced little more than ripples in these ridings. Only one of them, Pincher Creek-Crowsnest, gave the New Democrats half the votes polled by the winning Conservatives. In most of them, the New Democrats ran third and gained less than one third the votes received by the winner. The conservative tenor of these ridings, stretching from Lacombe to the American border, is very unlikely to diminish due to immigration or significant social change.

The second factor is the accumulated wealth at the disposal of the provincial government, which it can use to ease the burden of a static economy. Money from the Heritage Trust Fund will be available to fund programs such as capital works. It may also prove possible to avoid a provincial sales tax. These policies might prove very persuasive in demonstrating that the self-interest of Albertans continues to lie in supporting a conservative electoral option. More importantly, they will discourage Albertans from undertaking the process of questioning which might lead them to view non-conservative political options as relevant. Most of the Albertans who might be moved to reconsider their ideas—those who are not ideologically entrenched—will not feel a pressing need to do so. Alberta politics will continue as it has for the past several years, a process of "managing expectations". The goal of this exercise is to demonstrate, first, that the dreams nurtured during the boom were unrealistic and, second, that the leadership which guided the province during the boom remains the most effective choice for governing it when conditions have changed but still offer sufficient prospects for those whose expectations have been successfully lowered. In the end, the danger which this scenario poses for the NDP is a return after the next election to wandering in the wilderness.

An alternative scenario is that the oil and gas industry will decline sufficiently that the politics of electoral polarization cannot be stopped at the province's borders. In this instance, the government would confront the type of structural problem which is proving so difficult for other governments in Canada to address. In the same way that the boom in Alberta owed almost everything to a feature of the province's economic structure—its natural resources—rather than to successful policies of diversification or effective management of the business cycle, the decline will reflect the kind of structural problem which successive governments of Canada have failed to overcome. Indeed, it may be intensified if Ottawa responds to the structural problems in the national economy in ways which work against the interests of Alberta. For example, Ottawa might feel compelled in order to create a satisfactory free trade package with the United States to negotiate provisions which impair Alberta's freedom of action to assist its farmers or promote diversification. Perhaps, Ottawa might accede arrangements which directly harm industries which are important for Alberta's economic well being, without adequately providing the province with some countervailing benefit. It is also possible that Ottawa may respond to the difficulties encountered in 1985 by western financial institutions and enact banking legislation which harms regional banks or other financial institutions which are particularly sensitive to Alberta's capital needs.

The traditional individualism of Alberta[16], reinforced by the neoconservative tenor of the eighties, makes conservatives in Alberta, progressive or of other stripes, ideologically unprepared to intervene in the economy in ways which might substantially rationalize its structure. In any event, the province may not command the means to accomplish such a restructuring in the face of national and global market conditions. Given this context, the economic and political arena in which the NDP will find itself competing will come increasingly to resemble the political field of combat in Canada all told. To be sure, Alberta politics will not require the inter-regional accommodation found in Ottawa. Also, they will continue to be coloured by the persistently deep conservatism of much of rural Alberta. Still, a distressed economy will reproduce in Alberta the politics of fear and fragmentation taking shape elsewhere in Canada. Accepting the structural problems of the Alberta economy as given and immutable, the provincial government will make even more drastic choices between economic and social development programs than it is currently making. It will legitimize these choices by playing on Albertans' anxieties about their economic future and their belief that a publicly subsidized private sector represents the only hope of salvation. Personal income taxes will be increased, a variety of user fees created or increased, and services privatized to reduce pressure on government to improve inadequate standards of service. In addition, the terms of the marketplace, touching on such issues as labour relations and the rights and opportunities for capital, will be altered to assist business. Over a sufficient period of time, this emphasis on economic development over social development will create a real debate in Alberta, a debate which reflects the current debate between social democrats and conservatives nationally[17]. Electoral politics could come to reflect this debate. The provincial government's reinforced commitment to the rhetoric of the marketplace will inevitably intensify the grievances of a variety of groups of Albertans. This may lead them to realize that their longstanding belief in the identity of interests between themselves and those who represent the dominant commodity in the province no longer reflects reality.

In this way, repeated economic grievance could prove the solvent for the Alberta political consensus. It may compel people whose primary political identification in the past was with the mainstream of Alberta life to understand that they cannot expect to realize their ambitions as part of some vague and undifferentiated mass of Albertans. Increasingly they may define themselves first and foremost as workers who need jobs and the protection of more even-handed labour legislation; as public servants whose rights as organized workers demand recognition; as single parents whose various needs must be better served; as farmers who need more support; as native people who can only realize their goals of greater economic and political self-determination if provincial government policy becomes much more accommodating or as senior citizens who require a variety of improved services from government.

The key to understanding the new politics of Alberta, should the decline of the oil and gas sector create the kind of enduring, structurally-based, economic distress which characterizes Canada all told, will be the increased visibility of the differentiation in Alberta society. This differentiation will not be new; Alberta is already a highly urbanized, economically developed and differentiated society. However, this fact has been submerged in terms of public debates by the unity of identification of the mass of politically active Albertans with the province and its dominant economy. Once this identification weakens, Alberta's political culture will catch up with the social reality of the province. Social democratic appeals aimed at an electorate which will behave like a composite of interests, rather than a homogeneous mass, could begin to elicit a favourable response. Their identification with the mainstream broken, many Albertans may become willing to consider seriously arguments put forward by a social democratic party.

However, the evolution of their thinking is likely to be gradual and partial. It will depend on the performance of Alberta's economy and the shrewdness of the government of Alberta. More relevant to social democrats planning for the future, it will depend on how effectively they present themselves to Albertans whose difficult circumstances lead them to reject the Conservatives, but whose socialization discourages them from considering a social democratic alternative. These people, who swelled the ranks of the non-voters in 1986, need a reason to vote for a social democratic party. The psychological hold of political culture means that they will not respond to the social democratic rhetoric which they have traditionally rejected because this rhetoric represents a direct threat to their world view. They are much likelier to respond to programs aimed at their particular and tangible problems for which conservatism offers no solutions. Thus for the NDP to appeal to these newly accessible voters, it must present them with policies which address their new self-definitions.

Moreover, it must go farther than this. It must bring its policies as directly and personally as possible to these groups of voters and it must involve them individually in its policies. Aberhart did not succeed by merely addressing the mass of Albertans through radio broadcasts. He and his colleagues organized a great many small groups with which individual Albertans could identify, and which gave them the answers to the needs which they were feeling so intensely and which conventional politics were not meeting.

Alberta has changed in half a century. However, a pattern is repeating itself in the appearance of groups of Albertans who believe or could come to understand that conventional politics, controlled by the spokesmen of the dominant commodity, are not serving needs which they feel very strongly. As a result of better communications, greater urbanization and a more activist political culture than existed fifty years ago, these groups already exist. The NDP need not bring them into existence, as Aberhart had to do. Rather, the appropriate political strategy is to work with these groups, to develop the policies which respond to the fundamental political needs their members feel, be they parents who depend on out-of-school care for their children, feminists seeking a meaningful provincial advisory council on the status of women, or citizens wanting stronger laws against drunk drivers. Labour, as the logical constituency of a social democratic party, should receive ample attention, but it should be approached in terms of the specific needs which its members feel, rather than in terms of an appeal to social class with which, whatever the objective reality of its situation, it has not identified in the past. In any case, the failure of labour to support the NDP in past provincial elections warns that a winning strategy must reach many more Albertans than those encompassed by the labour movement, even if this means developing certain progressive policies which organized labour does not favour.

This broadening of appeal will require the direct approach outlined above. Mass media work most effectively when the electorate is neutral or favourably disposed toward a party or candidate. However, media alone cannot reverse the fortunes of a party struggling against a consensus, even one out of line with reality, because they are not sufficiently compelling. Voters will only change old patterns of thoughts if they are "hit where they live". They must be jarred loose from the *gestalt* of the consensus. The mass media lack the punch to motivate this fundamental intellectual reorganization. Voters find it psychologically easier to dismiss or ignore them than to deal with any messages they carry which contradict their world view.

Thus the psychology of political culture means that social democrats hoping to move Albertans to a fundamental rethinking of their political assumptions should build their strategy around responding to the specific and tangible concerns and grievances which Albertans are feeling increasingly deeply. A credible response can lead them to abandon their former thinking by exposing them to a favourable experience with social democrats which their old ideas cannot accommodate, but which affects an interest so personally important to them that they cannot dismiss it or rationalize it away. The only way to apply this lever is to work directly with these people. Indeed, the most profound sense in which the 1986 election results present an opportunity for the New Democrats is that it positions them to undertake precisely this kind of outreach. Private citizens can try to represent social democracy to Albertans, but social democratic MLAs can do the job so much better. They lack the resources of the government, but they enjoy the credibility of democratic election and they can raise the concerns of disaffected Albertans in the legislature. The division of portfolios in the caucus will enable them to master and to be identified with particular issue areas.

Those in need will know whom to seek out in the caucus. If its members out-hustle the cabinet ministers they are assigned to shadow, the service they provide can build strong links with Alberta's many interest groups, setting in motion the process of cultural change. In this way, when the economy improves or a right of centre alternative to the Conservatives emerges, the New Democrats will be able to meet the challenge.

To prepare for this challenge, the New Democrats elected in 1986 must define themselves as existential educators. They must give Albertans psychologically compelling experience of the benefits of social democratic politics to their lives. They must work with groups of Albertans on the issues which affect them so profoundly that they cannot retain their attachment to the Alberta consensus in the face of the contributions which New Democratic MLAs have made to their cause, or at least in the face of the understanding and active support which the New Democrats have shown. This strategy is laborious and runs the risk of distracting the caucus from its legislative responsibilities and media opportunities. However, it will test and improve the New Democrats' policies and offers the only way of animating enough Albertans to make a lasting electoral difference for the party.

None of this denies the relevance of an analysis based on social class. It will remain important for the party to develop policies which respond in a comprehensive and general way to the neo-conservatism of the Alberta government and to its regressive social policies. However, the complexity of the issues is sufficiently great that most Albertans are unlikely to base their voting decisions on comparisons among the macro-economic policies of various parties. They are likelier to respond to more easily understood issues, such as social programming and environment protection. However, because they are likelier to break deeply rooted voting patterns because of personal and tangible considerations, a strategy for turning around the fortunes of the NDP must pay particular attention to appealing to them at this level.

This strategy holds out some promise of success because the link between the twin pillars of the Alberta consensus may be breaking. The alienation against Ottawa and central Canada can be expected to endure. However, it is no longer certain to sustain Alberta's pattern of single party dominance in that the basic electoral question in Alberta will have changed. In the past, the question has been which party is the true or at least the most effective standard bearer for the provincial consensus. In the absence of a consensus, the question which will gain prominence is which party can command the allegiance of a winning coalition of the diverse interests which comprise a differentiated Alberta society. Alienation will probably produce something of a bandwagon effect; a party which can be identified as heading for electoral success will probably receive additional votes from uncommitted voters wishing to give the winner a strengthened mandate for dealing with Ottawa. However, this effect will not prove sufficient to produce single party dominance. Power will change hands more often than in the past, in an electoral system in which parties alternate rather than disappear after being defeated.

Even in this scenario, Alberta's political culture will limit the NDP's growth at the polls. The party will still face the certainty that it cannot compete in at least a quarter of the ridings in the province, the southern, rural ones. It will also have to face the fact that political culture changes slowly, hence that many Albertans will not revise their thinking on their relationship to the Alberta mainstream. Moreover, in operating in a more Canadian rather than Albertan context, the NDP will still have to answer neoconservative arguments which have proven persuasive elsewhere in Canada. Thus, the best which can be said for the prospects for social democracy in the context of Alberta's political culture is that the future may see that culture coming to reflect more closely the reality and divisions of Alberta's social structure. Such a change is most unlikely to lead to electoral victory for the NDP in the foreseeable future. However, particularly after the 1986 election, it does pose as realistic goals an end to the historic pattern of single party dominance and the creation of a real debate on social issues, such as tends to be found elsewhere in Canada. Social democrats may escape the Alberta wilderness if they are active enough. However, they will then have to confront a new wilderness, the wilderness of Canadian politics during the neo-conservative era.

---

[1]Doug Owram, "Reluctant Hinterland", in Larry Pratt and Garth Stevenson, eds., *Western Separatism* (Edmonton, Hurtig Publishers, 1981).

[2]L.H. Thomas, *The Struggle for Responsible Government in the Northwest Territories* (2nd edition, Toronto: University of Toronto Press, 1978).

[3]C.B. Macpherson, *Democracy in Alberta: Social Credit and the Party System* (2nd edition, Toronto: University of Toronto Press, 1962), pp. 6-10.

[4]Gerald Friesen, *The Canadian Prairies: A History* (Toronto: University

of Toronto Press, 1984) p. 349.

[5]*Ibid.*, p. 300.

[6]Warren Caragata, *Alberta Labour: A Heritage Untold* (Toronto: Lorimer, 1979).

[7]Myron Johnson, "The Failure of the CCF in Alberta: An Accident of History?" (unpublished M.A. thesis, University of Alberta, 1974) is devoted to this theme. The argument that CCF failure in Alberta was in significant measure a result of circumstances is reinforced by the role which circumstances played in the ultimate success of the Saskatchewan CCF. This subject is discussed in Nelson Wiseman, "The Pattern of Prairie Politics" in Hugh G. Thorburn, ed., *Party Politics in Canada* (5th edition, Scarborough: Prentice-Hall, 1985), pp. 252-3.

[8]James Marsh, ed., *The Canadian Encyclopedia* (Vol. 1, Edmonton: Hurtig Publishers, 1985), p. 40.

[9]*Ibid.*, p. 37.

[10]John Richards and Larry Pratt, *Prairie Capitalism*, (Toronto: McClelland and Stewart, 1979), pp. 235-6.

[11]Friesen, *op. cit.*, p. 454; Roger Gibbins, *Prairie Politics and Society*, (Toronto: Butterworths, 1980), pp. 195-97.

[12]Howard and Tamara Palmer, "The Alberta Experience" in *Journal of Canadian Studies*, Vol. 17, No. 3, pp. 31-2.

[13]Alberta Bureau of Statistics, *Alberta Statistical Review, Second Quarter, 1985*, p. 27.

[14]*Ibid.*, p. 41.

[15]Jack K. Masson and Peter Blaikie, "Labour Politics in Alberta", Carlo Caldarola, ed., *Society and Politics in Alberta* (Toronto: Methuen, 1979), p. 281.

[16]Palmer, *op. cit.*, p. 29.

[17]John Calvert, *Government, Limited* (Ottawa: Canadian Centre for Policy Alternatives, 1984) describes this debate.

Chapter 10

Class and Class Politics in Alberta*

Garth Stevenson

> There is not much evidence in Canadian provincial politics to justify the belief that truth and good sense will eventually overcome folly and rascality but it is to the credit of the Canadian people that such a belief is still accepted.
>
> J.R. Mallory, *Social Credit and the Federal Power in Canada*[1]

This essay is intended as a contribution to what should be, although in fact it is not, a vigorous debate on the past, present and future of the NDP in Alberta. As the NDP approaches the end of its first quarter century, the "New" in the party's name grows increasingly incongruous, which may explain why so many people outside the party assume that the "N" in its name must stand for "National." For parties, as for individuals, the approach of middle age is a good time for introspection, for examining the mistakes, and for honestly evaluating the achievements of the past, and for seeking to make better use of the opportunities that still remain. If it should not be a time for despair, still less should it be one for boastful celebration where none is warranted. The reflections that follow are offered in a constructive spirit, by one whose claim to be heard by his intended audience is based as much on his experience as a candidate for the NDP in provincial and federal elections as it is based on his presumed expertise as an academic political scientist.

By any normal standard the electoral failure of the NDP in Alberta has been impressive. In six general elections from 1963 to 1982 inclusive the party managed to win a total of five constituencies, or an average of less than one in each election. All but one of the victories were by exceedingly narrow margins, and all but one were accounted for by Grant Notley in Spirit River-Fairview. In thirteen by-elections the NDP has managed only two victories, one of which was also

---

*This analysis of social class and politics in Alberta was written prior to the provincial election of May 8, 1986, in which the NDP captured sixteen seats, including eleven in Edmonton and two in Calgary.

in Spirit River-Fairview, although it is a well-established fact of Canadian political life that most by-elections are won by the opposition rather than by the government. Only in New Brunswick, Newfoundland and Prince Edward Island, where desperate poverty helps to perpetuate a tradition of clientelistic politics that pre-dates Confederation, has the moderate left done as badly in Canadian provincial politics.

Despite the volume and quality of academic writing on Alberta politics, beginning with the seminal works of Macpherson, Mallory and Irving in the 1950s and continuing up to our own day, the reasons for this unhappy state of affairs remain somewhat obscure. Moreover, the social and economic changes in Alberta since the time when the province's political uniqueness began to attract academic attention have been so overwhelming that they seem to cast doubt on most of the traditional explanations without providing any new ones. Explanations based on cultural distinctiveness seem questionable when migrants from other provinces or other countries account for almost half the population, and explanations based on class homogeneity have even more obviously been overtaken by events. The preempting of radical dissent by the Social Credit movement in the 1930s cannot fully explain the impressive hegemony of an overtly conservative party in the 1980s. The petroleum-based prosperity of the 1970s declined sharply in the early 1980s, without any discernible effect on the behaviour of the electorate. Even federal-provincial conflict, although it temporarily reached extreme levels under both Aberhart and Lougheed, has not been as much of a constant factor in Alberta's history as is sometimes assumed. Furthermore, high and endemic levels of federal-provincial conflict in British Columbia have not prevented the social democratic left from being a major force in that province's politics for fifty years. One is almost tempted to conclude that Alberta's uniqueness, and its resistance to the NDP, are autonomous facts that can neither be explained nor corrected. It is certainly a tribute to the personal qualities of Grant Notley and other party activists that they persisted so valiantly in what seems so hopeless a task, despite abundant grounds for discouragement. Yet the meagre results of their efforts must give rise to uncomfortable questions: Is failure inevitable, and if so, why? Does the fault lie with the NDP itself or with external factors? If the latter, are they fundamental and permanent, or merely temporary and accidental?

While the relative failure of the NDP in Alberta makes the party's performance elsewhere in Canada look impressive, it should be remembered that the party across Canada has experienced disappointing results, relative to the high hopes that accompanied its foundation. The NDP was formed in 1961 in an effort to give new impetus to the old CCF dream of a political realignment on the British model, with a party of the left, backed by organized labour, competing for office against a party of the right, backed by organized business. The circumstances seemed propitious owing to the temporary eclipse of the federal Liberals, whose brief periods in opposition have generally been conducive to the flourishing of new parties. The transition from CCF to NDP promised a closer and more effective link with organized labour. In addition, the New Party clubs were expected to attract the educated "new middle class" of the growing cities, a class that was becoming bored and embarrassed by the rustic style and incompetent performance of the Diefenbaker regime.

As is well known, the dream was not fulfilled. The promised realignment did not occur in Ontario, and its occurrence in Quebec owed nothing to the NDP, which remained as irrelevant as the CCF had been. The new middle class multiplied, but it was a revived Liberal party that attracted their votes, at least in federal politics. The number of Canadians belonging to labour unions grew dramatically, but the newly organized, most of them in the public sector, did not affiliate with the NDP, whose organizational base has remained largely confined to auto and steel workers in Ontario and woodworkers in British Columbia. At the provincial level the only fundamental, dramatic and permanent improvement in NDP fortunes, relative to those of the CCF, was in Manitoba, a province with a small and rapidly declining share of Canada's population. At the federal level the party suffered the humiliation of a fourth-place showing in 1962 and 1963, followed by a modest improvement in 1965. Thereafter it remained at about the same level, winning approximately one fifth of the popular vote and occupying about one tenth of the seats in the House of Commons. There are few signs that a second, and perhaps longer, period of liberal eclipse at the hands of Brian Mulroney will bring about a significant improvement in the NDP's electoral performance. It is possible, therefore, that Alberta is not so much a deviant case as an extreme case of a general Canadian, or North American, phenomenon. If this is so, an examination of the NDP's failure in Alberta may have a significance that transcends the province's borders.

The fundamental purpose of a left-wing party is to transfer power, wealth and security to those who in a market economy are the least likely to gain these benefits, or in other words the working class.

Leftists argue that issues related to the distribution of power, wealth, and security—in other words, class issues—are the fundamental issues of politics. Thus Canadian leftists have always been critical of the Canadian party system, which has been characterized since its emergence in the nineteenth century by the alternation of two parties neither of which is conspicuously more egalitarian in sentiment than the other and both of which draw extensive support from the business community. The two major Canadian parties have differed at times in their views on foreign policy, the protective tariff, bilingualism, aid to Catholic schools, and federal-provincial relations, differences that reflect a combination of electoral opportunism, inherited bases of support, and genuine conflicts within the bourgeoisie whose interests are represented by both parties. Even in relation to these issues, however, both parties have been capable of astonishing reversals of policy, and the differences between them have rarely been consistently pursued over long periods. In fact some cynics have charged, probably incorrectly, that the only real purpose of the issues listed above is to mislead and confuse the voters.

Be that as it may, it is generally acknowledged by well-informed observers that the Liberals and Conservatives have differed hardly at all in their views on the distribution of wealth, power and security between classes. When competition between the two parties is vigorous, either one may seek electoral support by making concessions to the interests of the working class, but every such concession by one party which is offered as evidence of that party's more progressive character may be matched by citing a similar concession by the other party. When one party is so dominant as to be virtually immune from the possibility of electoral defeat, a circumstance that has often been found at the provincial level of politics, even these minimal concessions have been unnecessary, and the politics of inequality have reigned supreme.

Traditional textbooks in Canadian government applauded this lack of distinction between the major parties, arguing that political stability and national unity were best served by parties that were free of ideological commitments to reform and that sought to combine the divergent interests of different classes within one broad coalition of support.[2] Social democrats have derided such claims as mystifications and special pleading, and have identified two glaring weaknesses in the traditional argument. In the first place, the traditional theory does not explain why ideological commitments concerning foreign policy, religion or the tariff are less threatening to national harmony than those concerning public ownership, the welfare state, or the right of collective bargaining. In the second place, the traditional theory's endorsement of the alleged harmonization of divergent interests within the major parties glosses over the fact that both parties have been far more closely associated with the economically dominant class than with the working class, albeit seeking the votes of the latter, so that their neutrality is no more than a polite fiction.

In contrast to the traditional theory of "brokerage politics," Canadian social democrats have argued for what John Porter called "creative politics" and what Gad Horowitz has described as the democratic class struggle.[3] By this is meant a situation in which one major party (presumably the NDP) would draw most of its support from the working class and would emphasize the need for a more equal distribution of power, wealth and security. The other major party, either the sole survivor or a combination of the two existing ones, would draw most of its support from other classes and would espouse a less egalitarian position on economic issues. As a corollary, the electorate would presumably recognize these issues to be the major ones. However, it is not always made clear whether this development would be a cause or a consequence of the NDP's emergence as a major party, and the process by which the transition would take place remains somewhat obscure.

This particular vision of politics has been more evident in the writings of the NDP's academic supporters than in the behaviour of the party itself, a contrast that can be traced back to the days of the CCF, despite the romantic myth that that party was significantly more radical than its successor. In practice both the CCF and the NDP have lacked a clear and consistent approach to class politics and they have not always or even often identified the working class as their major target. Both have pursued votes wherever they could find them (which is understandable) but have not always known where best to look for them, given the party's policies, self-image, and presumed *raison d'etre*. Both have based their claim to be class parties rather than brokerage parties primarily on the fact that they didn't receive campaign funds from corporations. This claim, while true, has been mainly a case of making a virtue of necessity, and in any event the laws regarding electoral finance that now prevail in Canada and in most of the provinces have greatly reduced its importance.

In fact the image that the NDP has of itself as a working class party has been exceedingly blurred, to the point that many leading New Democrats have denied that the party could be, should be, or is a working class party at all. Partly for this reason, the party has demonstrably failed to win a majority of working class votes, and this fact has reinforced the tendency to argue that this should not be its objective. Specifically, the notion of the NDP as a working class party has faced a number of obstacles within the party itself, as follows:

1. The legacy of agrarian populism, which was an important component of the CCF.
2. A belief that the working class is a declining proportion of the population and is in any event too narrow a base on which to construct a political party.
3. The continuing pursuit of non-existent support from within the ranks of small business.
4. The mutual lack of empathy between middle class NDP activists and working class voters.

All of these problems are probably more pronounced in Alberta than elsewhere, and they contribute in no small measure to the NDP's weakness in that province. Since this essay is primarily about the Alberta NDP, the analysis that follows will concentrate on Alberta, but it should be borne in mind that the problems diagnosed herein exist in other provinces, albeit probably in less exaggerated form. It should also be conceded at the outset that the Alberta NDP faces environmental problems that are not the fault of the party itself, and that may not be encountered in other provinces to the same extent, if at all. These will be dealt with in a later section of the essay.

Populism is a rather confused amalgam of ideas, and arguably more a state of mind than a political philosophy. Its central idea, that the land is the source of all wealth and farmers the source of all virtue, has some respectable antecedents, including the French physiocrats, generally credited with inventing the discipline of economics, and Thomas Jefferson, who was perhaps the most intellectual of American presidents. Jefferson also would have approved the disdain for people who live in large cities and the belief in decentralized political power which are fundamental attributes of populist thought. As a mass movement in North American history, however, populism has had significant undercurrents of anti-intellectualism, puritanism, xenophobia and religious fundamentalism. The Idaho poet Ezra Pound, who became a fascist, the Alberta member of Parliament John Blackmore, who ranted about a "Turco-Mongolian conspiracy," and the Eckville schoolteacher James Keegstra, who systematically indoctrinated his students with anti-semitism, should be included in any honest appraisal of the populist tradition in North America.

Agrarian populism in Canada has deep roots, extending back to the Clear Grits of southwestern Ontario in the years before Confederation. Although it remained strong enough in Ontario for the United Farmers of that province to elect a minority government in 1919, its major stronghold in the twentieth century was in the prairie provinces. The peak of its electoral strength came immediately after the First World War, when the Liberal party was in disarray throughout English-speaking Canada. Progressive or United Farmers governments were elected in Ontario, Alberta and Manitoba, and sixty-four Progressives were elected to the House of Commons in 1921. In both Alberta and Saskatchewan the Progressives received a majority of the popular vote in that election. A second wave of populist sentiment gave Alberta the world's first Social Credit government in 1935 and contributed to the rise of the Saskatchewan CCF, which formed a provincial government in 1944. In Saskatchewan the CCF was a rural populist party rather than an urban labour or social democratic party as it was in Manitoba, Ontario, Nova Scotia and British Columbia.

Populists and social democrats have both been critical of the traditional Canadian party system, but for somewhat different reasons. Social democrats have argued that the system of two brokerage parties assumes an artificial unity and ignores the reality of divergent class interests. Populists have argued that the system of two brokerage parties, at least at the provincial level, assumes an artificial conflict where none really exists. The goal of social democrats is a party system polarized between left and right, nationally and within each province. The goal of populists is a quasi-party system, in C.B. Macpherson's phrase, which will eliminate interparty competition at the provincial level[4] This is based on the premise that there are no significant class conflicts within western Canada, that the fundamental conflict is between western Canada on the one hand and central Canada on the other, and that western Canada therefore can and should unite against the external foe. The populist party at the provincial level, like the brokerage party at the national level, claims that it can simultaneously and impartially represent the interest of farmers, businessmen, and the working class, and it seeks the support of all three groups. Macpherson demonstrated that the United Farmers of Alberta and the Social Credit movement represented two slightly different variations on this populist theme. Peter Lougheed's urban-based Progressive Conservatives, while breaking sharply with the populist tradition on matters of policy, retained the populist attitude towards the party system. In response to the argument that it would be healthy to have a larger opposition in the legislature, Alberta Tories argue that the Alberta version of democracy takes place not between government and opposition, but within the governing party, which everyone is free to join.[5]

CCF thinking about the party system owed something to both the populist and the social democratic elements of its heritage. On the one hand the CCF, for as long as it had hopes of becoming a major party, was committed to the social democratic dream of polarizing the party system between left and right. On the other hand it claimed to be a coalition of farmers and the working class, arguing rather unconvincingly that farmers and the working class had common interests. In fact any two classes may have some common interests: clean air, safe drinking water, and a reduction in the death toll from traffic accidents are examples of interests that are common to all classes. The notion that workers and farmers have any common interests more specific than these, however, is very dubious, and the history of the CCF suggests that neither Canadian workers nor Canadian farmers were convinced of its validity. As C.B. Macpherson pointed out in his classic study of Alberta populism, farmers are essentially small-scale businessmen who own their own land and equipment and work for themselves, while the working class consists of people who work for others in large scale organizations and have nothing to sell but their labour.[6] Except in very unusual circumstances, the farmer's interests and political attitudes have more in common with those of self-employed urban businessmen than with those of the working class, and this tendency increases as the average size of farms and the scale of their operations increases, a trend that has characterized Canadian agriculture for the last several decades.

By seeking to combine such divergent interests, the CCF risked becoming a brokerage party little different from its rivals. It was saved from complete incoherence by the federal structure of the Canadian state, since virtually all of its agrarian supporters were in Saskatchewan while virtually all of its working class supporters were in other provinces. Only at the federal level, where it was extremely weak, did the CCF actually have to worry about combining the interests of farmers with those of the working class, and there the working class got the short end of the stick. The over-representation of Saskatchewan in the federal caucus was partly a cause and partly a consequence of the CCF's failure as a working class party in national politics. Combined with the fact that the CCF controlled the Saskatchewan government, it gave the agrarian wing of the national party exaggerated influence, at a time when the proportion of Canadians living on farms was declining rapidly. Although Saskatchewan actually provided only about one fifth of the CCF popular vote in federal elections, the party acquired a rural image that handicapped it severely in its efforts to appeal to the working class of central Canada. CCF attacks on the legacy of John A. Macdonald's National Policy did not appeal to factory workers whose jobs depended on the protective tariff. Many Ontario voters even had difficulty distinguishing the CCF from Social Credit, a party which they associated with "funny money," fundamentalist religion, and generally eccentric behaviour.

Much ink has been spilled in efforts to explain why Alberta voted for Social Credit and Saskatchewan for CCF, parties that were ostensibly at opposite ends of the political spectrum. In fact the apparent paradox is based on the mistaken assumption that the Saskatchewan CCF was a social democratic rather than a populist party. There were admittedly some differences between the Alberta Social Credit version of populism and the Saskatchewan CCF version. These differences resulted partly from the fact that in Alberta the mainstream agrarian leadership had been discredited by the failure of the UFA government to cope with the depression and partly from the relationship, however tenuous, between the Saskatchewan CCF and the national party. However, there were also many similarities, so that the Saskatchewan CCF had more in common with Alberta Social Credit than it had in common with the CCF in Ontario or even Manitoba. In both Saskatchewan and Alberta the populist governments enacted legislation, almost identical in fact, to protect farmers from their creditors. Both extended social services to rural areas in the wheat belt, but ignored the native peoples in the north. Both had their problems with organized labour. Both reflected the puritanical aspect of the populist tradition in their liquor laws and their censorship of films and periodicals. Both began with radical economic policies but grew decidedly more conservative with advancing years. Both, ironically, presided over urbanization, the increasing concentration of ownership in agriculture, the rise of petroleum and the service industries, and the undermining of the social base of the populism which they both represented.

There was thus no contradiction in the fact that the Alberta CCF, and later NDP, attempted to model itself on both its successful rival, the Alberta Social Credit party, and its successful neighbour, the Saskatchewan CCF. Both inspired its envy and admiration, even if the admiration was somewhat grudging in the case of Social Credit. At the same time as it modelled itself after these two forms of populism, the Alberta CCF was the lineal descendant of yet another form of populism, the United Farmers of Alberta who had governed the province between 1921 and 1935. For these reasons, and because Alberta was still a predominantly agrarian province when the CCF was founded, the alternative model of an urban labour-based social democratic party had little influence on the CCF in Alberta. Until it subsided into total futility and irrelevance in the 1950s, the Alberta CCF aspired to replace Social Credit as a vehicle for agrarian protest, uniting all classes around what was presumed to be an agrarian majority. Its electoral efforts, such as they were, were concentrated in rural areas, although it did not elect a rural member to the legislature until 1952, when it was already in decline provincially as well as nationally. Under the system of proportional representation then used in Alberta's major cities it was able to win one Edmonton seat in 1944, 1948, and 1952, as well as one Calgary seat in 1944 and 1948, but its share of the urban popular vote was no higher than its provincial average.

As described by Robin Hunter and Larry Pratt elsewhere in this volume, the transition from CCF to NDP produced serious conflicts in Alberta, as it also did in Saskatchewan. Agrarian populists in the CCF of both provinces disliked the more urban, pro-labour and, in their opinion, less radical orientation of the new party. In Saskatchewan the damage was minimized by the choice of Premier Douglas as the first national leader of the NDP, but Hazen Argue, who had led the small CCF caucus in the House of Commons, ran an overtly anti-union leadership campaign against Douglas before defecting to the Liberals, and the provincial party retained the title of CCF for several years. In Alberta the moribund CCF refused to transform itself into the NDP and instead reorganized itself as the Woodsworth-Irvine Fellowship which did not affiliate with the NDP until 1972. The fears of the populists were exaggerated, for in both provinces the NDP continued to be more of a rural populist party than a labour party, despite its tenuous affiliation with a national party that was modelled after the British Labour Party and firmly based in Ontario.

In Saskatchewan the continued adherence to populism was understandable, for the province was still predominantly rural and agriculture employed about 37 per cent of the labour force in 1961, the year of the NDP's founding convention. In any event the old formula had demonstrably worked in Saskatchewan, since the CCF still controlled the provincial government. The adherence to a rural populist orientation was less explicable in Alberta. Although agriculture was still the largest single source of employment in Alberta in 1961, it was already down to 21 per cent of the labour force and falling fast. Edmonton and Calgary were rapidly approaching Winnipeg in size. In addition, the rural strategy had definitely not proved itself in Alberta, where the CCF had fallen to four per cent of the popular vote in the 1959 provincial election.

A sensible strategy for the Alberta NDP would have recognized the two major cities as the most vulnerable part of the Social Credit majority, as well as the most rapidly growing part of the province. Instead the NDP pursued a populist mirage which eventually won it a single seat in Spirit River-Fairview. It was left to Peter Lougheed's Progressive Conservatives to sweep the cities, win a narrow majority in the rest of the province, and bring the era of agrarian populism to an end in 1971. By that time Edmonton and Calgary had about half the province's population, although they were grossly underrepresented in the legislature.

The legacy of agrarian populism, internalized in the minds of the party's ruling circles, has thus weighed heavily on the Alberta NDP, and has discouraged the party from adapting to a rapidly changing society. The romantic fascination with, and mythologizing about, the province's tradition of rural radicalism is symbolized by the virtual beatification of William Irvine, whose name has been bestowed on the party's provincial headquarters and whose portrait hangs in its legislative office, conspicuously higher than that of the national party's founding saint, J.S. Woodsworth. Apart from this romantic tradition, the main reason for the persistence of a rural orientation in the Alberta NDP is the desire to emulate the success of the sister party in neighbouring Saskatchewan. Since Saskatchewan is roughly twenty years behind Alberta in the transition from a rural to an urban society, and proceeding inexorably in the same direction, it may seem strange that New Democrats in the more advanced province would seek to emulate its more backward neighbour, rather than the other way around. One is reminded of the famous last line of *The Great Gatsby*: "So we beat on, boats against the current, borne back ceaselessly into the past."

By the 1980s the industrial composition of Alberta had changed so drastically, as shown by Table 1, that the rural orientation of the NDP was becoming positively bizarre. At the same time the election results of 1982 revealed that the party was at last acquiring an urban electoral base, almost in spite of itself. Table 2 shows, for each provincial election, the constituencies in which the NDP received at least one-third of the votes cast. While the number of such constituencies in rural Alberta

Table 1

Distribution of the Alberta Labour Force by Sectors

	1961	1981
Agriculture	103,573	82,755
Forestry	2,784	4,050
Fishing and Trapping	839	280
Mining and Petroleum	17,350	76,950
Manufacturing	42,217	108,005
Construction	37,360	128,810
Transport/Communication/Utilities	47,435	100,365
Trade	80,096	202,680
Finance, Insurance, Real Estate	14,695	65,860
Services	93,424	336,740
Public Administration and Defence	38,627	88,680
Unspecified	11,111	4,795
Total	489,511	1,199,970

Sources: 1961 census, cat. 94-518, and 1981 census, cat. 95-941.

shows no consistent trend over the years, the trend in Edmonton is dramatic and significant, after dismal results in the NDP's first four elections. In the 1982 election Edmonton accounted for almost half of the NDP popular vote. Thus there would seem to be a possibility of the NDP building a strong base in the capital city and *then* expanding outwards into the poorer hinterlands of the province. The obvious prototype for such a strategy is the New Democratic Party of Manitoba, which dominated the working class ridings of North Winnipeg for years before it finally won a province-wide plurality in 1969.

In short, the central argument of this essay is that the Alberta NDP should view itself primarily as the party of the working class. But who are the working class? Pop sociology, and the rhetoric of the brokerage parties and the chambers of commerce, have so debased and confused the notion of class in contemporary North America that many people, including some New Democrats, are in genuine doubt as to whether the working class exists as a meaningful category. In addition, some people who are prepared to concede the existence of a substantial working class in Ontario or Manitoba are in doubt as to whether one exists in Alberta,

Table 2
Constituencies in which the Alberta NDP received at
least one-third of the votes cast

	Rural	*Urban*
1963	None	None
1967	Grouard Pincher Creek-Crowsnest Spirit River-Fairview Willingdon-Two Hills	None
1971	Smoky River Spirit River-Fairview	None
1975	Spirit River-Fairview	None
1979	Edson Redwater-Andrew Spirit River-Fairview St. Paul	Edmonton Beverly Edmonton Norwood Edmonton Strathcona
1982	Spirit River-Fairview St. Paul	Edmonton Beverly Edmonton Calder Edmonton Highlands Edmonton Kingsway Edmonton Norwood Edmonton Parkallen Edmonton Strathcona

owing to the peculiar nature of the province's economy. Finally, the changes in occupational patterns throughout the advanced capitalist countries in recent years have given rise to the notion of the "post-industrial society" in which the working class is doomed to erosion and eventual disappearance. Even some socialists now question whether the working class is still viable enough to play the role traditionally assigned to it in socialist theory as the agent of political change.

The most powerful North American myth about class is the myth of the middle class majority. Essentially this myth is based on a play on words, and a tautology. "Middle class" is equated with "middle income" which in turn is taken to mean average income. The surprising discovery is then announced that most people's incomes are fairly near the average. Therefore everyone, or almost everyone, must belong to the middle class. The only exceptions allowed for in the theory are the truly rich, whose fabulous lifestyles are depicted in television's prime time soap operas and in the writings of Peter C. Newman, and the truly poor, an embarrassing but inconsequential minority who fall below something called "the poverty line." Since none of us ordinary folks ever needs to encounter either the rich or the poor, except indirectly through reports in the media, they can be easily forgotten or, if remembered at all, can assume a somewhat fabulous character. Real life, and real politics, are assumed to be about the middle majority, which means people like ourselves. Within that middle majority, it is argued, there exists no class distinction of any consequence.

As a slight digression, it might be noted that this vision of society is very close to that held by agrarian populists in both nineteenth century Ontario and the twentieth century West. According to populists the farmers and small businessmen were the middle majority, a plausible view in the times and places where populism arose. The rich were the "family compact" or later the "fifty big shots" who controlled the banks, the grain trade, and the railways. In either version they were a fabulous collection of demons whose numerical insignificance inspired the hope that they could be easily destroyed. The poor were those who did not farm—or run a business—native Indians, derelicts, the unemployed and the handicapped—people with no property and no apparent role in the economy. While they might be objects of pity, such people were essentially marginal, and not really the stuff of serious politics. Fortunately, for the populist vision, they were so few and so inconspicuous in rural communities that they could safely be disregarded.

While the agrarian populist version of the middle majority myth was in its own time and place fairly plausible, the modern version is simply a fraud. It ignores the fact that the term "middle class" in its original and correct meaning had nothing to do with arithmetical means and averages, but rather referred to those who were intermediate in status between the economically dominant class, on the one hand, and the subordinate class who comprised the majority on the other. In other words they were people who did not fit neatly into the Marxist dichotomy of proletariat and bourgeoisie: professionals, small businessmen, government officials, and independent commodity producers among others. While the number of people who belong in this category has certainly increased since Marx's time, and contrary to his prediction, to the point where it may include the majority of people who will read this book, it is far from being a majority of the entire population, in Alberta or anywhere else.

Furthermore, as John Porter demonstrated in a Canadian context more than twenty years ago, the middle class majority model does not stand up to examination even when class is defined in terms of income and lifestyle. Porter estimated that in the 1950s only about ten per cent of Canadian families could actually afford the lifestyle depicted in popular magazines as the middle class ideal.[7] While the details of Porter's analysis have been overtaken by events, and while the percentage of Canadian families who can afford a middle class lifestyle may even have doubled, despite the fact that a middle class lifestyle is defined more generously today than in the 1950s, his general point remains valid. This may be illustrated with census data. The area included within the federal constituency of Edmonton South (roughly everything west of the Calgary Trail and south of the university) probably epitomizes the middle class ideal, although it contains a few pockets of genuine wealth and genuine poverty. In 1981 the average family income in Edmonton South was $40,898. However, Edmonton East at $25,052 and Edmonton North at $28,816 were much more typical of the living standards of Canadians, since the Canadian average was $26,748. In fact there were only eight federal constituencies in Canada (out of 282) where the average exceeded $40,000. At 1981 prices, $40,000 was a middle class income, while two thirds of that amount was a working class, and also an average, income. Very few parts of Canada are solidly middle class.

An important conceptual pitfall that must be avoided is the practice of equating the working class with "the poor." The poor may be defined as that group of people whose incomes and living standards are conspicuously below the average. Sometimes they are defined as those whose incomes fall below an arbitrary "poverty line" which is fixed well below the average level. By definition, "the poor" are a minority. For the most part they consist of people who, usually through no fault of their own, do not participate fully and continuously in the productive economy. As a result most of them are to some degree in a clientelistic relationship with the state, drawing a large part of their income from transfer payments of one kind and another. Far from being the working class, these unfortunate people are mainly those who dropped out of the working class because of age, poor health or some other adversity or who, like many of Canada's native peoples, never entered the working class at all. The "poor" are essentially the category of persons which Marx described as the "lumpenproletariat." Furthermore, as David Lewis pointed out in his memoirs, such persons rarely if ever vote for parties of the left, even in countries where "class politics" are well-established.[8] If we are seeking a class that can be mobilized for political purposes, we must look elsewhere.

Some who would accept most or all of the preceding analysis in a Canadian context would still argue that its applicability to Alberta is limited. According to this view, Alberta's political conservatism results from an untypical class structure, and specifically from a working class that is alleged to be unusually small in numbers, relative to the whole population. The small size of the working class in turn is attributed to the unusual structure of the economy and particularly the weakness of the manufacturing sector. The validity of this argument can be examined by referring to Tables 3 and 4.

Table 3
Distribution of Labour Force by Sector
Canada and Alberta, 1981 *(per cent)*

	Canada	Alberta
Agriculture	4.0	6.9
Forestry/Fishing/Trapping	1.2	0.4
Mining and Petroleum	1.8	6.4
Manufacturing	18.9	9.0
Construction	6.4	10.7
Transport/Communication/ Utilities	8.0	8.4
Trade	16.6	16.9
Finance/Insurance/Real Estate	5.3	5.5
Services	28.8	28.1
Public Administration and Defence	7.5	7.4

Source: Derived from 1981 census, cat. 95-941.

Table 3 shows that the structure of the Alberta economy does in fact deviate from the Canadian norm when measured in terms of employment. Agriculture, the only major sector of the economy in which most participants are self-employed and therefore not part of the working class, is still relatively much more important in Alberta than in Canada as a whole. On the other hand, it is interesting to note that even in Alberta, agriculture ranks in seventh place among sectors of the economy as a source of employment, while it ranks in eighth place for Canada as a whole. Manufacturing, as expected, is very weak in Alberta, employing less than one tenth of the labour force. Forestry, fishing and trapping, although relatively small sources of employment in Canada as a whole, are even weaker in Alberta. On the other hand Alberta has an unusually high proportion of its labour force in the mining and petroleum sector; more than one third of all Canadians employed in that sector live in Alberta. Finally, Alberta ranks well above the national norm in the percentage of its labour force that is employed in the construction sector.

While these data show that Alberta's economy is indeed different from that of other parts of Canada, they do not suggest that the working class is unusually small, merely that it is a different kind of working class from that of Quebec or Ontario. By even the narrowest definition of the working class, construction workers, transportation workers, oilfield workers and miners would have to be included. The working class is not confined to those in manufacturing, and in fact manufacturing workers have not typically been the most politically radical segment of the working class, in Canada or elsewhere.

A better appreciation of the strength of the Alberta working class can be derived from Table 4, which divides the labour force, as of 1981, horizontally into categories of occupations rather than vertically into sectors of the economy. It will be seen from this table that the real urban middle class comprises only about one quarter of the working population. Even when the farmers, practically all of whom are self-employed, and a scattering of self-employed people in other occupations are added to this number, it still leaves about two thirds of employed Albertans in the working class.

Some readers will undoubtedly object to the inclusion of the clerical, sales and service workers in the working class, and since these categories account for more than one third of the entire labour force in Alberta, the objection is an important one and must be dealt with. (Parenthetically, it might be pointed out that the large size of these categories is neither unique to Alberta nor a possible explanation for Alberta's conservatism; the percentage of the whole Canadian labour force in these categories is even higher). Some Marxists argue that clerical, sales and service workers are not "productive" and therefore not part of the working class, while many non-Marxists argue that these occupations are "white collar" and should therefore be included in the

Table 4
The Alberta Labour Force: 1981

	Male	Female	Total
Managerial and Administrative	88,885	29,905	118,790
Science/Engineering/Mathematics	46,735	8,170	54,905
Social Science	8,130	9,850	17,980
Religion	2,280	480	2,760
Teaching	16,745	27,520	44,265
Medicine and Health	9,275	37,085	46,360
Artistic, Literary and Recreational	7,750	5,930	13,680
Subtotal	179,800	118,940	298,740
Farming	62,440	17,770	80,210
Clerical	38,155	182,780	220,935
Sales	61,810	48,175	109,985
Service	56,050	76,295	132,345
Primary Resource Production	22,075	575	22,650
Processing	19,885	4,200	24,085
Machining	25,700	1,025	26,725
Fabricating, Assembling and Repairing	55,265	7,385	62,650
Construction Trades	113,750	2,775	116,525
Transport Equipment Operating	47,065	5,110	52,175
Material Handling	16,320	3,315	19,635
Other Crafts and Equipment Operating	10,165	2,665	12,830
Miscellaneous Occupations	13,750	1,945	15,695
Total: All Occupations	722,225	472,950	1,195,175

Source: 1981 census, cat. 95-941.

middle class. Both objections are old-fashioned and misguided. The Marxist one is based on a very narrow definition of productive work, more suited to the nineteenth century than to the twentieth, and the sartorial criterion of the non-Marxist objectors is even sillier. Clothes are no longer a reliable indicator of class, as shown by the fact that many professors do their work in faded blue jeans. In terms of income, job security, job satisfaction, possibilities for advancement, and power over their working environment, most clerical, sales and service workers have far more in common with the working class as traditionally defined than they have in common with the genuine middle class.

The most striking characteristic of these jobs, and particularly of those in the clerical category, is the extent to which they are performed by women. On the other hand women are very poorly represented in the traditional working class occupations related to the production of goods and commodities, and they scarcely appear at all in the construction industry. Assigning the clerical, sales and service occupations to the middle class leads to the absurd conclusion that only one out of every sixteen employed women, as compared to nearly half of employed men, belongs to the working class. In fact a very large proportion of the employed women in these categories belong to the same families and households as the men employed in traditional working class occupations.

This point is of more than academic importance, because working class women, suffering the double handicap of gender and class, have been a largely ignored group of Canadians. The feminist movement in Canada has been and remains predominantly middle class in its personnel and in the types of issues that it emphasizes. The trade union movement has been mainly oriented towards the male-dominated occupations in manufacturing, transportation, construction, and the resource industries. Neither has said much to, or about, working class women, who have understandably been somewhat apathetic about politics. The increased participation of working class women in the labour force in recent years, largely a response to the impact of unemployment, inflation and high interest rates on working class living standards, has made them somewhat more visible but has not fundamentally altered this situation. On the basis of personal observation the writer of this essay would estimate that fewer than half of the women in Edmonton's working class neighbourhoods even vote in federal or provincial elections. The party that first appeals to this large group of non-voters will gain a substantial advantage over its competitors.

The Alberta working class, if properly defined, is not particularly small and certainly in no danger of disappearing. In fact it now outnumbers the farmers by a ratio of about ten to one, even though this is not reflected in the legislature, still less in the rhetoric of Alberta politicians. Given the increasing conservatism of the farmers, and the ambiguity of their political activities and sentiments even at the height of their alleged radicalism, which in any event is more than half a century in the past, a strategy of concentration on the working class would seem much more sensible for the Alberta NDP than a strategy of concentrating on the farmers.

The CCF and NDP, in Alberta and elsewhere, have always had some support among elements of the middle class, particularly those engaged in social science, religion, teaching, and the arts. Elements of the middle class more closely associated with the profit-oriented sector of the economy, such as managers and administrators, doctors, lawyers, scientists and engineers, have not usually been sympathetic to left-wing politics, in Alberta or elsewhere. One of the reasons for the transition from CCF to NDP was the desire to attract more middle class support, at a time when the potentially sympathetic elements of the middle class were beginning to increase rapidly in numbers and influence. To a considerable extent the NDP has succeeded in this goal across English-speaking Canada, although its success has been far less dramatic in this regard than that of the Parti Quebecois in Quebec. Teachers, clergymen, and persons engaged in the humanities and social sciences have provided a large share of NDP candidates and other activists. Neighbourhoods popular with the radical fringe of the middle class, such as Garneau, Windsor Park, Groat Estate and Belgravia in Edmonton, have become fairly reliable NDP strongholds. Throughout North America the growth of this element, which former U.S. Vice-President Spiro Agnew once referred to as "the Volvo station wagon set," was largely a function of the economic boom of the 1960s, which permitted a vast expansion of public bureaucracies and of educational and cultural institutions of all kinds. Since about 1973, however, these institutions have faced an increasing scarcity of funds, and the rapid expansion in the numbers of their employees has ended. In any event they have always been a minority within the whole middle class, most of which works in the profit-oriented sector of the economy, while the middle class itself is a minority of the whole population.

This is particularly true in Alberta. Table 5 shows that the composition of the Alberta middle class differs from that of the Canadian middle class as a whole, and the differences are not such as to improve the prospects of the NDP in Alberta. Managers, administrators, scientists and engineers are a much higher proportion of the middle class in Alberta than elsewhere, while teachers, social scientists and those involved in

Table 5

Distribution of Middle Class Occupations by Sectors 1981 *(per cent)*

	Canada	Alberta
Managerial and Administrative	36.6	39.8
Science, Engineering and Mathematics	13.9	18.4
Social Science	6.6	6.0
Religion	1.2	0.9
Teaching	17.3	14.8
Medicine and Health	18.4	15.5
Artistic, Literary and Recreational	6.0	4.6

Source: derived from 1981 census, cat. 95-941.

cultural activities are underrepresented, perhaps because Alberta has not been a particularly congenial environment for persons in these occupations. The potentially sympathetic elements of the middle class are a very small minority in the Alberta electorate, being about as numerous overall as the farmers. While they will doubtless continue to play an important role in the Alberta NDP, they are too small a group to serve as the basis of an electoral strategy.

While the NDP across English-speaking Canada has enjoyed considerable support from the educated, salary-earning new middle class, particularly those who work outside the profit-oriented sector of the economy, it has received little support from what could be called the old middle class of self-employed entrepreneurs. This should come as no surprise, since the typical self-employed entrepreneur, or "small businessman" as politicians invariably describe him, regards labour unions as public enemy number one, with "big government" a close second. In fact throughout the twentieth century small businessmen in Europe and North America have been the backbone of all the major movements of right-wing extremism, a tendency that has increased as the trend to concentration and monopoly renders their situation more desperate.

Small business, however, has recently had a fatal fascination for the NDP, both nationally and, to an even greater extent, in Alberta. Great efforts have been made to demonstrate the party's sympathy for the struggling entrepreneur, and indeed this was a major theme of the party's federal election campaign in 1984. In Alberta the virtue and importance of small businessmen have been a theme of NDP rhetoric for years, although there is no evidence that the entrepreneurs themselves have reciprocated the party's good feelings. Apart from their natural conservatism, most small businessmen like to be on the winning side in provincial politics, since the provincial governments collectively are by far Canada's largest purchasers of goods and services. It is probably also for this reason, at least in part, that small businessmen have been the leading supporters of extreme provincialism and anti-centralism in Canada's constitutional debates. The Edmonton Chamber of Commerce, for example, produced constitutional position papers in 1971 and 1980 that would have reduced the federal government's powers over the economy almost to the vanishing point.[9]

The reasons for the NDP's fascination with small business are complex. It can certainly not be explained solely by the desire to win the votes of the small businessmen themselves, since self-employed persons, apart from farmers, comprise only two per cent of the Canadian labour force and about the same percentage in each province. Part of it is the legacy of populism, which viewed the rural entrepreneur (the farmer) and the urban entrepreneur (the small businessman) as allies against the banks and the railways. Another part is simple nostalgia: it would be interesting to draw a correlation between the popularity of Norman Rockwell commemorative plates and the political support for small business. Part of it is based on the proposition that small business is more labour intensive than big business, from which the corollary is drawn that encouraging small business will contribute to full employment. Finally, and perhaps most importantly, expressions of enthusiasm for small business are designed to counter the charge that the NDP is opposed to "free enterprise" and that its policies would discourage economic growth. In other words, they are believed to make the NDP more credible to an electorate saturated with anti-socialist ideology, and to do so without supporting "big business," something that most New Democrats are unwilling to do, at least publicly.

All of this begs some questions to which New Democrats, in Alberta and elsewhere, should give serious consideration. In the first place it is very difficult to draw the line between "small" and "large" business, and a successful small business, by definition, will inevitably become larger. Particularly in the petroleum industry, some very substantial Calgary-based enterprises are climbing on the "small business" bandwagon and using populist rhetoric to seek political support, mainly at the expense of Petro-Canada. Secondly, the belief that the economy will benefit by a reactionary reversal of the trend towards larger enterprises flies in the face of experience and common sense. Even the largest Canadian industrial enterprises are small by world standards, and if Canada is to survive in a harsh and unfriendly world, it needs firms that are large enough to develop and use the latest technology. Thirdly, the argument that small business is labour intensive, while true, ignores the other side of the coin: small business pays low wages. Precisely because they employ more persons per unit of output than do large firms, small firms can only survive by discouraging unions and keeping wages down, tasks with which their friendly provincial governments are only too happy to assist. Finally, the obsession with small business is a massive diversion of effort from more profitable electoral strategies, aimed at those who can realistically be expected to vote for the NDP. In the Alberta NDP specifically, it has caused a massive investment of time in the elaboration of complex and economically dubious industrial strategies, little different in fact from those espoused by the governing Progressive Conservatives.[10] While it can safely be assumed (and hoped) that no one outside of the NDP provincial council and the legislative press gallery has ever read these documents, many voters may be wondering whatever happened to the party that used to talk about pensions and medicare.

The industrial strategy documents are only one symptom of a psychological gap that separates the NDP from its potential supporters. Regrettably, there are no easy solutions to the problem. The Alberta NDP is far from being a party of the working class, and even if it adopted the goal of systematically seeking the votes of the working class it would not automatically become one, although that would be a major step in the right direction. Most NDP candidates in urban areas are drawn from the middle class, with a preponderance of secondary and post-secondary teachers. There are obvious reasons why social democratic parties recruit many of their candidates from this occupational group, similar to the reasons why the brokerage parties recruit such a preponderance of lawyers. Teachers and lawyers both tend to be reasonably adept at public speaking (although public speaking plays a smaller part in election campaigns now than it did fifty or a hundred years ago) and, even more important, they can usually find time to campaign without suffering a significant loss of income. In some provinces trade union officials have been effective candidates for the NDP, but trade unionism in Alberta is relatively weak and relations between the unions and the party have been less than ideal, in part because of the party's fascination with the vanishing tradition of agrarian populism. The only union that appears to play a conspicuous role in the Alberta NDP is the Alberta Union of Provincial Employees, and the low opinion which most Canadians have of civil servants makes this relationship a very dubious asset for the party.

Although an occupational gap between the candidates and the voters may be inevitable, at least in the short term, it can be overcome, or even turned into an advantage, if the candidate has some roots in the population which he seeks to represent. National NDP leader Ed Broadbent, who comes from a family of autoworkers in the company town which he represents in Parliament, is a classic example. Admittedly it may be difficult to identify the appropriate "roots," let alone find a suitable candidate who has them, in a society as heterogeneous as present-day Alberta. Half of the people in Edmonton, and three fifths of the people in Calgary, were born outside of Alberta, and the ethnic diversity of both cities, particularly in Edmonton, is proverbial. One suspects, however, that NDP candidates could be more representative of their intended clientele than they are. In the provincial election of 1982, for example, two thirds of the NDP candidates in Edmonton were apparently of British Isles ethnic origin, although persons of British Isles ethnic origin are probably less than one third of the city's working class (37.6 per cent of all Edmonton residents were of British Isles ethnic origin in 1981, but the percentage was higher in the south and west, where most of the middle class is concentrated, and lower in the working class north and east). The Progressive Conservatives produced a slate of Edmonton candidates that was far more representative in ethnic terms, and hardly less so in occupational terms, of the city's population.

Certain ideological issues also divide the NDP, in Alberta and elsewhere, from a large part of its intended clientele. The withdrawal of Canada from NATO and the removal of abortion from the criminal code are two goals deeply cherished by middle class NDP activists, but deeply offensive to large numbers of working class Canadians. Although both matters fall under federal jurisdiction, the hostile and emotional attitudes towards the party which they create spill over into provincial electoral contests as well. However much NDP provincial candidates may take refuge behind the allegedly watertight compartments of the constitution to avoid discussing these issues, it is not unreasonable that the voters should hold the party responsible for its views on them, since the party consists of the same people, and often the same candidates, at both levels of government. In the case of abortion the constitutional argument is particularly weak in any event, since criminal law, although enacted by Parliament, is administered by the provinces.

These ideological problems, it should be emphasized, are not unique to the Alberta section of the party. They exist in other sections as well and have probably contributed significantly to the NDP's failure to make any real progress in Ontario since the 1960s. However, the Alberta party's very weak ties with the trade union movement have prevented it from being the party of the working class in even the limited sense in which the Ontario NDP has been the party of the working class for the last two decades. Since it cannot possibly hope to become an agrarian party like its Saskatchewan counterpart, the Alberta party is thus left as the party of the Volvo station wagon set and little more. This in turn helps to give the policies that are least appealing to the working class a more prominent place on its agenda.

An alternative and superficially attractive explanation for the failure of the Alberta NDP might be based on the nature of the Alberta working class itself, and especially on its political attitudes. Unfortunately there has been very little systematic study of the Alberta working class as compared, for example, to the extensive literature on prairie farmers, or even on the working classes of Quebec and Ontario. Thus very little can be said with confidence about the ways in which the ideology of working class Albertans differs from that of their counterparts in other provinces, or the reasons for the differences, if any. Whether working-class Albertans are really less class-conscious, or more conservative, than their counterparts in provinces where the NDP has fared better is a question that deserves serious investigation. It would be wrong to assume that they are less class conscious or more conservative simply because they don't vote for the NDP.

One thing that is probably true about the Alberta working class is that it has little continuity or cohesion as a class. A large proportion of its members are newcomers to the working class, and an even larger proportion are newcomers to the province. Both facts are consequences of the rapid social and demographic change that has occurred in Alberta in recent decades. The number of working class Albertans in 1981 was roughly five times as large as the number in 1941, while the normal excess of births over deaths obviously accounted for only a fraction of this increase. The remainder came from three sources: migration from foreign countries, migration from other parts of Canada, and internal migration from the declining agricultural population of Alberta itself. These three sources of recruitment for the Alberta working class obviously more than compensated for the losses caused by migration of working class Albertans to other provinces (mainly British Columbia) and upward mobility into the middle class.

It is indicative of the way in which the Canadian state emphasizes geographical rather than class cleavages that the census measures geographical migration in considerable detail but does not measure mobility between classes, nor does it distinguish the geographical migrants on the basis of class. However, migrants from other parts of Canada comprised 29 per cent of Alberta's total population and migrants from other countries comprised 16 per cent at the time of the 1981 census. For the working class alone the percentages would probably be about the same. Migration between classes is of course almost impossible to estimate on the basis of census data, but since half of Alberta's population lived on farms as recently as 1941, the working class has obviously benefitted from one additional source of reinforcement, namely the surplus population of the rural areas. To counterbalance this there was undoubtedly some upward mobility from the working class into the middle class, but it should not be overestimated. The new recruits into Alberta's urban middle class have probably come from other provinces, other countries, and Alberta farms, in that order of importance, with the indigenous working class ranking a distant fourth as a source of recruitment.

All of this would seem likely to have two consequences for the political culture of working class Alberta. First, those whose class position has changed in the course of their lifetime (a group that would include many of the geographical migrants as well as those who grew up on Alberta farms) are unlikely to have a very clear sense of class identity. Secondly, the diversity of geographical and cultural origins among the Alberta working class is likely to inhibit the development of any sense of collective solidarity. This would be true even in the absence of any deliberate efforts by the state to manipulate cultural identities for that very purpose, but is obviously reinforced by the presence of such efforts.

The first point is of particular interest in the light of Macpherson's comments about the "petit bourgeois" ideology of prairie farmers, residues of which might be expected to survive in formerly rural persons who have made the transition to Alberta's urban working class. It should be remembered that this category includes substantial numbers from rural Saskatchewan and Manitoba, since Alberta attracted large numbers of migrants from both of those provinces between 1947 and 1980.

Alberta is not unique in the fact that diverse geographical and cultural origins inhibit a sense of solidarity among the working class. The province is actually close to the Canadian average both in the percentage of its population born outside of Canada and the percentage whose mother tongue is not the language of the province-wide majority. On the other hand in 1981 it did have an unusually large percentage of migrants from other provinces, a consequence of the oil and gas boom of the 1970s. In real terms Alberta is probably more of a melting pot than a mosaic. About two thirds of those who claim an ethnic origin other than "British Isles" have English as their mother tongue. The percentage of the population claiming "mixed" or "multiple" ethnic origins, an option available for the first time in the 1981 census, is at 12.2 per cent, the highest of any province. In terms of the ratio of "British Isles" to other ethnic origins Alberta ranks about midway between Ontario, where "British Isles" are still more than half the population, and the other two prairie provinces. Calgary is less ethnically diverse, and Edmonton more so, than the province as a whole, but Calgary has a disproportionately large share of the interprovincial migrants.

In terms of previous political allegiance the working class migrants to Alberta span the spectrum from Latin American Marxists to Ontario Tories, with perhaps even a few Liberals. Geographical migration *per se* is unlikely to have any effect on class consciousness or political beliefs, but it may create a consciousness of an ethnic, national or even regional identity that was previously taken for granted, and a disposition to associate with people who share it, even perhaps regardless of their class position. At the same time it may be difficult to develop much solidarity with members of one's own class who speak a different language or who differ in terms of other cultural characteristics. An ethnic identity may persist after the language is lost, as in the case of many Ukrainians in Alberta, but ethnic communities may be divided by ideological, religious and other cleavages. The Ukrainian community in Alberta, for example, spans the political spectrum from far right to far left. Despite the right-wing image given to Ukrainians by the media, they apparently support the NDP to at least as great an extent as their non-Ukrainian neighbours in all three prairie provinces.

Both the politics of multiculturalism and the multicultural aspects of politics are important subjects that require further investigation, in Alberta and in Canada generally. In recent years the concept of multiculturalism has been extensively touted by the federal, most provincial, and even some municipal governments in Canada. German and Ukrainian immersion classes are now offered in some Alberta public schools and ethnic historical sites of the most arcane significance are honoured with signposts along the provincial highways. The August civic holiday in Alberta, officially known as Heritage Day, has in effect become a festival of multiculturalism. In Edmonton it is celebrated in a park named after a deceased Ukrainian politician (but to which some anglo-Albertans still defiantly refer by its former, Anglo-Saxon, name) where an astonishing variety of ethnic associations, some with overlapping terms of reference, dispense food, entertainment, and handicrafts throughout the long weekend.

None of this activity alters the inter-ethnic inequalities of wealth and economic power that John Porter and others have documented, nor is it designed to do so. Two consequences that it does have are both damaging to the interests of the Alberta NDP. First, by reinforcing and artificially prolonging ethnic identities, and by drawing attention to inter-ethnic political and historical controversies, it inhibits the development of cross-ethnic solidarity among the working class. Events that occurred in Europe or Asia, in some cases before most of the voters were born, have a large and unhealthy impact on what passes for political discussion in Alberta. Secondly, state-sponsored multiculturalism reinforces the power of ethnic elites who, not unnaturally, are its strongest proponents. These people are doctors, dentists, lawyers and retailers who cater to a clientele largely drawn from their own ethnic group, political operators with a reputed ability to deliver the "ethnic" vote, and persons who derive their livelihood from cultural activities (in the broadest sense) of an ethnic nature. In Alberta almost all of these elites support, and most are closely associated with, the Progressive Conservative party, from which they received individual patronage of various kinds as well as the collective patronage of state-sponsored multiculturalism. The attraction of the Progressive Conservative party to ethnic elites is not only its right-wing ideology, which corresponds to their class interests as professionals and businessmen, but also the fact that it is in power and thus has the patronage at its disposal. As noted in an earlier part of this essay, the Alberta Progressive Conservatives have been shrewd enough since 1971 to recruit candidates for the legislature and cabinet who represent the ethnic diversity of the province and are largely drawn from within the ethnic elites. For an opposition party, especially one that seeks to unite the underprivileged on the basis of class, this situation creates a vicious circle from which there is no easy escape.

Another and more obvious way in which the political culture of the Alberta working class is affected by external manipulation is the stimulation of provincial and "western" chauvinism associated with anti-federal, anti-Ontario, and anti-Quebec sentiments. These sentiments of course have deep roots in prairie history, although most of the issues and events that gave rise to them in the first place have little or no relevance today. During the Lougheed-Trudeau era, however, the sentiments were revived and reinforced by the intragovernmental conflicts over energy policy, the prominence of francophones in the federal government, and the long-overdue efforts to make the federal state reflect the linguistic duality of the country. Alberta's Progressive Conservative rulers used Quebec's demands for more powers as a precedent and excuse to demand more for themselves, at the same time as they repeatedly denounced the federal government for allegedly promoting the interests of central Canada at the expense of Alberta or "the West." Many unsophisticated Albertans read between the lines of this discourse and perceived some sinister link between the economic and cultural sides of the Liberal government's agenda. Without overtly appealing to the latent francophobia of the electorate, the Lougheed government was able to benefit from it nonetheless. At the same time the Alberta Progressive Conservatives sought to identify their own economic and constitutional demands with the tradition of agrarian populist protest against the business interests of the east, a tradition that is a folk memory for the many Alberta residents who grew up on prairie farms. The fact that the Alberta government was itself closely associated with big business hardly seemed to matter. Lougheed's claim that Albertans should demonstrate their solidarity against the external foe by voting for his party, and that the province could not afford the luxury of a large opposition in the legislature, was squarely in the tradition of prairie populism, even if the economic and social policies of his government were not.

At the same time as the Alberta government and media systematically sought to make "Ottawa" the scapegoat for every real or imagined misfortune, a deliberate effort was made to promote a sense of solidarity and identity as "Albertans," rather than as Canadians, westerners, or members of a class.[11] No doubt this was in large part an effort to socialize the many newcomers to the province, more than half of whose adult residents by 1981 had been born somewhere else. In a province defined by no more than some arbitrary surveyors' lines on a map, and to which people were attracted only because its energy resources, in the short-lived economic circumstances of the 1970s, promised lower taxes and higher living standards than they could enjoy elsewhere, the creation of any genuine sense of community was and is an uphill struggle. Significantly, the artificial-sounding word "Albertan" has not really entered the common speech, despite the frequency with which it appears in the discourse of provincial politicians. The universal popularity achieved by the word "Quebecois," which is also of recent origin, makes a revealing contrast.

Undoubtedly there is a great deal of anti-Quebec and anti-Ontario prejudice among the Alberta working class, more of it based on ignorance than on genuine malice. Given the quality of what passes for political commentary in the newspapers and privately owned radio stations of Alberta, it could hardly be otherwise. Much of this prejudice is the residue of traditional prairie populist attitudes, and those working class Albertans who hold such beliefs to a significant degree almost always turn out, on examination, to be the first generation off the farm. However, the depth and extent of prejudice should not be overestimated. The separatist and populist Western Canada Concept, which many predicted would form the official opposition after the 1982 election, made little impression on the Alberta working class. The nine constituencies where it won more than 20 per cent of the vote were all in rural areas, and five of them were constituencies where Social Credit candidates had survived the Lougheed sweep in 1971. Its best showings in the major urban areas were in middle class Sherwood Park, where it had an exceptionally well-known candidate, and in the wealthy enclave of Edmonton Glenora.

The weakness of the Alberta NDP, in short, cannot be explained by provincial chauvinism or anti-eastern sentiment, both of which are equally prevalent, if not more so, in British Columbia, any more than it can be explained by the relatively insignificant differences between Alberta's class composition and that of other provinces. What rational explanation can be found for the distinctiveness of voting behaviour in Alberta?

Almost two decades ago, the Quebec sociologist Maurice Pinard attempted to answer some questions analogous to those raised in this essay: why was there no working class party in Quebec, and why had working class voters given such impressive support to the right-wing Union Nationale, despite the Duplessis government's frequent conflicts with organized labour.[12] The parallel between the Quebec of Maurice Duplessis and the Alberta of Peter Lougheed is in many ways remarkably close. Both Duplessis and Lougheed were lawyers of bourgeois background and conservative attitudes who assumed the leadership of moribund political parties and turned them into two of the most formidable electoral machines in Canadian history. Both overturned governing parties that had held office for nearly four decades. Both presided over rapid urbanization and economic growth. Both drew impressive electoral support from all classes and from both rural and urban voters. Both had similar views on economic and social policy, federal-provincial relations, and closer economic ties with the United States. Both used federal-provincial conflict, largely of their own making, for electoral purposes. Both ruled with an iron hand over cabinet colleagues whose mediocrity was conspicuous even by the standards of Canadian provincial politics. Both treated intellectuals, labour unions and the legislature with contempt. Both benefitted from the adulation of a servile press, although neither contributed significantly to the happiness and well-being of his fellow citizens. How did such men win such vast power, and hold it for so long?

In his study of working class voting in Quebec Pinard rejected two common assumptions: that the Quebec working class shared the conservative beliefs of the party that they voted for and that they voted for the Union Nationale because of its hostility to "Ottawa." He argued instead that Quebec workers were relatively class conscious and that they were neither as conservative nor as nationalistic as Quebec's elites. However, he pointed out that class sentiments among the masses do not necessarily become actualized and reflected in class organizations, such as unions, or in class parties. The relationship between class sentiments and class organizations or parties is mediated by elites, who determine what political options are available to the working class. Working class voters supported the Union Nationale at the outset because it was the only available alternative to the seemingly interminable rule of the Liberals. Thereafter their allegiance to the Union Nationale became fixed, even though they perceived no real ideological difference between it and the Liberal party. The cohesiveness and conservatism of Quebec elites at that time ensured that no more meaningful alternative would be made available.

In Alberta it is often assumed that the working class is unusually conservative in its attitudes or that its voting in provincial elections is influenced by hostility to the central government. The reasons for rejecting these assumptions have already been discussed. Just as the Quebec working class voted for Duplessis in 1936 as a protest against the Liberals, so it is likely that the Alberta working class voted for Lougheed in 1971 as a protest against Social Credit and not out of any positive feelings about Lougheed or his party. There is some circumstantial evidence for this in the fact that Edmonton was the area of strongest support for the Progressive Conservatives in 1971; they took every seat in Edmonton but only slightly more than half of the ridings in the rest of the province. In 1982, by contrast, Edmonton was the weakest area for the Progressive Conservatives, although they lost only one seat.

After 1971 the incorporation of virtually all of Alberta's elites into the Progressive Conservative party was facilitated by massive petroleum revenues, fear that the federal Liberals would prevent Alberta businessmen from increasing their share of the nation's wealth, and the farsighted and successful strategy of opening the party to ethnic businessmen and professionals. With elite cohesion attaining a level that even Quebec had never experienced, the working class voter was offered very little choice. The alternatives to the government were a Social Credit party that was literally dying of old age, a New Democratic Party led by a dissident, and powerless, fringe element of the middle class and, in 1982, the bizarre fantasies of the Western Canada Concept. Collectively these various alternatives and an assortment of other opposition candidates were supported by about a quarter of the electorate in 1975, 1979, and 1982, but in each case a far larger number of those eligible did not bother to vote at all. In Edmonton in 1982 more eligible persons abstained than voted for the Progressive Conservatives, and in Calgary almost as many.

The half million eligible voters who did not vote in 1982 are the untapped resource of Alberta politics, and the fact that more than two thirds of them live in Calgary and Edmonton suggests where the NDP should focus its efforts. To penetrate the layers of apathy and cynicism that are the legacy of Alberta's unfortunate political history will not be an easy task, and this essay can offer no simple recipe for success. Yet there was never more of a need for a viable progressive political alternative in Alberta than there is today. The inherent instability of the province's unbalanced economy, the juxtaposition of wealth and luxury with poverty and misery, the deterioration of social services, the degradation of the physical environment, the absence of civility and of a real sense of community, are all evidence of that need. It will take more than successful hockey teams, grandiose commercial emporia, the (temporary) absence of a retail sales tax and the self-serving hucksterism of a singularly crass and vulgar elite to make Alberta a community of which its residents can be proud. The emergence of competitive and creative politics is an essential first step. The question is whether the NDP will be equal to the challenge.

[1]Toronto, Univ. of Toronto Press 1954, reprinted 1976, p. 178.

[2]e.g., R. Macgregor Dawson, *The Government of Canada* (4th edition, Toronto, Univ. of Toronto Press, 1963) and J.A. Corry and J.E. Hodgetts, *Democratic Government and Politics* (3rd edition, Toronto, Univ. of Toronto Press, 1959).

[3]John Porter, *The Vertical Mosaic* (Toronto, Univ. of Toronto Press, 1965), pp. 366-385; Gad Horowitz, "Toward the Democratic Class Struggle," in T. Lloyd and J. McLeod, *Agenda 1970: Proposals for a Creative Politics* (Toronto, Univ. of Toronto Press, 1968), pp. 241-255.

[4]C.B. Macpherson, *Democracy in Alberta* (2nd edition, Toronto, Univ. of Toronto Press, 1962), pp. 237-250.

[5]Garth Stevenson, "Quasi-Democracy in Alberta," *The Canadian Forum*, LXII, 725 (February 1983).

[6]Macpherson, *op. cit.*, pp. 215-230.

[7]Porter, *op. cit.*, pp. 125-132.

[8]David Lewis, *The Good Fight* (Toronto, Macmillan, 1982), p. 157.

[9]"Submission by the Edmonton Chamber of Commerce on Constitutional Amendment" (Edmonton, August 1979) and "Submission by the Edmonton Chamber of Commerce on Constitutional Amendment: second report" (Edmonton, August 1980).

[10]e.g., *A New Democratic Future: Proposals for an Economic Strategy, 1985-1990* (Edmonton, 1984).

[11]Peter Puxley, "The Psychological Appeals of Separatism," in Larry Pratt and Garth Stevenson, *Western Separatism: The Myths, Realities and Dangers* (Edmonton, Hurtig, 1981), pp. 135-154.

[12]Maurice Pinard, "Working Class Politics: An Interpretation of the Quebec Case," *Canadian Review of Sociology and Anthropology*, VII (1970), 87-109.

Contributors

Ray Martin is Leader of the Alberta New Democrats and Leader of the Official Opposition in Alberta.

Larry Pratt is co-author of *Prairie Capitalism* and teacher in the Department of Political Science at the University of Alberta.

Olenka Melnyk is an Edmonton writer who is working on a grassroots history of the CCF in Canada.

Robin Hunter was a member of the CCF-Youth in the late 1950s and played a part in the founding of the Alberta NDP. He is writing a study of the Liberal Party of Alberta.

Allan Tupper is the author of *Public Money in the Private Sector* and chairman of the Department of Political Science at the University of Alberta.

Ed Shaffer is the author of *Canada's Oil and the American Empire* and teaches in the Department of Economics at the University of Alberta.

Ron Chalmers worked as Executive Assistant to the Leader of Alberta's Official Opposition, Robert Clark, in the late 1970s, and is now a reporter with *The Edmonton Journal*.

Tom Pocklington was active in the Alberta NDP and Waffle movement in the 1960s and '70s. The editor of *Liberal Democracy*, he teaches in the Department of Political Science at the University of Alberta.

Frederick C. Engelmann is co-author of *Canadian Political Parties* and past-President of the Canadian Political Science Association.

Gurston Dacks is the author of *A Choice of Futures* and teaches in the Department of Political Science at the University of Alberta.

Garth Stevenson has been an advisor to the New Democratic Party on constitutional questions and an NDP candidate. The author of *Unfulfilled Union*, he teaches in the Department of Political Science at the University of Alberta.